HOW I FILMED THE WAR

When I was in France I made arrangements with my friend Mr. Low Warren, at that time Editor of the Kinematograph Weekly, *to arrange the manuscript I sent him for publication in book form.*

The manuscript has in no way been altered in any material respect, and is in the form in which I originally wrote it.

GEOFFREY H. MALINS.

HOW I FILMED
:: THE WAR ::
A RECORD OF THE EXTRAORDINARY EXPERIENCES OF THE MAN WHO FILMED THE GREAT SOMME BATTLES ETC.

BY

LIEUT. GEOFFREY H. MALINS, O.B.E.

EDITED BY
LOW WARREN

INTRODUCTION BY
DR. NICHOLAS HILEY

The Naval & Military Press Ltd

Published by

The Naval & Military Press Ltd
Unit 10 Ridgewood Industrial Park,
Uckfield, East Sussex,
TN22 5QE England

Tel: +44 (0) 1825 749494
Fax: +44 (0) 1825 765701

www.naval-military-press.com
www.military-genealogy.com
www.militarymaproom.com

In reprinting in facsimile from the original, any imperfections are inevitably reproduced and the quality may fall short of modern type and cartographic standards.

FILMING THE PRELIMINARY BOMBARDMENT OF THE BIG PUSH, JULY 1ST, 1916. A FEW MINUTES AFTER THIS PHOTOGRAPH WAS TAKEN A SHELL BURST WITHIN SIX YARDS, SMASHING DOWN THE TRENCH WALLS AND HALF BURYING ME. NOTE THE SANDBAG ON A WIRE IN FRONT OF MY CAMERA FOR "CAMOUFLAGE"

CONTENTS

PART I

CHAPTER I
A FEW WORDS OF INTRODUCTION

CHAPTER II
WITH THE BELGIANS AT RAMSCAPELLE

I Reach the First Line Belgian Trenches—And become a Belgian Soldier for the Time Being—A Night Attack—An Adventure whilst Filming a Mitrailleuse Outpost—Among the Ruins of Ramscapelle—I Leave the Company and Lose my Way in the Darkness—A Welcome Light and a Long Sleep—How Little does the Public know of the Dangers and Difficulties a Film Operator has to Face 6

CHAPTER III
WITH THE GOUMIERS AT LOMBARTZYDE

A Morning of Surprises—The German Positions Bombarded from the Sea—Filming the Goumiers in Action—How these Tenacious Fighters Prepare for Battle—Goumier Habits and Customs—I Take the Chief's Photograph for the First Time—And Afterwards take Food with Him—An Interesting and Fruitful Adventure Ends Satisfactorily 15

CHAPTER IV
THE BATTLE OF THE SAND-DUNES

A Dangerous Adventure and What Came of It—A Race Across the Sand-dunes—And a Spill in a Shell-hole—The Fate of a Spy—A Battle in the Dunes—Of which I Secured Some Fine Films—A Collision with an Obstructive Mule . . . 22

CHAPTER V
UNDER HEAVY SHELL-FIRE

In a Trench Coat and Cap I again Run the Gauntlet—A Near Squeak—Looking for Trouble—I Nearly Find It—A Rough Ride and a Mud Bath—An Affair of Outposts—I Get Used to Crawling—Hot Work at the Guns—I am Reported Dead—But Prove Very Much Alive—And then Receive a Shock—A Stern Chase 30

CHAPTER VI
AMONG THE SNOWS OF THE VOSGES

I Start for the Vosges—Am Arrested on the Swiss Frontier—And Released—But Arrested Again—And then Allowed to Go My Way—Filming in the Firing Zone—A Wonderful French Charge Over the Snow-clad Hills—I Take Big Risks—And Get a Magnificent Picture 40

PART II

CHAPTER I
HOW I CAME TO MAKE OFFICIAL WAR PICTURES

I am Appointed an Official War Office Kinematographer—And Start for the Front Line Trenches—Filming the German Guns in Action—With the Canadians—Picturesque Hut Settlement Among the Poplars—"Hyde Park Corner"—Shaving by Candlelight in Six Inches of Water—Filming in Full View of the German Lines, 75 yards away—A Big Risk, but a Realistic Picture 51

CHAPTER II
CHRISTMAS DAY AT THE FRONT

Leave-taking at Charing Cross—A Fruitless Search for Food on Christmas Eve—How Tommy Welcomed the Coming of the Festive Season—" Peace On Earth, Good Will To Men" to the Boom of the Big Guns—Filming the Guards' Division—And the Prince of Wales—Coming from a Christmas Service—This Year and Next 61

CHAPTER III
I GET INTO A WARM CORNER

Boxing Day—But No Pantomime—Life in the Trenches—A Sniper at Work—Sinking a Mine Shaft—The Cheery Influence of an Irish Padre—A Cemetery Behind the Lines—Pathetic Inscriptions and Mementos on Dead Heroes' Graves—I Get Into a Pretty Warm Corner—And Have Some Difficulty in Getting Out Again—But All's Well that Ends Well 65

CHAPTER IV
THE BATTLEFIELD OF NEUVE CHAPELLE

A Visit to the Old German Trenches—Reveals a Scene of Horror that Defies Description—Dodging the Shells—I Lose the Handle of My Camera—And then Lose My Man—The Effect of Shell-fire on a Novice—In the Village of Neuve Chapelle—A Scene of Devastation—The Figure of the Lonely Christ . . . 72

CHAPTER V
FILMING THE PRINCE OF WALES

How I Made a " Hide-up "—And Secured a Fine Picture of the Prince Inspecting some Gun-pits—His Anxiety to Avoid the Camera—And His Subsequent Remarks—How a German Block-house was Blown to Smithereens—And the Way I Managed to Film it Under Fire 76

CHAPTER VI
MY FIRST VISIT TO YPRES AND ARRAS

Greeted on Arrival in the Ruined City of Ypres by a Furious Fusillade —I Film the Cloth Hall and Cathedral, and Have a Narrow

CONTENTS

Escape—A Once Beautiful Town Now Little More Than a Heap of Ruins—Arras a City of the Dead—Its Cathedral Destroyed—But Cross and Crucifixes Unharmed . . . 80

CHAPTER VII

THE BATTLE OF ST. ELOI

Filming Within Forty-five Yards of the German Trenches—Watching for " Minnies "—Officers' Quarters—" Something " Begins to Happen—An Early Morning Bombardment—Develops Into the Battle of St. Eloi—Which I Film from Our First-Line Trench—And Obtain a Fine Picture 85

CHAPTER VIII

A NIGHT ATTACK—AND A NARROW ESCAPE

A Very Lively Experience—Choosing a Position for the Camera Under Fire—I Get a Taste of Gas—Witness a Night Attack by the Germans—Surprise an Officer by My Appearance in the Trenches—And Have One of the Narrowest Escapes—But Fortunately Get Out with Nothing Worse than a Couple of Bullets Through My Cap 93

CHAPTER IX

FOURTEEN THOUSAND FEET ABOVE THE GERMAN LINES

The First Kinematograph Film Taken of the Western Front—And How I Took It Whilst Travelling Through the Air at Eighty Miles an Hour—Under Shell-fire—Over Ypres—A Thrilling Experience—And a Narrow Escape—A Five Thousand Foot Dive Through Space 107

CHAPTER X

FILMING THE EARTH FROM THE CLOUDS

Chasing an " Enemy " Aeroplane at a Height of 13,500 Feet—And What Came of It—A Dramatic Adventure in which the Pilot Played a Big Part—I Get a Nasty Shock—But am Reassured—A Freezing Experience—Filming the Earth as we Dived Almost Perpendicularly—A Picture that would Defy the Most Ardent Futurist to Paint 116

CHAPTER XI

PREPARING FOR THE "BIG PUSH"

The Threshold of Tremendous Happenings—General ——'s Speech to His Men on the Eve of Battle—Choosing My Position for Filming the " Big Push "—Under Shell-fire—A Race of Shrieking Devils—Fritz's Way of " Making Love "—I Visit the " White City "—And On the Way have Another Experience of Gas Shells 121

viii HOW I FILMED THE WAR

PAGE

CHAPTER XII
FILMING UNDER FIRE

The General's Speech to the Fusiliers Before Going Into Action—Filming the 15-inch Howitzers—A Miniature Earthquake—" The Day " is Postponed—Keeping Within " The Limits "—A Surprise Meeting in the Trenches—A Reminder of Other Days—I Get Into a Tight Corner—And Have An Unpleasantly Hot Experience—I Interview a Trench Mortar—Have a Lively Quarter of an Hour—And Then Get Off 135

CHAPTER XIII
THE DAWN OF JULY FIRST

A Firework Display Heralds the Arrival of " The Day "—How the Boys Spent Their Last Few Hours in the Trenches—Rats as Bedfellows—I Make an Early Start—And Get Through a Mineshaft into " No Man's Land "—The Great Event Draws Near—Anxious Moments—The Men Fix Bayonets—And Wait the Word of Command to " Go Over the Top " 151

CHAPTER XIV
THE DAY AND THE HOUR

A Mighty Convulsion Signalises the Commencement of Operations—Then Our Boys " Go Over the Top "—A Fine Film Obtained whilst Shells Rained Around Me—My Apparatus is Struck—But, Thank Goodness, the Camera is Safe—Arrival of the Wounded—" Am I in the Picture ? " they ask 162

CHAPTER XV
ROLL-CALL AFTER THE FIGHT

A Glorious Band of Wounded Heroes Stagger Into Line and Answer the Call—I Visit a Stricken Friend in a Dug-out—On the Way to La Boisselle I Get Lost in the Trenches—And Whilst Filming Unexpectedly Come Upon the German Line—I Have a Narrow Squeak of Being Crumped—But Get Away Safely—And later Commandeer a Couple of German Prisoners to Act as Porters . 169

CHAPTER XVI
EDITING A BATTLE FILM

The Process Described in Detail—Developing the Negative—Its Projection on the Screen—Cutting—Titling—Joining—Printing the Positive—Building Up the Story—It is Submitted to the Military Censors at General Headquarters—And After Being Cut and Approved by Them—Is Ready for Public Exhibition . . 178

CHAPTER XVII
THE HORRORS OF TRONES WOOD

Three Times I Try and Fail to Reach this Stronghold of the Dead—Which Has Been Described as " Hell on Earth "—At a Dressing Station under Fire—Smoking Two Cigarettes at a Time to Keep off the Flies—Some Amusing Trench Conversations by Men who had Lost Their Way—I Turn in for the Night—And Have a Dead Bosche for Company 183

CONTENTS

CHAPTER XVIII
FILMING AT POZIÈRES AND CONTALMAISON

Looking for " Thrills "—And How I Got Them—I Pass Through " Sausage Valley," on the Way to Pozières—You *May* and you *Might*—What a Tommy Found in a German Dug-out—How Fritz Got " Some of His Own " Back—Taking Pictures in What Was Once Pozières—" Proofs Ready To-morrow " . . . 196

CHAPTER XIX
ALONG THE WESTERN FRONT WITH THE KING

His Majesty's Arrival at Boulogne—At G.H.Q.—General Burstall's Appreciation—The King on the Battlefield of Fricourt—Within Range of the Enemy's Guns—His Majesty's Joke Outside a German Dug-out—His Memento from a Hero's Grave—His Visit to a Casualty Clearing Station—The King and the Puppy—Once in Disgrace—Now a Hospital Mascot 205

CHAPTER XX
KING AND PRESIDENT MEET

An Historic Gathering—In which King and President, Joffre and Haig Take Part—His Majesty and the Little French Girl—I Am Permitted to Film the King and His Distinguished Guests—A Visit to the King of the Belgians—A Cross-Channel Journey—And Home 214

CHAPTER XXI
THE HUSH! HUSH!—A WEIRD AND FEARFUL CREATURE

Something in the Wind—An Urgent Message to Report at Headquarters—And What Came Of It—I Hear for the First Time of the " Hush ! Hush ! "—And Try to Discover What It Is—A Wonderful Night Scene—Dawn Breaks and Reveals a Marvellous Monster—What Is It ? 222

CHAPTER XXII
THE JUGGERNAUT CAR OF BATTLE

A Weird-looking Object Makes Its First Appearance Upon the Battlefield—And Surprises Us Almost as Much as It Surprised Fritz—A Death-dealing Monster that Did the Most Marvellous Things—And Left the Ground Strewn with Corpses—Realism of the Tank Pictures 230

CHAPTER XXIII
WHERE THE VILLAGE OF GUILLEMONT WAS

An Awful Specimen of War Devastation—Preparing for an Advance —Giving the Bosche " Jumps "—Breakfast Under Fire—My Camera Fails Me Just Before the Opening of the Attack—But I Manage to Set it Right and Get Some Fine Pictures—Our Guns " Talk " Like the Crack of a Thousand Thunders—A Wonderful Doctor 234

x   HOW I FILMED THE WAR

PAGE

CHAPTER XXIV
FIGHTING IN A SEA OF MUD

Inspecting a Tank that was *Hors de Combat*—All that was Left of Mouquet Farm—A German Underground Fortress—A Trip in the Bowels of the Earth—A Weird and Wonderful Experience . 245

CHAPTER XXV
THE EVE OF GREAT EVENTS

A Choppy Cross-Channel Trip—I Indulge in a Reverie—And Try to Peer Into the Future—At Headquarters Again—Trying to Cross the River Somme on an Improvised Raft—In Peronne After the German Evacuation—A Specimen of Hunnish " Kultur " . 250

CHAPTER XXVI
AN UNCANNY ADVENTURE

Exploring the Unknown—A Silence That Could be Felt—In the Village of Villers-Carbonel—A Cat and Its Kittens in an Odd Retreat—Brooks' Penchant for " Souvenirs "—The First Troops to Cross the Somme 259

CHAPTER XXVII
THE GERMANS IN RETREAT

The Enemy Destroy Everything as They Go—Clearing Away the Débris of the Battlefield—And Repairing the Damage Done by the Huns—An Enormous Mine Crater—A Reception by French Peasants—" Les Anglais ! Les Anglais ! "—Stuck on the Road to Bovincourt 266

CHAPTER XXVIII
THE STORY OF AN "ARMOURED CAR" ABOUT WHICH I COULD A TALE UNFOLD

Possibilities—Food for Famished Villagers—Meeting the Mayoress of Bovincourt—Who Presides at a Wonderful Impromptu Ceremony—A Scrap Outside Vraignes—A Church Full of Refugees—A True Pal—A Meal with the Mayor of Bierne . 275

CHAPTER XXIX
BEFORE ST. QUENTIN

The "Hindenburg" Line—A Diabolical Piece of Vandalism—Brigadier H.Q. in a Cellar—A Fight in Mid-air—Waiting for the Taking of St. Quentin—*L'Envoi* 292

ILLUSTRATIONS

FILMING THE PRELIMINARY BOMBARDMENT OF THE "BIG PUSH," JULY 1ST, 1916	*Frontispiece*
	TO FACE PAGE
WITH A GROUP OF BELGIAN OFFICERS AT FURNES, BELGIUM, 1914	12
ON SKIS IN THE VOSGES MOUNTAINS JUST BEFORE THE FRENCH ATTACK, FEBRUARY AND MARCH, 1915	12
USING MY AEROSCOPE IN BELGIUM, 1914-15	22
HOW I CARRIED MY FILM IN THE EARLY DAYS OF THE WAR IN BELGIUM AND THE VOSGES MOUNTAINS	40
THE STATE OF THE TRENCHES IN WHICH WE LIVED AND SLEPT (?) FOR WEEKS ON END DURING THE FIRST AND SECOND WINTER OF WAR	52
OUR DUG-OUTS IN THE FRONT LINE AT PICANTIN IN WHICH WE LIVED, FOUGHT, AND MANY DIED DURING 1914-15, BEFORE THE DAYS OF TIN HATS	52
CHOOSING A POSITION FOR MY CAMERA IN THE FRONT LINE TRENCH AT PICANTIN. WITH THE GUARDS. WINTER, 1915-16	56
THE PRINCE OF WALES TRYING TO LOCATE MY "CAMOUFLAGED CAMERA"	62
THE PRINCE OF WALES LEAVING A TEMPORARY CHURCH AT LA GORGUE, XMAS DAY, 1915	62
ON THE WAY TO THE "MENIN GATE" WITH AN ARTILLERY OFFICER TO FILM OUR GUNS IN ACTION	76
TAKING SCENES IN DEVASTATED YPRES, MAY, 1916	80
IN YPRES, WITH "BABY" BROOKS, THE OFFICIAL STILL PHOTOGRAPHER, MAY, 1916	84
WITH MY AEROSCOPE CAMERA AFTER FILMING THE BATTLE OF ST. ELOI	90
IN THE MAIN STREET OF CONTALMAISON THE DAY OF ITS CAPTURE	96
LAUNCHING A SMOKE BARRAGE AT THE BATTLE OF ST. ELOI	96
IN THE TRENCHES AT THE FAMOUS AND DEADLY "HOHENZOLLERN REDOUBT," AFTER A GERMAN ATTACK	109
IN A SHELL-HOLE IN "NO MAN'S LAND" FILMING OUR HEAVY BOMBARDMENT OF THE GERMAN LINES	122
GEOFFREY H. MALINS, O.B.E., OFFICIAL KINEMATOGRAPHER TO THE WAR OFFICE	132
BOMBARDING THE GERMAN TRENCHES AT THE OPENING BATTLE OF THE GREAT SOMME FIGHT, JULY 1ST, 1916	138
MY OFFICIAL PASS TO THE FRONT LINE TO FILM THE BATTLE OF THE SOMME, JULY 1ST, 1916	138
THE PLAN OF ATTACK AT BEAUMONT HAMEL. JULY 1ST, 1916	146

	TO FACE PAGE
Over the Top of Beaumont Hamel. July 1st, 1916	146
In the Sunken Road at Beaumont Hamel, just before Zero Hour, July 1st, 1916	154
In a Trench Mortar Tunnel, during the Battle of the Somme, at Beaumont Hamel, July 1st, 1916	154
The Opening of the Great Battle of the Somme, July 1st, 1916	162
The Roll Call of the Seaforths at "White City," Beaumont Hamel, July 1st, 1916	168
Fagged out in the "White City" after we Retired to our Trenches, July 1st, 1916	168
The Germans make a Big Counter Attack at La Boisselle and Ovillers, July 3rd and 4th, 1916	176
Men of Scotland Rushing a Mine Crater at the Deadly "Hohenzollern Redoubt"	176
Filming the King during his Visit to France in 1916. He is Accompanied by President Poincaré, Sir Douglas Haig, General Joffre and General Foch	184
His Majesty the King, with President Poincaré, in France, 1916	206
Her Majesty, the Queen of the Belgians, taking a Snap of me at Work while Filming the King	218
The Prince of Wales Speaking with Belgian Officers at La Panne, Belgium	218
The First "Tank" that went into Action, H.M.L.S. "Daphne." September 15th, 1916	222
The Battlefield of "Ginchy"	224
Reserves Watching the Attack at Martinpuich, September 15th, 1916	224
Over the Top at Martinpuich, Sept. 15th, 1916	228
Two Minutes to Zero Hour at Martinpuich, Sept. 15th, 1916	228
The Highland Brigade going Over the Top at Martinpuich, September 15th, 1916	234
Lord Kitchener's Last Visit to France	256
Filming Our Guns in Action during the Great German Retreat to St. Quentin, March, 1917	268
The Quarry from which I Crawled to Film the German Trenches in Front of St. Quentin, 1917	290
Our Outpost Line within 800 Yards of St. Quentin	302

PART I

HOW I FILMED THE WAR

CHAPTER I

A FEW WORDS OF INTRODUCTION

FATE has not been unkind to me. I have had my chances, particularly during the last two or three years, and—well, I have done my best to make the most of what has come my way. That and nothing more.

How I came to be entrusted with the important commission of acting as Official War Office Kinematographer is an interesting story, and the first few chapters of this book recount the sequence of events that led up to my being given the appointment.

Let me begin by saying that I am not a writer, I am just a " movie man," as they called me out there. My mind is stored full to overflowing with the impressions of all I have seen and heard ; recollections of adventures crowd upon me thick and fast. Thoughts flash through my mind, and almost tumble over one another as I strive to record them. Yet at times, when I take pen in hand to write them down, they seem to elude me for the moment, and make the task more difficult than I had anticipated.

In the following chapters I have merely aimed at setting down, in simple language, a record of my impressions, so far as I can recall them, of what I have seen of many and varied phases of the Great

Drama which has now been played to a finish on the other side of the English Channel. Most of those recollections were penned at odd moments, soon after the events chronicled, when they were still fresh in mind, often within range of the guns.

It was my good fortune for two years to be one of the Official War Office Kinematographers. I was privileged to move about on the Western Front with considerable freedom. My actions were largely untrammelled; I had my instructions to carry out; my superiors to satisfy; my work to do; and I endeavoured to do all that has been required of me to the best of my ability, never thinking of the cost, or consequences, to myself of an adventure so long as I secured a pictorial record of the deeds of our heroic Army in France. I have striven to make my pictures worthy of being preserved as a permanent memorial of the greatest Drama in history.

That is the keynote of this record. As an Official Kinematographer I have striven to be, and I have tried all the time to realise that I was the eyes of the millions of my fellow-countrymen at home. In my pictures I have endeavoured to catch something of the glamour, as well as the awful horror of it all. I have caught a picture here, a picture there; a scene in this place, a scene in that; and all the time at the back of my mind has always been the thought: " That will give them some idea of things as they are out here." My pictures have never been taken with the idea of merely making pictures, nor with the sole idea, as some people think, of merely providing a " thrill." I regarded my task in a different light to that. To me has been entrusted the task of securing for the enlightenment and education of the people of to-day, and of future generations, such a picture as will stir their imaginations and thrill their hearts with pride.

This by way of introduction. Now to proceed

INTRODUCTION

with my task, the telling of the adventures of a kinematograph camera man in war-time.

From my early days I was always interested in photography, and boyish experiments eventually led me along the path to my life's vocation. In time I took up the study of kinematography, and joined the staff of the Clarendon Film Company (of London and Croydon), one of the pioneer firms in the industry. There I learned much and made such progress that in time I was entrusted with the filming of great productions, which cost thousands of pounds to make. From there I went to the Gaumont Company, and I was in the service of this great Anglo-French film organisation when war broke out.

During the early days of the autumn of 1914 I was busily occupied in filming various scenes in connection with the war in different parts of the country. One day when I was at the London office of the Company I was sent for by the Chief.

"We want a man to go out to Belgium and get some good 'stuff.' [Stuff, let me say, is the technical or slang term for film pictures.] How would you like to go?"

"Go?" I asked. "I'm ready. When? Now?"

"As soon as you like."

"Right, I'm ready," I said, without a moment's hesitation, little thinking of the nature of the adventure upon which I was so eager to embark.

And so it came about. Provided with the necessary cash, and an Aeroscope camera, I started off next day, and the following chapters record a few of my adventures in search of pictorial material for the screen.

CHAPTER II

WITH THE BELGIANS AT RAMSCAPELLE

I Reach the First Line Belgian Trenches—And become a Belgian Soldier for the Time Being—A Night Attack—An Adventure whilst Filming a Mitrailleuse Outpost—Among the Ruins of Ramscapelle—I Leave the Company and Lose my Way in the Darkness—A Welcome Light and a Long Sleep—How Little does the Public know of the Dangers and Difficulties a Film Operator has to Face.

LEAVING London, I crossed to France. I arranged, as far as possible, to get through from Calais to Furnes, and with the greatest of good luck I managed it, arriving at my destination at eleven o'clock at night. As usual, it was raining hard.

Starting out next day for the front line, I reached the district where a battalion was resting—I was allowed in their quarters. Addressing one of the men, I asked if he could speak English. "Non, monsieur," and making a sign to me to remain he hurried off. Back came the fellow with an officer.

"What do you want, monsieur?" said he in fine English.

"You speak English well," I replied.

"Yes, monsieur, I was in England for four years previous to the war." So I explained my position. "I want to accompany you to the trenches to take some kinema films."

After exchanging a few words he took me to his superior officer, who extended every courtesy to me. I explained to him what I was desirous of doing.

"But it is extraordinary, monsieur, that you should

AT RAMSCAPELLE

take such risks for pictures. You may in all probability get shot."

" Possibly, sir," I replied, " but to obtain genuine scenes one must be absolutely in the front line."

" Ah, you English," he said, " you are *extraordinaire*." Suddenly taking me by the arm, he led me to an outhouse. At the door we met his Captain. Introducing me, he began to explain my wishes. By the looks and the smiles, I knew things were going well for me.

Calling the interpreter, the Captain said, " If you accompany my men to the trenches you may get killed. You must take all risks. I cannot be held responsible, remember ! " And with a smile, he turned and entered the house.

Hardly realising my good fortune, I nearly hugged my new friend, the Lieutenant.

" Monsieur," I said, saluting, " I am un Belge soldat *pro tem*."

Laughingly he told me to get my kit ready, and from a soldier who could speak English I borrowed a water-bottle and two blankets. Going round to the back of the farm, I came upon the rest of the men being served out with coffee from a copper. Awaiting my turn, I had my water-bottle filled ; then the bread rations were served out with tinned herrings. Obtaining my allowance, I stowed it away in my knapsack, rolled up my blanket and fixed it on my back, and was ready. Then the " Fall in " was sounded. What a happy-go-lucky lot ! No one would have thought these men were going into battle, and that many of them would probably not return. This, unfortunately, turned out to be only too true.

In my interest in the scene and anxiety to film it, I was forgetting to put my own house in order. "What if I don't come back ? " I suddenly thought. Begging some paper, I wrote a letter, addressed to my firm, telling them where I had gone, and where to call at Furnes for my films in the event of my being shot. Addressing it, I left it in charge of an officer, to be posted if I did not return, and requested that if anything happened to me my stuff should be left at my café in Furnes. Shaking me by the hand, he said he sincerely hoped it would not be necessary. Laughingly I bade him adieu. Falling in with the other men we started off, with the cheers and good wishes of those left behind ringing in our ears.

It was still raining, and, as we crossed the fields of mud, I began to feel the weight of my equipment pressing on my shoulders, which with my camera and spare films made my progress very slow. Many a time during that march the men offered to help me, but, knowing that they had quite enough to do in carrying their own load, I stubbornly refused.

On we went, the roar of the guns getting nearer: over field after field, fully eighteen inches deep in mud, and keeping as close to hedges as possible, to escape detection from hostile aeroplanes. Near a bridge we were stopped by an officer.

"What's the matter?" I asked of my interpreter. Not knowing, he went to enquire.

An order was shouted. The whole regiment rushed for cover to a hedge which ran by the roadside. I naturally followed. My friend told me that the Germans had sent up an observation balloon, so we dare not advance until nightfall, or they would be sure to see us and begin shelling our column before we arrived at the trenches. In the rain we sat huddled close together. Notwithstanding the uncomfortable conditions, I was very thankful for the rest. Night came, and we got the word to start again. Progress was becoming more difficult than ever, and I only kept myself from many a time falling headlong by clinging on to my nearest companion; he did likewise.

Ye gods! what a night, and what a sight! Raining hard, a strong wind blowing, and the thick, black, inky darkness every now and then illuminated by the flash of the guns. Death was certainly in evidence to-night. One felt it. The creative genius of the weirdest, imaginative artist could not have painted a scene of death so truthfully. The odour arising from decaying bodies in the ground was at times almost overwhelming.

We had been conversing generally during the march, but now word was passed that we were not to speak under any circumstances, not until we were in the trenches. A whispered order came that every man must hold on to the comrade in front of him, and bear to the left. Reaching the trench allotted to us, we went along it in single file, up to our knees in water. Sometimes a plank had been thrown along it, or bricks, but generally there was nothing but mud to plough through.

"Halt!" came the command to the section I was with. "This is our shelter, monsieur," said a voice.

Gropingly, I followed the speaker on hands and knees. The shelter was about 12 feet long, 3 feet 6 inches high, the same in width, and made of old boards. On the top, outside, was about 9 inches of earth, to render it as far as possible shrapnel-proof. On the floor were some boards, placed on bricks and covered with soddened straw. There was just enough room for four of us.

Rolling ourselves in our blankets we lay down, and by the light of an electric torch we ravenously ate our bread and herrings. I enjoyed that simple meal as much as the finest dinner I have ever had placed before me. Whilst eating, a messenger came and warned us to be prepared for an attack. Heavy rifle-fire was taking place, both on the right and left of our position.

"Well," thought I, "this is a good start; they might have waited for daylight, I could then film their proceedings." At any rate, if the attack came, I hoped it would last through the next day.

Switching off the light, we lay down and awaited events. But not for long. The order came to man the trench. Out we tumbled, and took up our positions. Suddenly out of the blackness, in the direction of the German positions, came the rattle of rifle-fire, and the bullets began to whistle overhead. Keeping as low as possible, we replied, firing in quick succession at the flashes of the enemy rifles. This continued throughout the night.

Towards morning a fog settled down, which blocked out our view of each other, and there was a lull in the fighting. At midday the attack started again. Taking my apparatus, I filmed a section of Belgians in action. Several times bullets whistled unpleasantly near my head. Passing along the trench, I filmed a mitrailleuse battery in action, which was literally mowing down the Germans as fast as they appeared. Then I filmed another section of men, while the bullets were flying all around them. Several could not resist looking round and laughing at the camera.

Whilst thus engaged, several shells fell within thirty feet of me. Two failed to explode; another exploded and sent a lump of mud full in my face. With great spluttering, and I must admit a little swearing, I quickly cleaned it off. Then I filmed a large shell-hole filled with water, caused by the explosion of a German "Jack Johnson."

The diameter was 28 feet across, and, roughly, 6 feet deep in the centre. At the other end of the line I filmed a company damming the Canal, to turn it into the German trenches.

AT RAMSCAPELLE

Then I cautiously made my way back, and filmed a section being served with hot coffee while under fire. Coming upon some men warming themselves round a bucket-stove, I joined the circle for a little warmth. How comforting it was in that veritable morass. Even as we chatted we were subjected to a heavy shrapnel attack, and the way we all scuttled to the trench huts was a sight for the gods. It was one mad scramble of laughing soldiers. Plunk—plunk—plunk—came the shells, not 20–25 feet from where we were sitting by the fire. Six shells fell in our position, one failed to explode. I had a bet with a Belgian officer that it was 30 feet from us. He bet me it was 40 feet. Not to be done, I roughly measured off a yard stick, and left the shelter of the trench to measure the distance. It turned out to be 28 feet. Just as I had finished, I heard three more shells come shrieking towards me. I simply dived for the trench, and luckily reached it just in time.

Towards evening our artillery shelled a farm-house about three-quarters of a mile distant, where the Germans had three guns hidden, and through the glasses I watched the shells drop into the building and literally blow it to pieces. Unfortunately, it was too far off to film it satisfactorily.

That night was practically a repetition of the previous one. The trench was attacked the greater part of the time, and bullets continually spattered against the small iron plate.

Next morning I decided to try and film the mitrailleuse outpost on a little spot of land in the floods, only connected by a narrow strip of grass-land just high enough to be out of reach of the water. Still keeping low under cover of the trenches, I made my way in that direction. Several officers tried to persuade me not to go, but knowing it would make an excellent scene, I decided to risk it. On the side of the bank nearest our front line the ground sloped at a more abrupt angle, the distance from the trench to the outpost being about sixty yards. Rushing over the top of the parapet, I got to the edge of the grass road and crouched down. The water up to my knees, I made my way carefully along. Twice I stumbled over dead bodies. At last I reached the outpost safely, but during the last few yards I must have raised myself a little too high, for the next minute several bullets splashed into the water where I had been.

The outpost was very surprised when I made my appearance, and expressed astonishment that I had not been shot. "A miss is as good as a mile," I laughingly replied, and then I told them I had come to film them at work. This I proceeded to do, and got an excellent scene of the mitrailleuse in action, and the other section loading up. The frightful slaughter done by these guns is indescribable. Nothing can possibly live under the concentrated fire of these weapons, as the Germans found to their cost that day.

After getting my scenes, I thanked the officer, and was about to make my way back; but he forbade me to risk it, telling me to wait until night and return under cover of the darkness. To this I agreed, and that night left the outpost with the others when the relief party came up.

Shortly after news was received that we were to be relieved from duty in the trenches for the next forty-eight hours; the relief column was on its way to take our places. I was delighted, for I had been wet through during the days and nights I had been there, but was fully satisfied that I had got some real live films. Hastily packing up my equipment, I stood waiting the signal to move off. At last the relief came up. Holding each other's hands, we carefully made our way in Indian file along the trench, on to the road, and into Ramscapelle.

WITH A GROUP OF BELGIAN OFFICERS AT FURNES, BELGIUM, 1914.
ONE OF THEM USED TO ACT AS MY COURIER

ON SKIES IN THE VOSGES MOUNTAINS JUST BEFORE THE FRENCH ATTACK,
FEBRUARY AND MARCH, 1915

AT RAMSCAPELLE

What a terrible sight it was! The skeletons of houses stood grim and gaunt, and the sound of the wind rushing through the ruins was like the moaning of the spirits of the dead inhabitants crying aloud for vengeance. The sounds increased in volume as we neared this scene of awful desolation, and the groans became a crescendo of shrieks which, combined with the crash of shell-fire, made one's blood run cold.

Leaving the ruins behind we gained the main road, and on arriving at the bridge where we had stopped on our journey out, I parted with the company, thinking to make my way to a café by a short cut over some fields. I wished to heaven afterwards that I had not done so. I cut across a ditch, feeling my way as much as possible with a stick. But I had not gone far before I knew I had lost my way. The rain was driving pitilessly in my face, but I stumbled on in the inky darkness, often above my knees in thick clay mud. Several times I thought I should never reach the road. It was far worse than being under fire.

I must have staggered along for about two miles when I perceived a light ahead. Never was sight more welcome. Remember, I had about fifty to sixty pounds weight on my back, and having had little or no sleep for five nights my physical strength was at a low ebb. It seemed hours before I reached that house, and when at last I got there I collapsed on the floor.

I struggled up again in a few minutes, and asked the bewildered occupants to give me hot coffee, and after resting for an hour, I made again for Furnes reaching it in the early hours of the morning.

Going to my café, I went to bed, and slept for eighteen hours; the following day I packed up and returned to London.

A day or two afterwards I was sitting comfortably

in a cushioned chair in the private theatre at our London office watching these selfsame scenes being projected upon the screen. Ah! thought I, how little does the great public, for whom they are intended, know of the difficulties and dangers, the trials and tribulations, the kinematograph camera man experiences in order to obtain these pictures.

CHAPTER III

WITH THE GOUMIERS AT LOMBARTZYDE

A Morning of Surprises—The German Positions Bombarded from the Sea—Filming the Goumiers in Action—How these Tenacious Fighters Prepare for Battle—Goumier Habits and Customs—I Take the Chief's Photograph for the First Time—And Afterwards take Food with Him—An Interesting and Fruitful Adventure Ends Satisfactorily.

ONCE more I went to Furnes, and while sipping my coffee at the café I heard a remark made about the Goumiers (the Arab horsemen employed by the French as scouts). Quickly realising the possibilities in a film of such a body of men, I made enquiries of the speakers as to their whereabouts.

"Ah, monsieur, they are on the sand-dunes near Nieuport. They are veritable fiends, monsieur, with the Bosches, who run away from them like cats. They are terrible fighters."

After such a glowing account, I thought the sooner I interviewed these fighters the better.

Starting out next morning, I made a bee-line for the coast.

I soon began to hear the sharp crackle of rifle-fire, and artillery on my right opened fire on the German position, and then the heavy boom, boom of the guns from the sea. Looking in that direction, I discerned several of our battleships opening fire, the shells giving a fearful shriek as they passed overhead. The Germans were certainly in for it that day.

Keeping along the bottom of the dunes, I observed

a Goumier encampment in the distance. At that moment there came a rasping voice on my right.

"Halt!" This certainly was a morning of surprises.

"Ah," I said, with a laugh, "you startled me."

"I am sorry, monsieur," he said. "The password, if you please?"

"It is not necessary," I replied. "I wish to speak to your officer. I will go by myself to the officer in charge, it is not necessary for you to leave your post. Direct me to Headquarters, and tell me your captain's name."

"Captain ——, monsieur. He is billeted in that house which is half destroyed by shell-fire. Be careful, monsieur, and keep low, or you will draw the fire on you." He saluted, and turned back to his post.

Making straight for the ruined house in question, I observed a sentry on guard at the door. This, I perceived, led to a cellar. I asked to see the Captain. The man saluted and entered the house, appearing in a few minutes with his chief. I saluted, and bade him "good morning," extending my hand, which he grasped in a hearty handshake. I straightway explained my business, and asked him for his co-operation in securing some interesting films of the Goumiers in action.

He replied that he would be glad to assist me as far as possible.

"You will greatly help me, sir," I said, "if you can roughly give me their location."

"That I cannot do," he replied, "but follow my directions, and take your chance. I will, however, accompany you a short distance."

We started out, keeping as much to the seashore as possible.

"Keep low," the Captain said, "the place is thick with Bosche snipers." I certainly needed no

THE GOUMIERS AT LOMBARTZYDE 17

second warning, for I had experienced those gentry before. " Our Goumiers are doing splendid work here on the dunes. It is, of course, like home to them among the sand-heaps."

Our conversation was suddenly cut short by the shriek of a shell coming in our direction. Simultaneously we fell flat on the sand, and only just in time, for on the other side of the dune the shell fell and exploded, shaking the ground like a miniature earthquake and throwing clouds of sand in our direction.

" They have started on our encampment again," the Captain said, " but our huts are quite impervious to their shells; the sand is finer than armourplate."

Several more shells came hurtling overheard, but fell some distance behind us. Looking over the top of the dune, I expected to see an enormous hole, caused by the explosion, but judge my surprise on seeing hardly any difference. The sides of the cavity had apparently fallen in again. A short distance further on the Captain said he would leave me.

"You can start now," and he pointed in the distance to a moving object in the sand, crawling along on its stomach for all the world like a snake. " I will go," he said, " and if you see the Chief of the Goumiers, tell him I sent you." With a handshake we parted. I again turned to look at the Goumier scout, his movements fascinated me. Keeping low under the top of the dune, I made for a small hill, from which I decided to film him. Reaching there, I did so.

I then saw, going in opposite directions, two more scouts, each proceeding to crawl slowly in the same fashion as the first.

" This film certainly will be unique," I thought. Who could imagine that within half an hour's ride of this whirling sand, with full-blooded Arabs moving about upon it, the soldiers of Belgium are fighting in two feet of mud and water, and have been doing so for months past. No one would think so to look at it.

A rattle of musketry on my right served as a hint that there were other scenes to be secured. Making my way in the direction of the sound, I came upon a body of Goumiers engaged in sniping at the Germans. I filmed them, and was just moving away when the interpreter of the company stopped and questioned me. I told him of my previous conversation with the Captain, which satisfied him.

"Well," he said, "you are just in time to catch a troop going off on a scouting expedition," and he led the way to a large dune looking down on the sea, and there just moving off was the troop.

What a magnificent picture they made, sitting on their horses. They seemed to be part of them. Veritable black statues they looked, and their movements were like a finely tensioned spring. Hastily filming the troop, I hurried across and succeeded in obtaining some scenes of another detachment proceeding further on the flank, and as they wound in and out up the sand-hills, I managed to get into a splendid point of vantage, and filmed them coming towards me. Their wild savage huzzas, as they passed, were thrilling in the extreme. Looking round, I perceived a curious-looking group a short distance away, going through what appeared to be some devotional ceremony.

Hastening down the hill, I crossed to the group, which turned out to be under the command of the Chief of the Goumiers himself, who was going through a short ceremony with some scouts, previous to their meeting the Germans. It was quite impressive. Forming the four men up in line, the Chief gave each of them instructions, waving signs and symbols over their heads and bodies, then with

THE GOUMIERS AT LOMBARTZYDE 19

a chant sent them on their journey. The actual obeisance was too sacred in itself to film. I was told by the interpreter afterwards that he was glad I did not do so, as they would have been very wrath?

A few words about the customs of the Goumiers may not be out of place. These men are the aristocracy of the Algerian Arabs; men of independent means in their own land. At the outbreak of war they patriotically combined under their chief, and offered themselves to the French Government, which gladly accepted their services for work on the sand-dunes of Flanders. The troop bore the whole cost of their outfit and transport. They brought their own native transport system with them. The men obey none but their chief, at whose bidding they would, I believe, even go through Hell itself. All arguments, quarrels, and discussions in the troop are brought before the Chief, whose word and judgment is law.

On the dunes of Northern Flanders they had their own encampment, conducted in their own native style. They looked after their horses with as much care as a fond mother does her child. The harness and trappings were magnificently decorated with beautiful designs in mother-of-pearl and gold, and the men, when astride their horses and garbed in their long flowing white *burnouses*, looked the very personification of dignity. The Chief never handles a rifle, it would be beneath his position to do so. He is the Head, and lives up to it in every respect possible.

I filmed him by the side of his horse. It was the first time he had been photographed.

Returning to the point where the scouts were leaving, I decided to follow close behind them, on the chance of getting some good scenes. Strapping my camera on my back, and pushing a tuft of grass under the strap, to disguise it as much as possible if viewed from the front, I crawled after them. One may think that crawling on the sand is easy; well, all I can say to those who think so is, " Try it." I soon found it was not so easy as it looked, especially under conditions where the raising of one's body two or three inches above the top of the dune might be possibly asking for a bullet through it, and drawing a concentrated fire in one's direction.

I had crawled in this fashion for about 150 yards, when I heard a shell come shrieking in my direction. With a plunk it fell, and exploded about forty feet away, choking me with sand and half blinding me for about five minutes. The acrid fumes, too, which came from it, seemed to tighten my throat, making respiration very difficult for some ten minutes afterwards. Cautiously looking round, I tried to locate the other scouts, but nowhere could they be seen. I crawled for another thirty yards or so, but still no sign of them. Deciding that if I continued by myself I had everything to lose and nothing to gain, I concluded that discretion was the better part of valour. Possibly the buzzing sensation in my throat, and the smarting of my eyes, helped me in coming to that decision, so I retraced my steps, or rather crawl. Getting back to the encampment, I bathed my eyes in water, which quickly soothed them.

In a short time news came in that the scouts were returning. Hurrying to the spot indicated, I was just in time to film them on their arrival. The exultant look on their faces told me that they had done good work.

I then filmed a general view of the encampment, and several other interesting scenes, and was just on the point of departing when the Chief asked me to partake of some food with him. Being very hungry, I accepted the invitation, and afterwards, over a cup of coffee and cigarettes, I obtained through an interpreter some very interesting information.

The night being now well advanced, I bade the Chief adieu, and striking out across the dunes I made for Furnes. The effect of the star-shells sent up by the Germans was very wonderful. They shed a vivid blue light all round, throwing everything up with startling clearness.

After about a mile I was suddenly brought up by the glitter of a sentry's bayonet. "Password, monsieur." Flashing a lamp in my face, the man evidently recognised me, for he had seen me with his officer that day, and the next moment he apologised for stopping me. "Pardon, monsieur," he said. "Pass, Monsieur Anglais, pardon!"

Accepting his apologies, I moved off in the direction of Furnes, where, after reviewing the events of the previous days, I came to the conclusion that I had every reason to be thankful that I had once more returned from an interesting and fruitful adventure with a whole skin.

CHAPTER IV

THE BATTLE OF THE SAND-DUNES

A Dangerous Adventure and What Came of It—A Race Across the Sand-dunes—And a Spill in a Shell-Hole—The Fate of a Spy—A Battle in the Dunes—Of which I Secured Some Fine Films—A Collision with an Obstructive Mule.

I ARRIVED at Oost-Dunkerque, which place I decided to use as a base for this journey, chiefly because it was on the main route to Nieuport Bain. Having on my previous visit proceeded on foot, and returned successfully, I decided that I should go by car. To get what I required meant that I should have to pass right through the French lines.

Finding out a chauffeur who had previously helped me, I explained my plans to him.

"Well, monsieur," he said, "I will try and help you, but for me it is not possible to get you through. I am stationed here indefinitely, but I have a friend who drives an armoured car. I will ask him to do it." We then parted; I was to meet him with his friend that night.

I packed my things as close as possible, tying two extra spools of film in a package round my waist under my coat, put on my knapsack, and drew my Balaclava helmet well down over my chin.

Anxiously I awaited my friends. Seven o'clock—eight o'clock—nine o'clock. "Were they unable to come for me?" "Was there some hitch in the arrangement?" These thoughts flashed through my mind, when suddenly I heard a voice call behind me.

"Monsieur, monsieur!"

USING MY AEROSCOPE CAMERA IN BELGIUM, 1914-15

THE BATTLE OF THE SAND-DUNES 23

Turning, I saw my chauffeur friend beckoning to me. Hurrying forward, I asked if all was well.

"Oui, monsieur. I will meet you by the railway cutting."

This was the beginning of an adventure which I shall always remember. I had been up at the bridge some two minutes, when the armoured car glided up. "Up, monsieur," came a voice, and up I got. Placing my camera by the side of the mitrailleuse, I sat by my chauffeur, and we started off for the French lines.

Dashing along roads covered with shell-holes, I marvelled again and again at the man's wonderful driving. Heaps of times we escaped a smash-up by a hair's-breadth.

On we went over the dunes; the night was continuously lighted up by flashes from the big guns, both French and German. We were pulled up with a jerk, which sent me flying over the left wheel, doing a somersault, and finally landing head first into a lovely soft sandbank. Spluttering and staggering to my feet, I looked round for the cause of my sudden exit from the car, and there in the glare of the headlight were two French officers. Both were laughing heartily and appreciating the joke. As I had not hurt myself, I joined in. After our hilarity had subsided they apologised, and hoped I had not hurt myself. Seeing that I was an an Englishman, they asked me where I was going. I replied, "to Nieuport Bain." They asked me if my chauffeur might take a message to the Captain of the —— Chasseurs. "Yes, yes," I replied, "with pleasure."

Thinking that by staying every second might be dangerous, I asked the officers to give the message, and we would proceed. They did so, and again apologising for their abrupt appearance, they bade us "good night."

I hurriedly bade the driver start off, and away we went. He evidently had not got over his nervousness, for, after going about three-quarters of a mile, we ran into a large, partially filled shell-hole, burying the front wheels above the axle. To save myself from a second dive, I clutched hold of the mitrailleuse.

This was a position indeed! Scooping away as much sand as possible from the front wheels, we put on full power, and tried to back the car out of it. But as the rear wheels were unable to grip in the sand it would not budge.

While there the Germans must have seen our light, for suddenly a star-shell shot up from their position, illuminating the ground for a great distance. I swiftly pinched the tube of our headlight, so putting it out, then dropped full length on the sand. I observed my companion had done the same.

We lay there for about ten minutes, not knowing what to expect, but luckily nothing happened. It was obvious that we could not move the car without assistance, so shouldering my apparatus we started to walk the remaining distance. Twice we were held up by sentries, but by giving the password we got through. Enquiring for the headquarters of Captain ——, we were directed to a ruined house which had been destroyed by German shell-fire. " Mon Capitaine is in the cellar, monsieur."

Thinking that it would be a better introduction if I personally delivered the message to the Captain, I asked my chauffeur to let me do so. Asking the sentry at the door to take me to his Captain, we passed down some dozen steps and into a comfortably furnished cellar. Sitting round a little table were seven officers. I asked for Captain ——.

" He is not here, monsieur," said one. " Is it urgent ? "

" I do not know," I replied. I was trying to form

BATTLE OF THE SAND-DUNES

another reply in French, when an officer asked me in English if he could be of any service. I told him that an officer had given me a message to deliver on my journey here, but owing to an accident to the car I had had to walk. Taking the letter, he said he would send a messenger to the Captain with it.

"You must be hungry, monsieur. Will you share a snack with us?" Gladly accepting their hospitality, I sat down with them. "Are you from London?" he asked.

"Yes," I said. "Do you know it?"

"Yes, yes," he replied. "I was for three years there. But are you *militaire?*" he enquired.

"Well, hardly that," I confess. "I am here to take kinema records of the war. I have come in this direction to film an action on the sand-dunes. Will you help me?"

"I will do what I can for you," he replied. "We expect to make a sortie to-morrow morning. It will be very risky for you."

"I will take my chance," I replied, "with you."

Whilst our conversation proceeded, I noticed a scuffling on the cellar steps, then into the room came four soldiers with a man in peasant's clothes. He turned out to be a spy caught signalling in the dunes. They brought him in to have a cup of coffee before taking him out to be shot. He was asked if he would take sugar; his reply was "No."

Presently there was a shot outside, and there was one spy the less.

The Captain returned and, after explanations, made me understand that he would accept no responsibility for my safety. Those conditions I did not mind a scrap. Rolling myself in a blanket, I tumbled in. "What would the morrow bring forth?" I wondered.

I was up next morning at four o'clock. Everywhere there was a state of suppressed excitement.

Outside the men were preparing, but there was not the least sign of confusion anywhere. To look at them one would not imagine these men were going out to fight, knowing that some of them at least would not return again. But it is war, and sentiment has no place in their thoughts.

The order came to line up. Hours before the scouts had gone out to prepare the ground. They had not returned yet. Personally, I hoped they would not turn up till the day was a little more advanced. Eight o'clock; still not sufficient light for filming. A lieutenant came to me, and said if I would go carefully along the sand-dunes in the direction he suggested, possibly it would be better; he would say no more. I did so; and I had only gone about half a kilometre when, chancing to turn back, I spied coming over the dunes on my right two scouts, running for all they were worth.

Quietly getting my camera into position, I started exposing, being certain this was the opening of the attack. I was not mistaken, for within a few minutes the advance guard came hurrying up in the distance; the attack was about to begin. Suddenly the French guns opened fire; they were concealed some distance in the rear. Shells then went at it thick and fast, shrieking one after the other overhead.

The advance guard opened out, clambered up the dunes, and disappeared over the top, I filming them. I waited until the supporting column came up, and filmed them also. I followed them up and over the dunes. Deploying along the top, they spread out about six metres apart, with the object of deceiving the Germans as to their numbers, until the supporting column reached them. The battle of musketry then rang out. Cautiously advancing with a company, I filmed them take the offensive and make for a large dune forty yards ahead. Successfully reaching it they lay down and fired in

BATTLE OF THE SAND-DUNES   27

rapid succession. Crawling up, I managed to take a fine scene of the attack, showing the explosion of two French shells over the ruins of the town. The Germans evidently found our range, for several shells came whistling unpleasantly near me.

What followed was a succession of scenes, showing the covering columns advancing and others moving round on the flank. The Germans lost very heavily in this engagement, and great progress was made by the gallant French. While filming a section of the flanking party, I had the nearest acquaintance with a shell that I shall ever wish for. I don't think it would have been the good fortune of many to have such an experience and come scathless out of it.

I was kneeling filming the scene, when I heard a shell hurtling in my direction. Knowing that if I moved I might as likely run into it as not, I remained where I was, still operating my camera, when an explosion occurred just behind me, which sounded as if the earth itself had cracked. The concussion threw me with terrific force head over heels into the sand. The explosion seemed to cause a vacuum in the air for some distance around, for try as I would I could not get my breath. I lay gasping and struggling like a drowning man for what seemed an interminable length of time, although it could have only been a few seconds.

At last I pulled round; my first thought was for my camera. I saw it a short distance away, half buried in the sand. Picking it up, I was greatly relieved to find it uninjured, but choked with sand round the lens, which I quickly cleared. The impression on my body, caused by the concussion of the exploding shell, seemed as if the whole of one side of me had been struck with something soft, yet with such terrible force that I felt it all over at the same moment. That is the best way I can describe it, and I assure you I don't wish for a second interview. Noticing some blood upon my hand, I found a small wound on the knuckle. Whether or no it was caused by a small splinter from the shell, I cannot say; in all probability it was, for I do not think striking the soft sand would have caused it.

Turning back, I made for the sea road, and filmed the reserves coming up to strengthen the positions already won. Hurrying across in the direction of another column, I filmed them steadily advancing, while their comrades kept the Germans employed from the top of a large dune. The main body then came up and lined the top for a considerable distance, and at the word of command the whole body arose as one man. For the fraction of a second they were strikingly silhouetted against the sky-line; then with a cheer they charged down the other side.

Darkness was now closing in, making it impossible for me to film any further developments, so I proceeded back to the cellar with an officer and some men. After resting awhile, I decided to go back to Furnes that night with my films and get home with them as quickly as possible. Meeting a small transport car going in the desired direction after some stores, I begged a ride, and getting up beside the driver, we started off. Owing to the enormous shell-holes it was impossible to proceed along the road without a light.

What a magnificent sight it was. Magnesium star-shells were continually being sent up by the Germans. They hung in the air alight for about thirty seconds, illuminating the ground like day. When they disappeared the guns flashed out; then the French replied; after that more star-shells; then the guns spoke again, and so it continued. We were suddenly stopped by an officer warning us to put out our lamp immediately, and proceed

BATTLE OF THE SAND-DUNES

cautiously for about three hundred yards. While doing so a shell came screaming by. We knew then that the Germans had seen our light. We immediately rushed to a shell-proof shelter in the sand. I had barely reached it when a shell exploded close by the car, half destroying the body of it. That was the only one that came anywhere near. Running to see what damage was done, I was pleased to see, by the aid of a covered light, that the chassis was practically uninjured. So starting up we once more proceeded on our journey.

We had several narrow squeaks in negotiating corners and miniature sand-banks, and once we bumped into a mule that had strayed on to the road—but whether it will do so again I don't know, for after the bump it disappeared in a whirl of sand, making a noise like a myriad of fiends let loose. But the remainder of the journey was uneventful, and after a long night's rest I left for Calais.

CHAPTER V

UNDER HEAVY SHELL-FIRE

In a Trench Coat and Cap I again Run the Gauntlet—A Near Squeak—Looking for Trouble—I Nearly Find It—A Rough Ride and a Mud Bath—An Affair of Outposts—I Get Used to Crawling—Hot Work at the Guns—I am Reported Dead—But Prove Very Much Alive——And then Receive a Shock—A Stern Chase.

TIME after time I crossed over to France and so into Belgium, and obtained a series of pictures that delighted my employers, and pleased the picture theatre public. But I wanted something more than snapshots of topical events.

Unfortunately, I had been unable to make previous arrangements for a car to take me into Belgium. The railroad was barred to me, and walking quite out of the question. A motor-car was the only method of travelling. After two days of careful enquiries, I at last found a man to take me. He was in the transport department, taking meat to the trenches. I was to meet him that evening on the outskirts of Calais. And I met him that night at an appointed rendezvous, and started on our journey.

Eventually we entered Furnes. Making my way into a side street, I told my chauffeur to call at a certain address whenever he passed through the town, and if I should require his services further, I would leave a letter to that effect.

I was awakened next morning by being vigorously shaken by my Belgian friend, Jules.

"Quick, monsieur, the Germans are bombarding us," he cried.

Jumping out of bed, I rushed to the window. The next second I heard the shriek of shells coming nearer. With a crash and a fearful explosion they burst practically simultaneously on the houses opposite, completely demolishing them, but luckily killing no one. Hastily dressing, I grabbed my camera and went out into the square and waited, hoping to film, if possible, the explosion of the shells as they fell on the buildings. Two more shells came shrieking over. The few people about were quickly making for the cover of their cellars. Getting my camera into position, ready to swing in any direction, I waited. With deafening explosions the shells exploded in a small street behind me. The Germans were evidently trying to smash up the old Flemish town hall, which was in the corner of the market-place, so I decided to fix my focus in its direction. But though I waited for over an hour, nothing else happened. The Germans had ceased firing for that morning at least. Not till I had gone to my café did I realise the danger I had exposed myself to, but somehow I had seemed so confident that I should not get hit, that to film the explosions entirely absorbed all my thoughts.

Next morning I decided to tour the front line, if possible from Dixmude to Nieuport, making Ramscapelle a centre. I hoped to drop in with an isolated action or a few outpost duels, for up to the present things were going exceedingly slow from my point of view.

Arranging for a dispatch rider to take me along to Ramscapelle, away I went. The roads were in a frightful condition after months of rain, and shell-holes were dotted all over the surface. It is marvellous these men do not more frequently meet death by accident, for what with the back wheel sliding and skidding like an unbroken mule, and dodging round shell-holes as if we were playing musical chairs, and hanging round the driver's waist like a limpet to keep our balance, it was anything but a comfortable experience. In the end one back wheel slipped into a shell-hole and pitched me into a lovely pool of water and mud. Then after remounting, we were edged off the road into the mud again by a heavy transport lorry, and enjoyed a second mud-bath. After that I came to the conclusion that I would rather film a close view of a bayonet charge than do another such journey.

By now I was the most abject-looking specimen of humanity imaginable. My camera in its case was securely fastened on my shoulders as a knapsack, and so, with the exception of a slight derangement, which I soon readjusted, no damage was done. But the motor-cycle suffered considerably, and leaving it alongside the road to await a breakdown lorry to repair it—or a shell to finish it—I proceeded on foot to Ramscapelle.

Within a hundred yards of the ruined town, from the shelter of a wrecked barn came the voice of a Belgian soldier peremptorily ordering me to take cover. Without asking questions, I did so by sprawling full length in a deep wheel-rut, but as I had previously had a mud-bath, a little more or less did not matter. I wriggled myself towards the cover of the barn, when a sharp volley of rifle-fire broke out on my left. Gaining shelter, I asked the soldier the reason of the fusillade.

"Uhlan outposts, monsieur," replied the man laconically.

Keeping under cover, I crawled towards the back of the barn, and ensconced behind some bales of straw, on a small bridge, I filmed this Belgian outpost driving off the Uhlans, and peeping through one of the rifle slots, I could see them showing a clean pair of heels, but not without losing one of their number. He was brought into our lines later, and I was lucky enough to secure the pennon from his lance as a souvenir.

I made my way by various means into the town. The place was absolutely devoid of life. It was highly dangerous to move about in the open. To be seen by the German airmen was the signal for being shelled for about three hours.

Whilst filming some of the ruins, I was startled by a sharp word of command. Turning round, I saw a Belgian soldier, with his rifle pointing at me. He ordered me to advance. I produced my permit, and giving the password, I quite satisfied him. Bidding me come inside he indicated a seat, and asked me to have some soup. And didn't it smell appetising! A broken door served as a table; various oddments, as chairs and the soup-copper, stood in the centre of the table. This proved one of the most enjoyable meals of the campaign.

The soldier told me they had to be very careful to guard against spies. They had caught one only that morning, " but he will spy no more, monsieur," he said, with a significant look.

I rose, and said I must leave them, as I wanted to take advantage of the daylight. I asked my friend if he could give me any information as to the whereabouts of anything interesting to film, as I wanted to take back scenes to show the people of England the ravages caused in Belgium by the Huns, and the brave Belgians in action. He was full of regrets that he was not able to accompany me, but being on duty he dare not move.

With a hearty shake of the hand and best wishes we parted, and, keeping under cover of the ruined buildings as much as possible, I made my way through Ramscapelle. Hardened as I was by now to sights of devastation, I could not help a lump rising in my throat when I came upon children's toys, babies' cots, and suchlike things, peeping out from among the ruins caused by the German guns.

These scenes caused me to wander on in deep thought, quite oblivious to my immediate surroundings. This momentary lapse nearly proved disastrous. By some means I had passed the sentries, and wandered practically on top of a Belgian concealed heavy gun battery. I was quickly brought to my senses by being dragged into a gun trench, absolutely invisible both from the front and above.

Compelled to go on hands and knees into the dug-out, I was confronted by a rather irate Belgian officer, who demanded why I was there walking about and not taking cover. Did I know that I had drawn the enemy's fire, which was very nearly an unpardonable offence?

Quickly realising the seriousness of my position, I thought the best thing to do was to tell him my mission, and so I explained to the officer that I had unconsciously wandered there.

"There, monsieur," he said, "that is what you have done," and at that moment I heard two shells explode fifteen yards behind us. "We dare not reply, monsieur," he said, "because this is a secret battery. Mon Dieu!" he exclaimed, "I hope they cease firing, or they may destroy our defences." Fortunately, the Germans seeing no further sign of life, evidently thought it was a case of an isolated soldier, and so ceased their fire. Imagine my thankfulness.

I enquired if there was anyone there who could speak English. A messenger was sent out and returned with a Belgian, who before the war broke out was a teacher of languages in England. With his aid I gave the chief officer full explanation, and pledged my word of honour that neither names, districts, nor details of positions should ever be mentioned.

Wishing to film some scenes of big guns in action, I enquired whether he was going to fire. He was expecting orders any minute, so making myself as comfortable as possible in the dug-out, I waited. But nothing happened, and that night, and the one following, I slept there.

Early next morning (about 3 a.m.) I was awakened by the noise of a terrific cannonading. Together with the officer I crawled out on to the top of our embankment and viewed the scene. The Germans had started a night attack, the Belgian guns had caught them in the act and were shelling them for all they were worth.

As soon as it was daylight I strapped my camera on my back, and, lying flat in the mud, I edged away in the direction of the battery. Before leaving, the officer gave me a final warning about drawing the Germans' fire. Alternately crawling and working my way on hands and knees, and taking advantage of any little bit of cover, I drew nearer to the guns. While I was lying here, there crashed out a regular inferno of rifle-fire from the German trenches. The bullets sang overhead like a flight of hornets. This certainly was a warm corner. If I had filmed this scene, all that would have been shown was a dreary waste of mud-heaps, caused by the explosion of the shells, and the graves of fallen soldiers dotted all over the place. As far as the eye could see the country was absolutely devoid of any living thing.

Thousands of people in England, comfortably seated in the picture theatre, would have passed this scene by as quite uninteresting except for its memories. But if the sounds I heard, and the flying bullets that whizzed by me, could have been photographed, they might take a different view of it.

Death was everywhere. The air was thick with it.

To have lifted my head would have meant the billet for a bullet. So there I had to lie soaked through to the skin, and before I had been there twenty minutes I was literally lying in water. The German fusillade seemed interminable. Suddenly with a roar the Belgian guns spoke. About fifty shells were fired, and gradually the rifle-fire ceased. With a sigh of relief I drew myself out of the hole which my body had made, and on my elbows and knees, like a baby crawling, I covered the intervening ground to the battery. Getting up, and bending nearly double, I ran under cover of the barricades.

The men were astounded to see me run in. I went in the direction of a group of officers, who looked at me in amazement. Saluting me, one of them came forward and asked who I wanted. Explaining my business, I told him I had permission from headquarters to film any scenes of interest. The officer then introduced me to his friends, who asked me how in the world I had crossed the district without getting hit. I described my movements, and they all agreed that I was exceedingly lucky.

Once more the guns started, so getting my camera ready I commenced filming them in action, one scene after another. I changed from the firing of one gun to the full battery in action. The men were working like mad. All the time they were baling water out of the gun trenches with buckets. In some cases after the gun had fired it sank back about eighteen inches in the mud, and had to be dug out and set again. These poor devils had been doing this for nearly four months, every man of them was a hero.

While taking these scenes, my compressed air cylinders ran out. Looking round for somewhere solid on which to put my machine and foot-pump, I found some bricks, and made a little foundation. Then I started to pump up. At every six strokes of the pump, it was necessary to pack under it more bricks, and still more, for the ground was a veritable morass. In the ordinary way my camera takes ten minutes to refill. On this occasion it took me forty-five minutes, and all the time guns were thundering out.

Making my way in a semi-circle, under cover of the communication trenches, to the most advanced outpost, I filmed a party of Belgian snipers hard at work, cheerfully sniping off any German unwise enough to show the smallest portion of his head. Several times while I was watching, I noticed one of the men mark upon his rifle with the stub of a pencil. I asked why he did it.

"That, monsieur," he replied, "is a mark for every Bosche I shoot. See," he said, holding the butt-end for me to look at, and I noticed twenty-eight crosses marked upon it. Snatching it up to his shoulder he fired again, and joyfully he added another cross.

By this time it was getting dark, and quite impossible to take any more scenes, so I returned to the battery, where the officer kindly invited me to stay the night. Getting some dry straw from a waterproof bag, we spread it out on the boards of the trench-hut, rolled our blankets round our shoulders, and lighted our cigarettes. Then they asked me about England. They told me that as long as Belgium existed they would never forget what England had done for her people. While talking our candle went out, and as we had no other we sat in the darkness, huddled together to keep warm. Heavy rain again came on, penetrating through the earth roof and soaking into my blanket.

I must have dozed off, for after a little while I awoke with a start and, looking towards the entrance, I noticed a blue-white glare of light. As my companions were getting out, I followed them, in time to see the Germans sending up star-shells, to guard against any attack on our part.

The following day I filmed several scenes connected with the Belgian artillery and outposts. I waited during the remainder of the day to catch, if possible, some scenes of German shells exploding, but again I was doomed to disappointment, for, with the exception of a few at a distance, I was never able to get the close ones in my field of view.

Having exhausted my stock of film, I decided to return to my base, but on bidding adieu to the Commandant he begged me to return under cover of darkness. That night I set out for Furnes, and after walking about an hour, I was lucky enough to get a lift in an ambulance waggon, which set me down in the market-place.

Entering the café by a side door, my Belgian friend seemed to me to be astounded at my appearance. He immediately rushed up to me, shook my hands and pummelled my back. His friends did the same. After I had got over my astonishment, I ventured to ask the reason for this jubilation.

"We thought you were dead," he cried; "we heard you had been shot by the Germans, and as you had not turned up for the last five days, we came to the conclusion that it was true. But, monsieur, we cannot tell you how pleased we are to see you again alive and well."

Seeing the condition I was in, they heated water for a bath, and assisted me in every way possible. When I was once more comfortable, I asked my friend, over a cup of coffee, to tell me the exact report, as it highly amused me.

"Well, monsieur," he said, " your motor cyclist came rushing in the other evening, saying that Monsieur Malins, the Englishman, had been shot while crossing ground between the two batteries. He told us that you had been seen attempting the crossing; that you suddenly threw up your arms, and pitched forward dead. And, monsieur, we were preparing to send your bag to London, with a letter explaining the sad news. The Colonel was going to write the letter."

"Well," I replied with a laugh, "I am worth a good many dead men yet. I remember crossing the ground you mention—but, anyway, the 'eye-witness' who saw my death was certainly 'seeing things.'"

CHAPTER VI

AMONG THE SNOWS OF THE VOSGES

I Start for the Vosges—Am Arrested on the Swiss Frontier—And Released—But Arrested Again—And then Allowed to Go My Way—Filming in the Firing Zone—A Wonderful French Charge Over the Snow-clad Hills—I Take Big Risks—And Get a Magnificent Picture.

THE man who wants to film a fight, unlike the man who wants to describe it, must be really on the spot. A comfortable corner in the Hôtel des Quoi, at Boulogne, is no use to the camera man.

"Is it possible to film actual events with the French troops in the Vosges and Alsace?" I was asked when I got back after my last adventure.

"If the public wants those films," I replied, "the public must have them." And without any previous knowledge of the district, or its natural difficulties, apart from the normal military troubles to which by that time I was hardened, I set out for Paris, determined to plan my route according to what I learned there. And for the rest I knew it would be luck that would determine the result, because other camera men had attempted to cover the same district, men who knew everything there was to be known in the way of getting on the spot, and all had been turned back with trifling success.

For various reasons, among them the claims of picturesqueness, St. Dié struck me as the best field, and to get there it is necessary to make a detour into Switzerland. From Geneva, where I arranged for transport of my films in case of urgent need, much

HOW I CARRIED MY FILM IN THE EARLY DAYS OF THE WAR IN BELGIUM AND THE VOSGES MOUNTAINS

THE SNOWS OF THE VOSGES 41

as an Arctic explorer would leave supplies of food behind him on his way to the Pole, I arranged in certain places that if I was not heard from at certain dates and certain times, enquiries were to be made, diplomatically, for me.

From Basle I went to the Swiss frontier, and had a splendid view of the Alsace country, which was in German possession. German and Swiss guards stood on either side of the boundary, and they made such a picturesque scene that I filmed them, which was nearly disastrous. A gendarme pounced on me at once, took me to general headquarters and then back to Perrontruy, where I was escorted through the streets by an armed guard.

At the military barracks I was thoroughly examined by the chief of the staff, who drew my attention to a military notice, prohibiting any photographing of Swiss soldiery. He decided that my offence was so rank that it must go before another tribunal, and off I was marched to Delemont, where a sort of court-martial was held on me. My film, of course, was confiscated; that was the least I could expect, but they also extracted a promise in writing that I would not take any more photographs in Switzerland, and they gave me a few hours to leave the country, by way of Berne.

That didn't suit me at all. Berne was too far away from my intended destination, and, after a hurried study of the map, I decided to chance it, and go to Biel. I did. So did the man told off to watch me. And when I left the train at Biel he arrested me. I am afraid I sang " Rule Britannia " very loudly to those good gentlemen before whom he took me, claiming the right of a British citizen to do as he liked, within reason, in a neutral country.

In the result they told me to get out of the country any way I liked, if only I would get out, and, as my opinion was much the same, we parted good friends.

I had lost a week, and many feet of good film, which showed me that the difficulties I should have to face in my chosen field of operations were by far the greatest I had up to then encountered in any of my trips to the firing line. I pushed on through Besançon on the way to Belfort.

Now Belfort, being a fortified town, was an obviously impossible place for me to get into, because I shouldn't get out again in a hurry. So I took a slow train, descended at a small station on the outskirts, prepared to make my way across country to Remiremont. This I achieved, very slowly, and with many difficulties, by means of peasants' carts and an occasional ride on horseback.

This brought me into the firing zone, and the region of snow. My danger was increased, and my mode of progress more difficult, because for the first time in my life I had to take to skis. So many people have told the story of their first attempts with these that I will content myself with saying that, after many tumbles, I became roughly accustomed to them, and that when sledge transport was not available, I was able to make my way on ski. I don't suppose anyone else has ever learned to ski under such queer conditions, with the roar of big guns rumbling round all the time, with my whole expedition trembling every moment in the balance.

The end of my journey to St. Dié was the most dramatic part of the whole business. Tired out, I saw a café on the outskirts of the village, which I thought would serve me as a reconnoitring post, so I went in and ordered some coffee. I had not been there five minutes when some officers walked in, and drew themselves up sharply when they saw a stranger there, in a mud-stained costume that might have been a British army uniform. I decided to take the bold course. I rose, saluted them, and in my Anglo-French wished them good evening. They returned my greeting and sat down, conversing in an undertone, with an occasional side-flung glance at me. I saw that my attack would have to be pushed home, especially as I caught the word "*espion*," or my fevered imagination made me think I did.

I rose and crossed to their table, all smiles, and in my best French heartily agreed with them that one has to be very careful in war time about spies. In fact, I added, I had no doubt they took me for one.

This counter-attack—and possibly the very noticeable Britishness of my accent—rather confused them. Happily one of them spoke a little English, and, with that and my little French, satisfactory explanations were made.

I affected no secrecy about my object, and asked them frankly if it would be possible for pictures of their regiment to be taken. One of them promised to speak to the Commandant about it. I begged them not to trouble about it, however, as really all I wanted was a hint as to when and where an engagement was probable, and then I would manage to be there.

They shrugged their shoulders in a most grimly expressive way.

"If you do that it will be at your own risk," they said.

I gladly accepted the risk, and they then told me of one or two vantage points in the district from which I might manage to see something of the operations, taking my chance, of course, of anything happening near enough to be photographed, as they could not, and quite rightly would not, say anything as to the plans for the future.

It was not quite midday. I had at least four hours of daylight, and I determined not to lose them. It was obvious that my stay in St. Dié would be very brief at the best. I hired a sledge and persuaded the driver to take me part of the way at least to the nearest point which the officers had mentioned.

But neither he nor his horse liked the way the shells were coming around, and at last even his avarice refused to be stimulated further at the expense of his courage. So I strapped on my skis, thankful for my earlier experience with them, and sped towards a wood which French soldiers were clearing of German snipers. I managed to get one or two good incidents there, though occasional uncertainty about my skis spoiled other fine scenes, and in my haste to move from one spot to another, I once went head over heels into a snowdrift many feet deep.

The ludicrous spectacle that I must have cut only occurred to me afterwards, and the utterly inappropriate nature of such an incident within sight of men who were battling in life and death grip was a reflection for calmer moments. I do not mind confessing that my sole thought during the whole of that afternoon was my camera and my films. The lust of battle was in me too. I had overcome great difficulties to obtain not merely kinema-pictures, but actual vivid records of the Great War, scenes that posterity might look upon as true representations of the struggle their forefathers waged. Military experts may argue as to whether this move or that was really made in a battle: the tales of soldiers returned from the wars become, in passing from mouth to mouth, fables of the most wondrous deeds of prowess. But the kinema film never alters. It does not argue. It depicts.

The terrific cannonade that was proceeding told me that beyond the crest of the hill an infantry attack was preparing. It was for me a question of finding both a vantage point and good cover, for shells had already whizzed screaming overhead and exploded not many yards behind me. There were the remains of a wall ahead, and I discarded my skis in order to crawl flat on my stomach to one of the larger remaining fragments, and when I got behind it I found a most convenient hole, which would allow me to work my camera without being exposed myself.

In the distance a few scouts, black against the snow, crawled crouching up the hill.

The attack was beginning.

The snow-covered hillside became suddenly black with moving figures sweeping in irregular formation up towards the crest. Big gun and rifle fire mingled like strophe and antistrophe of an anthem of death. There was a certain massiveness about the noise that was awful. Yet there was none of the traditional air of battle about the engagement. There was no hand to hand fighting, for the opponents were several hundred yards apart. It was just now and then when one saw a little distant figure pitch forward and lie still on the snow that one realised there was real fighting going on, and that it was not manœuvres.

The gallant French troops swept on up the hill, and I think I was the only man in all that district who noted the black trail of spent human life they left behind them.

I raised myself ever so little to glance over the top of my scrap of sheltering wall, and away across the valley, on the crest of the other hill, I could see specks which were the Germans. They appeared to be massing ready for a charge, but the scene was too far away for the camera to record it with any distinctness.

I therefore swept round again to the French lines, to meet the splendid sight of the French reserves dashing up over the hill behind me to the support. Every man seemed animated by the one idea—to take the hill. There was a swing, an air of irresistibility about them that was magnificent. But even in the midst of enthusiasm my trained sense told me that my position must have been visible to some of them, and that it was time for me to move.

I edged my way along the broken stumps of wall to the shelter of a wood, and there, with bullets from snipers occasionally sending twigs, leaves, and even branches pattering down around me, with shells bursting all round, I continued to film the general attack until the spool in the camera ran out. To have changed spools there would have been the height of folly, so I plunged down a side path, where in the shelter of a dell, with thick undergrowth, I loaded up my camera again, and utterly careless of direction, made a dash for the edge of the wood again, emerging just in time to catch the passage of a French regiment advancing along the edge of the wood to cut off the retreat of the little party of Germans who had been endeavouring to hold it as an advanced sniping-post.

Snipers seemed to be in every tree. Bullets whistled down like acorns in the autumn breeze, but the French suddenly formed a semi-circle and pushed right into the wood, driving the enemy from their perches in the trees or shooting them as they scrambled down.

Through the wood I plunged, utterly ignoring every danger, both from friend or foe, in the thrill of that wonderful " drive." Luck, however, was with me. Neither the French nor the Germans seemed to see me, and we all suddenly came out of the wood at the far side, and I then managed to get a splendid picture of the end of the pursuit, when the French, wild with excitement at their success in clearing the district of the enemy, plunged madly down the hill in chase of the last remnants of the sniping band.

A few seconds later I darted back into the cover of the trees.

My mission was accomplished. I had secured pictures of actual events in the Vosges. But that was the least part of my work. I had to get the film to London.

The excitement of the pursuit had taken me far from my starting-point, and with the reaction that set in when I was alone in the wood, with all its memories and its ghastly memorials of the carnage, I found it required all my strength of nerve to push me on. I had to plough through open spaces, two feet and more deep in snow, through undergrowth, not knowing at what moment I might stumble across some unseen thing. Above all, I had but the barest recollection of my direction. It seemed many hours before I regained my stump of wall and found my skis lying just where I had cast them off.

It was a race against time, too, for dusk was falling, and I knew that it would be impossible to get out of St. Dié by any conveyance after dark.

I had the luck to find a man with a sledge, who was returning to a distant village, some way behind the war zone, and he agreed for a substantial consideration to take me. We drove for many hours through the night, and it was very late when at last, in a peasant's cottage, I flung myself fully dressed on a sofa, for there was no spare bed, and slept like a log for several hours.

It was by many odd conveyances that I made my way to Besançon, and thence to Dijon. I had managed to clean myself up, and looked less like an escaped convict than I had done; but I was very wary all the way to Paris, where I communicated with headquarters, and received orders to rush the films across to London as fast as ever I could.

Having overcome the perils of the land, I had to face those of the sea, for the German submarines were just beginning their campaign against merchant shipping, and cross-Channel steamers were an almost certain mark. So the boat service was suspended for a day or two, and there was I stranded in Dieppe with my precious films, as utterly shut off from London as the German army.

I was held up there for three days, during which time I secured pictures of the steamer *Dinorah*, which limped into port after being torpedoed, of a sailing vessel which had struck a mine, and some interesting scenes on board French torpedo boat destroyers as they returned from patrolling the Channel.

I spent most of my time hanging around the docks, ready to rush on board any steamer that touched at an English port. At last I heard of one that would start at midnight. My films were all packed in tins, sealed with rubber solution to make them absolutely watertight, and the tins were strung together, so that in the event of the ship going down I could have slipped them round my waist. If they went to the bottom I should go too, but if I was saved I was determined not to reach London without them.

As it happened, my adventures were at an end. We saw nothing of any under-water pirates, and my trip to the fighting line ended in a prosaic taxi-cab through London streets that seemed to know nothing of war.

PART II

CHAPTER I

HOW I CAME TO MAKE OFFICIAL WAR PICTURES

I am Appointed an Official War Office Kinematographer—And Start for the Front Line Trenches—Filming the German Guns in Action—With the Canadians—Picturesque Hut Settlement Among the Poplars—"Hyde Park Corner"—Shaving by Candlelight in Six Inches of Water—Filming in Full View of the German Lines, 75 yards away—A Big Risk, but a Realistic Picture.

DURING the early days of the war I worked more or less as a free lance camera man, both in Belgium and in France, and it was not till the autumn of 1915 that I was appointed an Official Kinematographer by the War Office, and was dispatched to the Front to take films, under the direction of Kinematograph Trade Topical Committee. When offered the appointment, I did not take long to decide upon its acceptance. I was ready and anxious to go, and as I had had considerable experience of the work, both in Belgium and in the Vosges, I knew pretty well what was expected of me. Numerous interviews with the authorities and members of the Committee followed, and for a few days I was kept in a fever of expectation.

Eventually arrangements were completed, and the announcement was then made that Mr. Tong (of Jury's Imperial Pictures) and myself had been appointed Official War Office Kinematographers. I was in the seventh heaven of delight, and looked forward to an early departure for the Front in my official capacity. This came soon enough, and on the eve of our going Tong and I were entertained to dinner by the members of the Topical Committee, and during the post-prandial talk many interesting and complimentary things were said.

We left Charing Cross on an early morning in November, and several members of the Committee were there to see us off, and wish us God-speed. We reached the other side safely, after a rather choppy crossing, and soon I was on my way to the Front—and the front line trenches, if possible.

Passing through Bailleul, Armentières and Plœgsteert, I was able to film some hidden batteries in action. As the whole road was in full view of the German lines we had to go very carefully. Several shells dropped close by me when running across the open ground. I managed at last to get into a house, and from a top window, or rather what was once a window, filmed the guns in action.

While doing so an artillery officer came and told me not to move too much as the Germans had been trying to find this battery for some considerable time, and if they saw any movement they would undoubtedly start to shell heavily. Not wishing to draw a cloud of shells on me, needless to say, I was very careful. Eventually I obtained the desired view, and making my way through the communication trenches to the front of the guns, I obtained excellent pictures of rapid firing. I had to keep very low the whole of the time. About forty yards on my right a small working party of our men had been seen, and they were immediately " strafed."

During the next few days it rained the whole of the time, and there was little opportunity for photography; but I obtained some excellent scenes, showing the conditions under which our men were living and fighting, and their indomitable cheerfulness.

About this time I arranged to go to the Canadian front trenches, in their section facing Messines. Arriving at the headquarters at Bailleul, I met

THE STATE OF THE TRENCHES IN WHICH WE LIVED AND SLEPT (?) FOR
WEEKS ON END DURING THE FIRST AND SECOND WINTER OF WAR

OUR DUG-OUTS IN THE FRONT LINE AT PICANTIN IN WHICH WE LIVED,
FOUGHT, AND MANY DIED DURING 1914-15, BEFORE THE DAYS OF TIN HATS

Lieutenant-Colonel ——, and we decided to go straight to the front line. Leaving in a heavy rain, we splashed our way through one continuous stream of mud and water. Mile after mile of it. In places the water covered the entire road, until at times one hardly knew which was the road and which was the ditch alongside. Several times our car got ditched. Shell-holes dotted our path everywhere.

Apart from the rotten conditions, the journey proved most interesting; vehicles of all kinds, from motor-buses to wheelbarrows, were rushing backwards and forwards, taking up supplies and returning empty. Occasionally we passed ambulance cars, with some poor fellows inside suffering from frost-bite, or "trench-foot" as it is generally called out here. Though their feet were swathed in bandages, and they were obviously in great pain, they bore up like true Britons. Line after line of men passed us. Those coming from the trenches were covered in mud from head to foot, but they were all smiling, and they swung along with a word and a jest as if they were marching down Piccadilly. Those going in to take their places: were they gloomy? Not a bit of it! If anything they were more cheerful, and quipped their mud-covered comrades on their appearance.

We drew up at a ruined farm-house, which the Colonel told me used to be their headquarters, until the position was given away by spies. Then the Germans started shelling it until there was hardly a brick standing. Luckily none of the staff were killed. Leaving the farm, we made our way on foot to Plœgsteert Wood. A terrible amount of "strafing" was going on here. Shells were exploding all round, and our guns were replying with "interest." As we made our way cautiously up to the side of the wood, with mud half way up to our knees, we scrambled, or rather waddled, round the base of the much-contested hill, which the Germans tried their hardest to keep, but which, thanks to the Canadians, we wrested from them.

Under cover of canvas screens, which in many places were blown away by shell-fire, and bending low to save our heads from the snipers' bullets, we gained the communication trenches. Again wading knee-deep in mud and water, we eventually reached the firing trench.

The German front line was only sixty-five yards away, and the town of Messines could be seen in the distance.

Staying in this section of trench, I filmed several scenes of the men at work repairing and rebuilding the sides which the night previous had been destroyed by shell-fire and the heavy rains. Then followed scenes of relief parties coming in, and working parties hard at it trying to drain their dug-outs. This latter seemed to me an almost superhuman task; but through it all, the men smiled. Bending low, I raced across an open space, and with a jump landed in an advanced sniper's post, in a ruined farm-house. I filmed him, carefully and coolly picking off the Germans foolish enough to show their heads.

Then I set my camera up behind what I thought quite a safe screen, to film a general view of our front line, but I had hardly started exposing when, with murderous little shrieks, two bullets whizzed close by my head—quite as near as I shall ever want them. Dropping as low as possible, I reached up, and still turning the handle finished the scene. Then followed several pictures of scouts and snipers making their way across the ground, taking advantage of any slight cover they could get, in order to take up suitable positions for their work.

By this time the light was getting rather bad, and as it was still raining hard I made my way back.

During the return journey, an officer who accompanied me showed himself unknowingly above the parapet, and " zipp " came a bullet, which ripped one of the stars off his coat.

" Jove! " said he, with the greatest of *sang-froid*, " that's a near thing ; but it's spoilt my shoulder-strap " : and with a laugh we went on our way.

Again we had to cross the open ground to the covered way. Accordingly we spread out about fifty yards apart, and proceeded. Careful as we were, the Germans spotted us, and from thence onwards to the top of the hill shrapnel shells burst all round us and overhead. Several pieces fell almost at my feet, but by a miracle I escaped unscathed.

For some minutes I had to lie crouching in a ditch, sitting in water. It was a veritable inferno of fire. I cautiously worked my way along. Where the rest of the party had gone I did not know. I hugged my camera to my chest and staggered blindly on. In about half an hour I gained the cover of some bushes, and for the first time had a chance to look about me. The firing had momentarily ceased, and from various ditches I saw the heads of the other officers pop out. The sight was too funny for words. With a hearty laugh they jumped up and hurried away. My chauffeur, who incidentally used to carry my tripod, was the most sorry spectacle for he was absolutely covered from head to foot with clay, and my tripod was quite unrecognisable. Hurrying over the top of the hill we gained our cars, and rapidly beat a retreat for headquarters.

The following day I went to film the ruins of Richebourg St. Vaaste. What an awful spectacle! A repetition of the horrors of Ypres on a smaller scale. Nothing left, only the bare skeletons of the houses and the church. With great difficulty, I managed to climb to the top of the ruined tower, and filmed the town from that point. I was told by an observation officer to keep low, as the Germans had the church still under fire. Naturally I did so, not wishing for a shell that might bring the tower down, and myself with it.

Remarkable to relate, the figure of Christ upon the Cross was untouched in the midst of this terrible scene of devastation. Subsequently the tower was completely destroyed by German shells.

Hearing that the Canadian guns were going to bombard Petite Douve, a large farmstead which the Germans had fortified with machine-guns and snipers, I started off from headquarters in the company of a lieutenant-colonel and a captain. A few passing remarks on the conditions of the road as we went along to Hill 63 will be interesting. No matter where one looked there was mud and water. In several places the roads were flooded to a depth of six inches, and our cars several times sank above the front axle in hidden shell-holes. The whole district was pitted with them. Entire sections of artillery were stuck in the mud on the roadside, and all the efforts of the men failed to move them.

All around us hidden guns, 4·5 and 9·2, were hurtling their messengers of death with a monotonous regularity. Passing a signpost, marked " Hyde Park Corner," which looked incongruous in such a place, we entered Plœgsteert Wood. But what a change ! It was as if one had suddenly left France and dropped unceremoniously into the western woods of America, in the times of the old pioneers. By the wood-side, as far as one could see, stretched a series of log-huts. To the right the same scene unfolded itself. Our cars came to a stop. Then I had a chance to study the settings more closely.

What a picture ! Amidst all the glamour of war, these huts, surrounded by tall poplars, which stood grim, gaunt and leafless—in many places branchless, owing to the enemies' shells, which tore their way

CHOOSING A POSITION FOR MY CAMERA IN THE FRONT LINE TRENCH AT PICANTIN. WITH THE GUARDS. WINTER, 1915-16

OFFICIAL WAR PICTURES 57

through them—presented the most picturesque scene I had come across for many a long day. Upon the boards fixed over the doorposts were written the names of familiar London places. As the time of the bombardment was drawing near I could not stay at the moment to film anything, but decided to do so at an early opportunity.

Sharing my apparatus with two men, we started climbing through eighteen inches of slimy mud towards the top of Hill 63. The effort was almost backbreaking. At last we got through and paused, under cover of the ruins of an old château, to gain breath. To negotiate the top needed care as it was in full view of the German front. I went first with the Captain, and both of us kept practically doubled up, and moved on all fours. The men behind us waited until we had covered about one hundred yards, then they followed. We decided to make for a point in the distance which was at one time a grand old château. Now it was nothing more than a heap of rubble. We waited for the remainder of the party to come up before proceeding, the idea being that in case either of us was hit by shrapnel, or picked off by a sniper, no time would be lost in rendering assistance.

Resting awhile, we again proceeded in the same order as before. We were held up by a sentry, and warned to take to the communication trenches down the hill, as German snipers had been picking off men in the working parties the whole of the morning, and shrapnel was continually bursting overhead. We entered the trench, and as usual sank up to our knees in mud.

How in the world we got through it I don't know! Every time I lifted my foot it seemed as though the mud would suck my knee-boot off. After going along in this way for about three hundred yards, and occasionally ducking my head to avoid being hit by bursting shells, we came to a ruined barn. The cellars had been converted, with the aid of a good supply of sandbags, into a miniature fort. A sloping tunnel led to the interior, and the Captain going in front, we entered.

There by the light of a candle, and standing in a good six inches of water, was a captain shaving himself. This officer the previous week had led his party of bombers into the German trenches, killed over thirty and captured twelve, and only suffered one casualty. For this action he was awarded the D.S.O. I was introduced, and sitting on the edge of a bench we chatted until the others came up. A few minutes later the Colonel entered.

We then started off in single file down the other side of Hill 63. I had to take advantage of any bit of cover that offered itself during the descent. At one point we had to cross an open space between a ruined farm and a barn. The Germans had several snipers who concentrated on this point, and there was considerable risk in getting across. Bending low, however, I started, and when half-way over I heard the whistle of a bullet overhead. I dropped flat and crawled the remainder of the distance, reaching cover in safety.

At that moment our big guns started shelling the German trenches, and knowing that the diversion would momentarily occupy the snipers' attention the others raced safely across in a body. The remainder of the journey was made in comparative safety, the only danger being from exploding shrapnel overhead. But one does not trouble very much about that after a time. Reaching the front trenches, I made my way along to a point from which I could best view the Petite Douve. Obtaining a waterproof sheet we carefully raised it very, very slowly above the parapet with the aid of a couple of bayonets. Without a doubt, I thought, the Germans would be

OFFICIAL WAR PICTURES 59

sure to notice something different on that section after a few seconds. And so it proved. Two rifle-shots rang out from the enemy trench, and right through the sheet they went.

Our object in putting up this temporary screen was to hide the erection of my tripod and camera, and then at the moment the bombardment began it was to be taken away, and I would risk the rest.

Just when the bullets came through I was bending to fasten the tripod legs. A few seconds earlier and one or other of them would have surely found my head. Getting some sandbags, we carefully pushed them on to the parapet, in order to break the contact as much as possible, and we put one in front of the camera in a direct line to cover the movement of my hand while exposing. I was now ready. Raising my head above the parapet for a final look, I noticed I was fully exposed to the right German trenches, and was just on the point of asking Captain —— if there was any possibility of getting sniped from that direction when with a "zipp" a bullet passed directly between our heads. Having obtained such a practical and prompt answer to my enquiry, though not exactly the kind I had expected, I had some more sandbags placed, one on top of the other, to shelter my head as much as possible.

All I had to do now was to focus, and to do that I lifted the bottom edge of the screen gently. In a few seconds it was done, and dropping the screen, I waited for the first shot. I was warned by an observing officer that I had still five minutes to spare. They were not bombarding until 2.15. German shells were continually dropping all round. The part of the hill down which we came was getting quite a lively time of it. The enemy seemed to be searching every spot. On the right a Canadian sniper was at work, taking careful aim. Turning to me, he said:

" Wall, sir, I bet that chap won't want any more headache pills."

The remark caused a good deal of laughter.

Boom—boom—boom. In rapid succession came two shells from our guns. Every one was alert. I sprang to my camera. Two men were standing by me, ready to take down the screen. Boom came another shell, and at a sign the men dropped the screen.

I was exposed to the full view of the German lines, from my shoulders upwards.

I started exposing; the shells came in rapid succession, dropping right in the middle of the Petite Douve. As they fell clouds of bricks and other débris were thrown in the air; the din was terrific. Nothing in the world could possibly have lived there. After about thirty shells had been dropped there was a slight pause for about half a minute, during which I continued turning the handle. The Germans were too occupied in getting under cover to notice the fine target my head offered, for not a single shot was fired at me.

Once more our guns rang out, and in as many seconds—at least so it seemed to me—another thirty shells dropped into the buildings and tore them wall from wall. Word was then passed to me that this was the finishing salvo.

With the same suddenness as it had begun, the firing ceased. Dropping quickly, and dragging the camera after me, I stood safely once more in the bottom of the trench and, to tell the truth, I was glad it was over. To put one's head above the parapet of a trench, with the Germans only seventy-five yards away, and to take a kinematograph picture of a bombardment, is not one of the wisest—or safest—things to do!

CHAPTER II

CHRISTMAS DAY AT THE FRONT

Leave-taking at Charing Cross—A Fruitless Search for Food on Christmas Eve—How Tommy Welcomed the Coming of the Festive Season—" Peace On Earth, Good Will To Men " to the Boom of the Big Guns—Filming the Guards' Division—And the Prince of Wales—Coming from a Christmas Service—This Year and Next.

ON December 23rd I met an officer, a captain, at Charing Cross Station. We were leaving by the 8.50 train, and we were not the only ones to leave Christmas behind, for hundreds of men were returning to the Front. Heartbreaking scenes were taking place, and many of the brave women-folk were stifling their sobs, in order to give their men a pleasant send-off, possibly for the last time.

Amidst hurried good-byes and fond kisses from mothers, sisters, sweethearts and wives, and with shouts of good luck from hundreds of throats, the train started off. Handkerchiefs were waved from many windows, cheerful heads were thrust out, and not until the train had cleared the platform, and the " hurrahs " had faded away in the distance, did we take our seats. Then with set faces, grim with determination, we resigned ourselves to the fate that awaited us on the battlefields of France. Reaching Boulogne, after a rather choppy voyage, our car conveyed us to G.H.Q., which we reached late in the evening.

The following morning I was told to leave for La Gorgue, to film scenes connected with the Guards' Division. Late that afternoon, the Captain and

I set out for our destination, reaching there about 8 o'clock. I was billeted in a private house, and immediately enquired for some food, but it was impossible to obtain any there. Going out I walked through the town, in the hope of finding a place to get something. But none could be found. Feeling very tired, I began to retrace my steps, with the intention of going to bed.

On my way back I had reason to change my mind. Quite an interesting scene unfolded itself. The boom of the guns rang out sharp and clear. The moon was shining brightly, and at intervals there flashed across the sky the not-far-distant glare of star-shells. In the houses, lining both sides of the road, there was music, from the humble mouth-organ to the piano, and lusty British voices were singing old English tunes with the enthusiasm of boyhood.

On the pavement clusters of our Tommies were proceeding towards their billets, singing heartily at the top of their voices. Some batches were singing carols, others the latest favourites, such as "Keep the Home Fires Burning."

No matter where one went, the same conditions and the same sounds prevailed; just happy-go-lucky throngs, filled with the songs and laughter born of the spirit of Christmas. And yet as I reached my room, despite the scenes of joyousness and hilarity rampant, I could still hear the crash of the guns.

This was my second Christmas at the Front, although not in the same district. Last year I was with the brave Belgian army. This year was certainly very different in all respects except the weather, and that was as poisonous as ever. A miserable, misty, drifting rain, which would soak through to the skin in a few minutes anyone not provided with a good rainproof. Donning my Burberry, I proceeded towards a small chapel, or rather to a building which is now used as one. It

THE PRINCE OF WALES TRYING TO LOCATE MY "CAMOUFLAGED CAMERA"

THE PRINCE OF WALES LEAVING A TEMPORARY CHURCH AT LA GORGUE,
XMAS DAY, 1915

was originally a workshop. On three sides it was entirely surrounded by the floods. The front door was just clear, but I had to paddle through mud half-way up to my knees to get there. I intended to obtain a film of the Guards' Division attending the Christmas service.

Fixing up my camera, I awaited their arrival. After a short time they came along, headed by their band. What a fine body of men! Swinging along with firm stride, they came past. Thinking I had got sufficient I packed my camera, when, to my astonishment, I saw the Prince of Wales, with Lord Cavan, coming up at the rear. Rushing back to my old position, I endeavoured to fix up again, to film them coming in, but I was too late. " Anyway," I thought, " I will get him coming out."

Fixing up my machine at a new and advantageous point of view, I waited. The service began. I could hear the strains of the old, old carols and Christmas hymns. Surely one could not have heard them under stranger conditions, for as the sound of that beautiful carol, " Peace on Earth, Good Will to Men!" swelled from the throats of several hundreds of our troops, the heavy guns thundered out round after round with increasing intensity. Strange that at such a moment so terrific a bombardment should have taken place. It seems as if some strange telepathic influence was at work, commanding all the guns in the vicinity to open fire with redoubled fury. And high in the air, our steel " birds " were hovering over the enemy lines, directing the fire, and flecked all round them, like flakes of snow, was the smoke from the shrapnel shells fired on them by the Germans.

" Peace on earth, good will to men," came the strains of music from the little church. Crash! went the guns again and again, throwing their shrieking mass of metal far overhead. I fell into a deep reverie, and my thoughts naturally strayed to those at home.

Returning to my room, I donned my thick woollen coat, as I intended to rush off to G.H.Q. to see Tong, who had got a bad attack of dysentery, and try and cheer him up. Getting into my car, I told the chauffeur to drive like the wind. I had fifty kilometres to go. Away we rushed through the night, and as we went through villages where our Tommies were billeted, the strains of the old home songs—Irish, Scotch and English—were wafted to my ears. Except for the incessant shelling, the flash of guns, and the distant glare from the star-shells, it was almost impossible to believe we were in the terrible throes of war. I arrived at G.H.Q. about 8.30 p.m.

Poor Tong was very queer and feeling dejected. Not being able to speak French, he could not let the people of the hotel know what he wanted. I soon made him as comfortable as possible, and sat beside his bed chatting about this, the strangest Christmas Day I had ever experienced. After remaining with him for about an hour and a half, I again started for the front line, where I arrived about 1 a.m., dog-tired, and at once turned in.

So ended my second Christmas Day at the Front, and, as I dozed off to sleep, I found myself wondering whether the next Christmas would find me still in France. Should I be listening to carols and guns at the Front, or would the message of the bells peal from a church in an adjacent street at home, and announce the coming of another Christmas to me and mine?

CHAPTER III

I GET INTO A WARM CORNER

Boxing Day—But No Pantomime—Life in the Trenches—A Sniper at Work—Sinking a Mine Shaft—The Cheery Influence of an Irish Padre—A Cemetery Behind the Lines—Pathetic Inscriptions and Mementoes on Dead Heroes' Graves—I Get Into a Pretty Warm Corner—And Have Some Difficulty in Getting Out Again—But All's Well that Ends Well.

BOXING DAY! But nothing out of the ordinary happened. I filmed the Royal Welsh Fusiliers en route for the trenches. As usual, the weather was impossible, and the troops came up in motor-buses. At the sound of a whistle, they formed up in line and stopped, and the men scrambled out and stood to attention by the roadside. They were going to the front line. They gave me a parting cheer, and a smile that they knew would be seen by the people in England—perchance by their own parents.

I went along the famous La Bassée Road—the most fiercely contested stretch in that part of the country. It was literally lined with shell-destroyed houses, large and small; châteaux and hovels. All had been levelled to the ground by the Huns. I filmed various scenes of the Coldstreams, the Irish and the Grenadier Guards. At the furthermost point of the road to which cars are allowed shells started to fall rather heavily, so, not wishing to argue the point with them, I took cover. When the "strafing" ceased I filmed other interesting scenes, and then returned to my headquarters.

The next day was very interesting, and rather

exciting. I was to go to the front trenches and get some scenes of the men at work under actual conditions. Proceeding by the Road, I reached the Croix Rouge crossing, which was heavily " strafed " the previous day. Hiding the car under cover of a partly demolished house, and strapping the camera on my back, my orderly carrying the tripod, I started out to walk the remaining distance. I had not gone far when a sentry advised me not to proceed further on the road, but to take to the trench lining it, as the thoroughfare from this point was in full view of the German artillery observers. Not wishing to be shelled unnecessarily, I did as he suggested. " And don't forget to keep your head down, sir," was his last remark. So bending nearly double, I proceeded. As a further precaution, I kept my man behind me at a distance of about twenty yards. Several times high explosives and shrapnel came unpleasantly near.

Presently I came upon a wooden tramway running at right angles to the road. My instructions were to proceed along it until I came to " Signpost Lane." Why it was so dubbed I was unable to discover, but one thing I was certainly not kept in ignorance of for long, and that was that it was perpetually under heavy shell-fire by the Germans. They were evidently under the impression that it was the route taken by our relief parties going to the trenches at appointed times during the day, and so they fairly raked it with shell-fire.

Unfortunately I happened to arrive on one of these occasions, and I knew it. Shells dropped all round us. Hardly a square yard of ground seemed untouched. Under such conditions it was no good standing. I looked round for cover, but there was none. The best thing to do under the circumstances was to go straight on, trust to Providence, and make for the communication trenches with all speed. I

I GET INTO A WARM CORNER

doubled like a hare over the intervening ground, and I was glad when I reached the trenches, for once there, unless a shell bursts directly overhead, or falls on top of you, the chances of getting hit are very small.

I was now in the sniping zone, and could continually hear the crack of a Hun rifle, and the resulting thud of a bullet striking the mud or the sandbags, first one side then the other. The communication trenches seemed interminable, and, as we neared the front line, the mud got deeper and parts of the trench were quite water-logged.

Plod, plod, plod; section after section, traverse after traverse. Suddenly I came upon a party of sappers mending the parapet top with newly filled sandbags. At that particular section a shell had dropped fairly near and destroyed it, and anyone walking past that gap stood a very good chance of having the top of his head taken off. These men were filling up the breach. "Keep your head well down, sir," shouted one, as I came along. "They" (meaning the Germans) "have got this place marked."

Down went my head, and I passed the gap safely.

We were now well up in the firing trench. Fixing the camera, and the rest of the apparatus, I began taking scenes of actual life and conditions in the trenches—that mysterious land about which millions have read but have never had the opportunity of seeing. No mere verbal description would suffice to describe them. Every minute the murderous crack of rifles and the whir of machine-guns rang out. Death hovered all round. In front the German rifles, above the bursting shrapnel, each shell scattering its four hundred odd leaden bullets far and wide, killing or wounding any unfortunate man who happened to be in the way.

The trenches looked as if a giant cataclysm of

Nature had taken place. The whole earth had been upheaved, and in each of the mud-hills men had burrowed innumerable paths, seven feet deep. It was hard to distinguish men from mud. The former were literally caked from head to foot with the latter. I filmed the men at work. There were several snipers calmly smoking their cigarettes and taking careful aim at the enemy.

Crack—crack—crack—simultaneously.

" Sure, sir," remarked one burly Irish Guardsman, " and he'll never bob his —— head up any more. It's him I've been afther this several hours ! " And as coolly as if he had been at a rifle range at home, the man discharged the empty cartridge-case and stood with his rifle, motionless as a rock, his eyes like those of an eagle.

All this time it was raining hard. I worked my way along the never-ending traverses. Coming upon a mount of sandbags, I enquired of an officer present the nature and cause of its formation. He bade me follow him. At one corner a narrow, downward path came into view. Trudging after him, I entered this strange shelter. Inside it was quite dark, but in a few seconds, when my eyes had got used to the conditions, I observed a hole in the centre of the floor about five feet square.

Peering over the edge, I saw that the shaft was about *twenty-five feet deep*, and that there was a light at the bottom. It then dawned upon me what it really was. It was a mine-shaft. At the bottom, men worked at their deadly occupation, burrowing at right angles under our own trenches (under " No Man's Land ") and under the German lines. They laid their mines, and at the appointed time exploded them, thus causing a great amount of damage to the enemy's parapets and trenches, and killing large numbers of the occupants.

Retracing my steps, I fixed the camera up and

I GET INTO A WARM CORNER   69

filmed the men entering the mines and others bringing up the excavated earth in sandbags and placing them on the outside of the barricade. Then I paused to film the men at work upon a trench road. Thinking I could obtain a better view from a point in the distance, I started off for it, bent nearly double, when a warning shout from an officer bade me be careful. I reached the point. Although about fifty yards behind the firing trench, I was under the impression that I was still sheltered by the parapet. Evidently I had raised my head too high while fixing up the tripod, for with a murderous whistle two bullets " zipped " by overhead. I must be more careful if I wanted to get away with a whole skin ; so bending low, I filmed the scene, and then returned.

While proceeding along the line, I filmed the regimental padre of the Irish Guards wading through the mud and exchanging a cheery word with every man he passed. What a figure he was ! Tall and upright, with a long dark beard, and a voice that seemed kind and cheery enough to influence even the dead. He inspired confidence wherever he went. He stayed awhile to talk to several men who were sitting in their dug-outs pumping the water out before they could enter. His words seemed to make the men work with redoubled vigour. Then he passed on.

Along this section, at the back of the dug-outs, were innumerable white crosses, leaning at all angles, in the mud. They were the last resting-place of our dead heroes. On each cross a comrade had written a short inscription, and some of these, though simple, and at times badly spelt, revealed a pathos and a feeling that almost brought tears to the eyes. For all its slime and mud it was the most beautiful cemetery I have ever seen. On some of the graves were a few wildflowers. No wreaths ; no marble headstones ; no elaborate ornamentation ; but in their place a battered cap, a rusty rifle or a mud-covered haversack, the treasured belongings of the dead.

I had barely finished filming this scene when with a shriek several shells came hurtling overhead from the German guns and burst about a hundred yards behind our firing line. Quickly adjusting the camera, I covered the section with my lens. In a few seconds more shells came over, and turning the handle I filmed them as they burst, throwing up enormous quantities of earth. The Huns were evidently firing at something. What that something was I soon found out. An enemy observer had seen a small working party crossing an open space. The guns immediately opened fire. Whether they inflicted any casualties I do not know, but a few minutes later the same party of men passed me as though nothing had happened.

The rain was still falling, and the mist getting heavy, so I decided to make my way back to headquarters. Packing up, and bidding adieu to the officers, I started on the return journey through the communication trenches. One officer told me to go back the same way, via " Signpost Lane." " You will manage to get through before their evening ' strafing,' " he called out. After wearily trudging through nearly a mile of trenches, I came out at " Signpost Lane," and I am never likely to forget it.

We had left the shelter of the trench, and were hurrying, nearly doubled, across a field, when a German observer spotted us. The next minute " whizzbangs " started falling around us like rain. No matter which way I turned, the tarnation things seemed to follow and burst with a deafening crash. At last, I reached the crossing, and was making my way down the trench lining the road, when a shell dropped and exploded not thirty feet ahead. But

I GET INTO A WARM CORNER

on I went, for a miss is as good as a mile. About a hundred yards further on was the battered shell of a farm-house. When almost up to it a couple of shells dropped fairly in the middle of it and showered the bricks all round. A fairly warm spot!

I had just reached the corner of the building when I heard the shriek of a shell coming nearer. I guessed it was pretty close, and without a moment's hesitation dropped in the mud and water of a small ditch, and not a moment too soon for with a dull thud the shell struck and burst hardly seven feet from me. Had I not fallen down these lines would never have been written. Picking myself up, I hurried on. Still the shells continued to drop, but fortunately at a greater distance. When I reached Croix Rouge, I was literally encased in mud. Our progress along the road had been anxiously watched by the sentries and by my chauffeur.

"Well, sir," said the latter, with a sigh of relief, "I certainly thought they had you that time."

CHAPTER IV

THE BATTLEFIELD OF NEUVE CHAPELLE

A Visit to the Old German Trenches—Reveals a Scene of Horror that Defies Description—Dodging the Shells—I Lose the Handle of My Camera—And then Lose My Man—The Effect of Shell-fire on a Novice—In the Village of Neuve Chapelle—A Scene of Devastation—The Figure of the Lonely Christ.

IT occurred to me that an interesting film might be made out of scenes of the battlefield of Neuve Chapelle. The very thought of it conjured up a reeking, whirling mass of humanity, fighting with all the most devilish, death-dealing weapons that had ever been conceived by the mind of man. I decided to do a picture of the scene, and took with me an orderly who had never been under fire before.

We proceeded along the La Bassée Road, and at the Croix Rouge proceeded on foot towards Neuve Chapelle. As usual, Bosche shelling was so consistent in its intensity that we thought it advisable to spread out a bit in case a shell burst near us. My guide was Major ——, who commanded one of the regiments holding the ground on the other side of Neuve Chapelle.

Eventually I reached the assembly trenches, where our men concentrated for the great attack. In shape they were just ordinary trenches, branches off a main gallery, but they were in an awful state of decay, and literally torn to shreds by shell-fire. What tales these old sandbags might tell if only they could speak, tales of our brave boys and our Indian troops that would live for ever in the history of man-

BATTLEFIELD OF NEUVE CHAPELLE 73

kind. Standing upon one of the parapets, I looked round, and marvelled that it was possible in so small a section of ground so many men were hidden there. Quickly formulating my programme, I decided to begin at the assembly trenches, and follow in imagination the path of the troops during the battle, ending up in the ruins of Neuve Chapelle village itself, which I could see in the distance.

"Be careful," came the warning voice of a major, "the whole of the ground here is in view of the Bosche artillery observers. If they see anyone moving about they'll start 'strafing' like anything, and I assure you they do it very conscientiously."

I therefore kept as low as possible.

Fixing up the camera, I started to film the scenes from the assembly trenches to the old first line trench, and then into the stretch of ground known as "No Man's Land." Finishing this particular picture, we went along to the old German trenches, and during the whole time we bent nearly double, to keep under the line of the old parapets. In the old German trenches the frightful effect of modern shell-fire was only too apparent. The whole line, as far as one could see, was absolutely smashed to atoms. Only the bases of the parapets were left, and in the bottom of the trenches was an accumulation of water and filth. It was a disgusting sight. The whole place was littered with old German equipment, and whilst wading and splashing along through the water I saw such things, and such stenches assailed my nostrils, as I shall not easily forget. Dotted all over the place, half in and half out of the mud and water, were dead bodies.

But why recount the horrors of the scene? Imagine the sights and the smell. How I got through that section of trench Heaven only knows. It was simply ghastly.

To escape from the scene I hurried to the end of

the trench and again crossed "No Man's Land." The sight here was not so bad as in the trenches. To obtain a good view of the spot I got up very gingerly on top of the parapet, fixed the machine, and filmed the scene. But this enterprise nearly put an end to my adventure, *and also to the other members of the party.* I had finished taking, and had got my camera down on the stand, in the bottom of the trench, and was on the point of unscrewing it, when two shells came hurtling overhead and exploded about forty feet away. The Major ran up to me and shouted that I had been seen, and told me to take cover at once. He and the others, suiting the action to the word, dived below the parapets. Snatching the camera off its stand, I followed, and paddled as close as possible to the mud. The shells began falling in quick succession. Nearer and nearer they came. Some just cleared the parapet top; some burst in front, some immediately behind.

"They have got our line; let's shift along further," some one said.

From one point of the trench to the other we dodged. The shells seemed to follow us wherever we went. Crash! One struck the crumbling parapet on the very spot where, a few seconds before, I had been sheltering. In the rush for cover I had lost the handle of the camera, and as it was the only one I had there, I began to work my way back to find it.

"Don't be a fool," called the Major. "If you show yourself they'll have you, as sure as eggs are eggs." But my anxiety to obtain pictures of the bursting shells was too much for me. I set to to make a handle of wood. Looking round, I spotted an old tree-trunk, behind which I could take cover. Doubling towards it, I crouched down, and finding a piece of wood and an old nail I fashioned a handle of a sort.

At this moment a funny incident occurred. I had

BATTLEFIELD OF NEUVE CHAPELLE

momentarily forgotten the existence of the other members of the party. I was hoping against hope that they had escaped injury. What had happened to them ? Where were they ? It almost seemed as if my thoughts were communicated by telepathy to one of them, for just above the parapet in front of me rose the head of Captain ——.

"I say, Malins," he said, "did you find your handle ? "

The words were barely out of his mouth when a shell shot by. Captain ——'s head went down like a jack-in-the-box. The sight was too funny for words. If he hadn't ducked the shell would have taken his head off, for it struck the ground and exploded, as we found out afterwards, only ten feet away.

For three-quarters of an hour this " strafing " continued, then giving Bosche ten minutes to settle down we came out of our holes and corners. What sights we were !

Collecting my apparatus, I again crossed " No Man's Land," and carefully made my way into the village of Neuve Chapelle itself. To describe it would only be to repeat what I said of the devastated city of Ypres. There was nothing whole standing. The place was smashed and ground down out of all recognition. And yet, from its solitary high position upon the cross, the figure of Christ looked down upon the scene. It was absolutely untouched. It stood there—this sacred emblem of our Faith—grim and gaunt against the sky. A lonely sentinel. The scene was a sermon in itself, and mere words fail to describe the deep impression it made upon me.

CHAPTER V

FILMING THE PRINCE OF WALES

How I Made a " Hide-up "—And Secured a Fine Picture of the Prince Inspecting some Gun-pits—His Anxiety to Avoid the Camera—And His Subsequent Remarks—How a German Block-house was Blown to Smithereens—And the Way I Managed to Film it Under Fire.

TO-DAY has certainly been most interesting, and not without excitement. I was to film the bombardment of a concrete German block-house from the Guards' trenches at ——. Previous to starting out from —— news came through from headquarters that the Prince of Wales was going to inspect some guns with Lord Cavan.

The staff officer who told me this knew the trouble I had previously experienced in trying to obtain good films of the Prince, and warned me to be very careful. I enquired the time of his arrival at the gun-pits. So far as I could ascertain, it was to be at 11.30 a.m. I therefore decided to be there half an hour earlier, and make a " hide-up " for myself and camera. I was determined to succeed this time. Proceeding by way of ——, which place has suffered considerable bombardment, the church and surrounding buildings having been utterly destroyed, I stayed awhile to film the interior and exterior of the church, and so add another to the iniquitous record of the Bosche for destroying everything held sacred.

A short distance outside the town I came upon the gun positions, and crossing a field—or rather shall I say a mud-pond, for the mud very nearly reached my knees—I selected a point of vantage at

ON THE WAY TO THE "MENIN GATE" WITH AN ARTILLERY OFFICER, TO FILM OUR GUNS IN ACTION

FILMING THE PRINCE OF WALES

one side of a hedge which ran at right angles to the gun-pits. There was only one path fit to traverse, and getting hold of an officer, I asked him if we could so arrange it that the Prince started from the further end of the path and came towards camera. He said he would try. Fixing up the camera, I got in front of the hedge facing the path, and completely hid all signs of the machine with bracken and branches of trees. Pushing the lens well through the hedge, I ripped open an old sandbag, cut a hole in it and hung it on the hedge, with my lens pointing through. By such means it was quite impossible for anyone in front to see either myself or the camera, and having completed my preparations, I settled down to patiently await the arrival of the Prince.

In about half an hour he came along with Lord Cavan, a general, and other officers of the staff. True to his promise, Captain —— got the Prince to follow the path I had indicated. When he arrived at the further end of the row of guns, I started filming. He came direct towards the camera, but when within fifteen feet of it the noise of handle turning attracted his attention. He stood fully fifteen seconds gazing in my direction, evidently wondering what it was on the other side of the hedge. Then he passed out of range. I hurried across the field with my aeroscope (an automatic camera), and stood at the end of the path waiting for him to pass.

In a few moments he came along, and I started filming. The smiles of the staff officers were pleasing to behold. One of them remarked to the Prince that it was quite impossible to escape this time. As he passed inside the farm-house, I heard him remark: " That was the man I tried to dodge on Christmas Day. How did he know I was coming here ? Who told him ? " The enquiry was followed by some good-natured laughter, and feeling satisfied with my work, I hurried away.

I had now to proceed to the front line trenches, taking the car, as far as possible, along the road. I had hidden it under cover of some ruined buildings, and taking the camera, and bidding my chauffeur bring the tripod, I started out. A captain conducted me. We quickly got to the communication trenches. As usual, a good deal of "strafing" was going on, and the German snipers were very busy. When we reached the first line firing trenches, I peered over the parapet through a periscope, but found I was too far south of the block-house. So I proceeded higher up, and about eight hundred yards further on came a traverse, which I had chosen, and the loophole through which I was going to film the scene. The distance to the German block-house from where I was standing was about 150 yards.

The thickness of the parapet, I should say, was roughly four feet; and through the parapet was a conical, square-shaped, wooden cylinder. In front, under cover of darkness, the night previous, I had had two sandbags placed, so that when everything was ready, and my camera fixed, a slight push from the back with a stick would shift them clear of the opening. Fixing up the camera, I very carefully pinned an empty sandbag over the back of the aperture, with the object of keeping any daylight from streaming through. I placed a long stick ready to push the sandbags down. I intended doing that after the first shell had fallen.

This particular loophole had been severely sniped all the morning, the Germans evidently thinking it was a new Maxim-gun emplacement. Time was drawing near. I thought I would try with the stick whether the sandbags would fall easily. Evidently I gave them too vigorous a push, for the next moment they came toppling down. Knowing such a movement as that was certain to attract the German snipers' attention, I quickly ducked my head down,

FILMING THE PRINCE OF WALES

and hoped our 9·2's would soon open fire. I did not relish the idea of having a bullet through my camera.

Sure enough the Germans had seen the movement, for bullets began battering into sandbags around the loophole. At that moment the C.O. withdrew the whole of the men from that section of the trench, and I was left alone. But the prospect of getting a fine film drove all other thoughts from my mind.

A few minutes later the first shell came hurtling over and exploded within ten yards of the block-house. I started filming. Shell after shell I recorded as it exploded, first on one side then on the other, until at last the eighth shell fell directly on top of the block-house, and with a tremendous explosion the whole fabric disappeared in a cloud of smoke and flame. Debris of every description rattled in the trench all round me, and continued to fall for some moments, but luckily I was not hit. Being unable to resist the temptation of looking over the parapet, I jumped up and gazed at the remains of the building which now consisted of nothing more than a twisted, churned-up mass of concrete and iron rails. Our artillery had done its work, and done it well.

CHAPTER VI

MY FIRST VISIT TO YPRES AND ARRAS

Greeted on Arrival in the Ruined City of Ypres by a Furious Fusillade—I Film the Cloth Hall and Cathedral, and Have a Narrow Escape—A Once Beautiful Town Now Little More Than a Heap of Ruins—Arras a City of the Dead—Its Cathedral Destroyed—But Cross and Crucifixes Unharmed.

TO Ypres! This was the order for the day. The news gave me a thrill of excitement. The thunder of the big guns grew louder as we approached the front line, until they seemed to merge into one continuous roar.

Stopping on the road, I asked if the Germans were " strafing " to-day.

" Yes," said one of our military police, " they were shelling us pretty heavily this morning: you will have to be very careful moving about inside. Bosche machines are always up in the air, taking bearings for the guns."

Arriving at the outskirts of the ruined town, we were pulled up by a sentry, who, finding our papers in order, allowed us to proceed. At that moment a furious fusillade of gun-fire attracted our attention, and three shrill blasts of a whistle rang out; then we heard a cry, " Every one under cover ! " Stopping the car, I immediately jumped out, and stood under cover of a broken-down wall, and looking up, could see the cause of this activity.

High in the air, about eight to ten thousand feet, was a Bosche aeroplane, and while I was watching it shrapnel shells from our anti-aircraft guns were

TAKING SCENES IN DEVASTATED YPRES, MAY, 1916

exploding round it like rain. A great number were fired at it. The whole sky was flecked with white and black patches of smoke, but not one hit was recorded. The machine seemed to sail through that inferno as if nothing were happening, and at last it disappeared in the haze over its own lines. Only then were we allowed to proceed.

I had made a rough programme of what to film, and decided to start from the Grand Place. In a few words, I may say that I filmed the Place from the remains of the Cloth Hall, the Cathedral, and various districts of the town, but to try and describe the awful condition of what was once the most beautiful town in Belgium would be to attempt the impossible. No pen, and no imagination, could do justice to it. The wildest dreams of Dante could not conjure up such terrible, such awful scenes.

The immensity of the outrage gripped me perhaps more completely when I stood upon the heap of rubble that was once the most beautiful piece of architecture of its kind in all the world. The Cloth Hall, and the Cathedral, looked exactly as if some mighty scythe had swept across the ground, levelling everything in its path. The monster 15-inch German shells had dismembered and torn open the buildings brick by brick. Confusion and devastation reigned everywhere, no matter in what direction you looked. It was as if the very heavens and the earth had crashed together, crushing everything between them out of all semblance to what it had been.

The ground was literally pock-marked with enemy shell-holes. The stench of decaying bodies followed me everywhere. At times the horror of it all seemed to freeze the understanding, and it was difficult to realise that one was part and parcel of this world of ours. Literally, horror was piled upon horror. And this was the twentieth century of which men boasted; this was civilisation! Built by men's hands, the result of centuries of work. Now look at them; those beautiful architectural monuments, destroyed, in a few months, by the vilest spawn that ever contaminated the earth. A breed that should and would be blotted out of existence as effectively as they had blotted out the town of Ypres.

Beneath one large building lay buried a number of our gallant soldiers, who were sheltering there, wounded. The position was given away by spies, with the result that the Germans poured a concentrated fire of shells upon the helpless fellows, and the shelling was so terrific that the whole building collapsed and buried every living soul beneath the debris.

As I stood upon the heap tears came into my eyes, and the spirits of the brave lads seemed to call out for vengeance. And even as I stood and pondered, the big guns rang out, the very concussion shaking bricks and dust upon me as I stood there. While filming the scene, German shells came hurtling and shrieking overhead, exploding just behind me and scattering the debris of the ruins high above and whizzing in my direction.

To obtain a good view-point, I clambered upon a mount of bricks nearly fifty feet high, all that was left of the Cathedral Tower. From that eminence I could look right down into the interior, and I succeeded in taking an excellent film of it. While doing so, two German shells exploded a short distance away. Whether it was the concussion or pieces of shell that struck it, I do not know—probably the latter—but large pieces of stone and granite fell at my feet, and one piece hit my shoulder. So I quickly made my way to more healthy quarters, and even as I left the shells overhead began to shriek with redoubled fury, as if the very legions of hell were moaning, aghast at the terrible crime which the fiendish Huns had perpetrated.

Arras, although not by any means as badly damaged as Ypres, is one of the most historical and beautiful places systematically destroyed by the Germans. The Cathedral, the wonderful Museum, the Hôtel de Ville, once the pride of this broken city, are now no more. Arras provides yet another blasting monument of the unspeakable methods of warfare as practised by the descendants of Attila, the Hun. The city was as silent as the tomb when I visited it. It was dead in every sense of the word; a place only fit for the inhabitants of the nether world. Only when the German shells came screaming overhead with unearthly noise, in an empty street, was the silence broken in this city of the dead.

I visited the ruined Cathedral, and filmed various scenes of the interior and exterior, having to climb over huge mounds of fallen masonry to obtain my best view-points. In places all that was left standing was the bare walls. The huge columns, with their beautiful sculptures, no longer able to support the roof, still stood like grim sentinels watching over their sacred charge. And yet, despite the unholy bombardment to which the building had been subjected, three things remained unharmed and untouched in the midst of this scene of awful desolation. The three crucifixes, with the figures of Christ still upon them, gazed down upon this scene of horror. And high upon the topmost joint of the south wall stood the cross, the symbol of Christianity —unharmed. The united endeavours of the Powers of Evil could not dislodge that sacred emblem from its topmost pinnacle.

I left the Cathedral and walked along the grass-covered streets, pock-marked by innumerable shell-holes, and every now and then I had to dive into some cellar for shelter from falling shells. At the Hôtel de Ville the same sight presented itself. The bombardment had reduced its walls to little more than a tottering shell, which fell to pieces at the merest touch.

IN YPRES, WITH "BABY" BROOKS, THE OFFICIAL STILL PHOTOGRAPHER, MAY, 1916

CHAPTER VII

THE BATTLE OF ST. ELOI

Filming Within Forty-five Yards of the German Trenches—Watching for "Minnies"—Officers' Quarters—"Something" Begins to Happen—An Early Morning Bombardment—Develops Into the Battle of St. Eloi—Which I Film from Our First-Line Trench—And Obtain a Fine Picture.

A BOMBARDMENT was to take place. A rather vague statement, and a common enough occurrence ; but not so this one.

I had a dim idea—not without foundation, as it turned out—that there was more in this particular bombardment than appeared on the surface. Why this thought crossed my mind I do not know. But there it was, and I also felt that it would somehow turn out seriously for me before I had finished.

I was to go to a certain spot to see a general—and obtain permission to choose a good view-point for my machine. My knowledge of the topography of this particular part of the line was none too good.

Reaching the place I met the General, who said, in a jocular way, when I had explained my mission :

" Have you come to me to-day by chance, or have you heard something ? "

This remark, " Had I heard something ? " confirmed my opinion that something *was* going to happen. Without more ado, the General told me the bombardment would take place on the morrow, somewhere about 5.30 a.m.

" In that case," I said, " it will be quite impossible to obtain any photographs. Anyway," I added, " if you will permit me, sir, I will sleep in the front line trenches to-night, and so be ready for anything that may happen. I could choose a good spot for my machine this afternoon."

",Well," he replied, " it's a hot corner," and going to the section maps he told me our front line was only forty-five yards away from the Bosche. " You will, of course, take the risk, but, honestly speaking, I don't expect to see you back again."

This was anything but cheerful, but being used to tight corners I did not mind the risk, so long as I got some good films.

The General then gave me a letter of introduction to another general, who, he said, would give me all the assistance he could. Armed with this document, I started out in company of a staff officer, who was to guide me to the Brigade headquarters. Arriving there (it was the most advanced point to which cars were allowed to go), I obtained two orderlies, gave one my aeroscope the other the tripod, and strapping another upon my back, we started off on a two-mile walk over a small hill, and through communication trenches to the section.

At a point which boasted the name of " Cooker Farm," which consisted of a few dug-outs, well below ground level, and about five by six feet high inside by seven feet square, I interviewed two officers, who 'phoned to the front line, telling them of my arrival. They wished me all good luck on my venture, and gave me an extra relay of men to get me to the front. A considerable amount of shelling was going on overhead, but none, fortunately, came in my immediate neighbourhood. The nearest was about fifty yards away.

From our front line trenches the Bosche lines were only forty-five yards away, therefore dangers were

THE BATTLE OF ST. ELOI

to be anticipated from German snipers. A great many of our men had actually been shot through the loophole of plates. I immediately reported myself to the officer in charge, who was resting in a dug-out, built in the parapet. He was pleased to see me, and promised me every assistance. I told him I wished to choose a point of vantage from which I could film the attack. Placing my apparatus in the comparative safety of the dug-out, I accompanied him outside. Rifle-fire was continuous; shells from our 60-pounders and 4·2's were thundering past overhead, and on either side " Minnies " (German bombs) were falling and exploding with terrific force, smashing our parapets and dug-outs as if they had been the thinnest of matchwood.

Fortunately for us these interesting novelties could be seen coming. Men are always on the lookout for " Minnies," and when one has been fired from the Bosche it rises to a height of about five hundred feet, and then with a sudden curve descends. At that point it is almost possible to calculate the exact whereabouts of its fall. Every one watches it; the space is quickly cleared, and it falls and explodes harmlessly. Sometimes the explosion throws the earth up to a height of nearly 150 feet.

While I was deciding upon the exact point of the parapet upon which I would place the camera, a sudden cry of " Minnie " was heard. Looking up, I saw it was almost overhead, and with a quick rush and a dive I disappeared into a dug-out. I had barely got my head into it before " Minnie " fell and blew the mud in all directions, covering my back plentifully, but fortunately doing no other damage.

Eventually I decided upon the position, and looking through my periscope saw the German trenches stretching away on the right for a distance of half a mile, as the ground dipped into a miniature valley.

From this point I could get an excellent film, and if the Germans returned our fire I could revolve the camera and obtain the resulting explosions in our lines.

The farm-house where I spent the night was about nine hundred yards behind the firing track. All that now remained of a once prosperous group of farm buildings were the battered walls, but with the aid of a plentiful supply of sandbags and corrugated iron the cellars were made comparatively comfortable.

By the time I reached there it was quite dark, but by carefully feeling my way with the aid of a stick I stumbled down the five steps into the cellar, and received a warm welcome from Captain ——, who introduced me to his brother officers. They all seemed astounded at my mission, never imagining that a moving picture man would come into the front battle line to take pictures.

The place was about ten feet square; the roof was a lean-to, and was supported in the centre by three tree-trunks. Four wooden frames, upon which was stretched some wire-netting, served as bedsteads; in a corner stood a bucket-fire, the fumes and smoke going up an improvised chimney of petrol tins. In the centre was a rough table. One corner of it was kept up by a couple of boxes; other boxes served as chairs.

Rough as it was, it was like heaven compared with other places at which I have stayed. By the light of two candles, placed in biscuit tins, we sat round, and chatted upon kinematograph and other topics until 11.30 p.m. The Colonel of another regiment then came in to arrange about the positions of the relieving battalions which were coming in on the following day. He also arranged for his sniping expert and men to accompany the patrolling parties, which were going out at midnight in "No Man's

THE BATTLE OF ST. ELOI

Land " to mend mines and spot German loopholes.

A message came through by 'phone from Brigade headquarters that the time of attack was 5.45 a.m. I could have jumped for joy ; if only the sky was clear, there would be enough light for my work. The news was received in quite a matter-of-fact way by the others present, and after sending out carrying parties for extra ammunition for bomb guns, they all turned in to snatch a few hours' sleep, with the exception of the officer on duty.

At twelve o'clock I turned in. Rolling myself in a blanket and using my trench-coat and boots as a pillow, I lay and listened to the continual crack of rifle-fire, and the thud of bullets striking and burying themselves in the sandbags of our shelter. Now and then I dozed, and presently I fell asleep. I suddenly awakened with a start. What caused it I know not ; everything seemed unnaturally quiet ; with the exception of an isolated sniper, the greatest war in history might have been thousands of miles away. I lit a cigarette, and was slowly puffing it (time, 4.15 a.m.), when a tremendous muffled roar rent the air ; the earth seemed to quake. I expected the roof of our shelter to collapse every minute. The shock brought my other companions tumbling out. " Something " was happening.

The rumble had barely subsided, when it seemed as if all the guns in France had opened rapid battery fire at the same moment. Shells poured over our heads towards the German positions in hundreds. The shrieking and earsplitting explosives were terrific, from the sharp bark of the 4·2 to the heavy rumble and rush of the 9-inch " How." The Germans, surprised in their sleep, seemed absolutely demoralised. They were blazing away in all directions, firing in the most wild and extraordinary manner, anywhere and everywhere. Shells were crashing and smashing their way into the remains of the outbuildings, and they were literally exploding all round.

Captain —— instructed his officers to see what had happened to the ammunition party. They disappeared in the hell of shell-fire as though it were quite an every-day incident. I opened the door, climbed the steps, and stood outside. The sight which met my eyes was magnificent in its grandeur. The heavens were split by shafts of lurid fire. Masses of metal shot in all directions, leaving a trail of sparks behind them; bits of shell shrieked past my head and buried themselves in the walls and sandbags. One large missile fell in an open space about forty feet on my left, and exploded with a deafening, ear-splitting crash. At the same moment another exploded directly in front of me. Instinctively I ducked my head. The blinding flash and frightful noise for the moment stunned me, and I could taste the exploding gas surrounding me. I stumbled down the steps into the cellar, and it was some minutes before I could see clearly again. My companions were standing there, calmly awaiting events.

The frightful din continued. It was nothing but high explosives, high explosive shrapnel, ordinary shrapnel, trench bombs, and bullets from German machine-guns. One incessant hail of metal. Who on earth could live in it? What worried me most was that there was not sufficient light to film the scene; but, thank Heaven, it was gradually getting lighter.

It was now 5 a.m. The shelling continued with increasing intensity. I got my apparatus together, and with two men decided to make my way to the position in the front line.

Shouldering my camera I led the way, followed by the men at a distance of twenty yards. Several

WITH MY AEROSCOPE CAMERA AFTER FILMING THE BATTLE OF ST. ELOI

THE BATTLE OF ST. ELOI 91

times on the journey shrapnel balls and splinters buried themselves in the mud close by. When I reached the firing trench all our men were standing to arms, with grim faces, awaiting their orders. I fixed up the tripod so that the top of it came level with our parapet, and fastened the camera upon it. It topped the parapet of our firing trench (the Germans only forty-five yards away), and to break the alignment I placed sandbags on either side of it.

In this position I stood on my camera case, and started to film the Battle of St. Eloi.

Our shells were dropping in all directions, smashing the German parapets to pulp and blowing their dug-outs sky-high. The explosions looked gorgeous against the ever-increasing light in the sky. Looking through my view-finder, I revolved first on one section then on the other; from a close view of 6-inch shells and "Minnies" bursting to the more distant view of our 9·2. Then looking right down the line, I filmed the clouds of smoke drifting from the heavy (woolly bears) or high shrapnel, then back again. Shells—shells—shells—bursting masses of molten metal, every explosion momentarily shaking the earth.

The Germans suddenly started throwing "Minnies" over, so revolving my camera, I filmed them bursting over our men. The casualties were very slight. For fully an hour I stood there filming this wonderful scene, and throughout all the inferno, neither I nor my machine was touched. A fragment of shrapnel touched my tripod, taking a small piece out of the leg. That was all!

Shortly after seven o'clock the attack subsided, and as my film had all been used up, I packed and returned to my shelter.

What a "scoop" this was. It was the first film that had actually been taken of a British attack. What a record. The thing itself had passed. It had gone; yet I had recorded it in my little 7- by 6-inch box, and when this terrible devastating war was over, and men had returned once again to their homes, business men to their offices, ploughmen to their ploughs, they would be able to congregate in a room and view all over again the fearful shells bursting, killing and maiming on that winter's morning of March 27th, 1916.

CHAPTER VIII

A NIGHT ATTACK—AND A NARROW ESCAPE

A Very Lively Experience—Choosing a Position for the Camera Under Fire—I Get a Taste of Gas—Witness a Night Attack by the Germans—Surprise an Officer by My Appearance in the Trenches—And Have One of the Narrowest Escapes—But Fortunately Get Out with Nothing Worse than a Couple of Bullets Through My Cap.

THE weather was very fine when I left G.H.Q., but on reaching ——, to interview Colonel —— in reference to the mining section, rain fell heavily. I arrived soon after midday, and went to the Intelligence Department to report; the C.O. telephoned to the C. of M. for an appointment. It was made for nine o'clock that night. Having plenty of time at my disposal, I returned to ——, and passed a few hours with some friends. In the evening I returned for my appointment at the hour named. The Colonel was exceedingly interested in my project, and was willing to do anything to help me. He gave me a letter of introduction to the Corps Commander of the —— Army, Brigadier-General ——; also one to Captain ——, C.O. of the —— Mining Section. I was to proceed to General —— first, and obtain the permission.

At eight o'clock the following morning I rushed off to the Company H.Q. I met the General leaving his château. Having read my letter of introduction, he promptly gave his consent. I was to report to Major ——, at H.Q., saying it was quite all right. Thanking the General, I hastened to H.Q., and showing his letter and delivering his message, I was given a note to Captain ——, asking him to give me every assistance. Before leaving, the Major wished me success, and asked me whether I was prepared to wait until a " blow " came off ?

" Yes, sir," I replied, " for five or six days in the trenches, if necessary."

The Colonel had made arrangements with several Companies that they were to report immediately to ——th Company when they were going to " blow," in order to give me time to go immediately to the spot and film it.

Leaving the Company H.Q., I proceeded to ——, and duly presented the Captain's letter.

" You have the Corps' permission," said the Colonel; " it will now be necessary to obtain the Divisional C.O. permit."

This I eventually obtained. Now if by any chance a " blow " took place opposite either of the other Companies, it would be necessary to obtain their permission, as they were in another Division. Therefore, calling upon a major of that Division, I secured the final permit.

Next morning I left for the front line trenches. Reaching ——, which was smashed out of all recognition, we drew up under cover of some ruined walls. Shells were falling and bursting among the ruins, but these diversions were of such ordinary, everyday occurrence that hardly any notice was taken of them. If they missed—well, they were gone. If they hit—well, it was war !

The Miners, gathering near the " Birdcage " (a spot which derives its name from a peculiar iron cage erection at the corner of the road), formed up, and proceeded for about three hundred yards to the beginning of " Quarry Ally," the ammunition trench leading to their particular part of the front line. They filed in one by one ; I filmed them meanwhile.

The journey of thirteen hundred yards to the

front line was quite an ordinary walk. It was interesting to note the different tones of the heavy and light shells as they flew overhead, from the dull rush of a 9·2 to the shriek of the 18-pounder. I reached a Company dug-out. It was certainly one of the best I have ever seen. Going down three steps, then turning sharply at right angles, I disappeared through a four-foot opening; down more steps to a depth of ten feet, then straight for three paces. At the end was the main gallery, about twenty-five feet long, five feet in width, and five feet six inches high. Half of it was used for the telephone operator, and sleeping accommodation for the orderlies, the other half was used as officers' quarters. Several officers were busy discussing plans when I arrived. The conversation might sound strange and callous to an ordinary listener.

"Well, what's the news? How's Brother Bosche?"

"Bosche reported quite near," was the reply. "Our shaft is practically finished, and ready for charging. This morning you could distinctly hear Bosche speaking. His gallery was getting nearer to ours. I told the Sergeant to work only when Bosche was doing so."

"When are you going to 'blow' ——?"

"I am not sure of the date, but 'Dinkie' is going to 'poop' in a few days. He's got two tons under Bosche. It will be a —— fine show; right under his trenches. Ought to snip a hundred or so."

"Well," said another, "I was down in C shaft, and could hear Bosche working very hard, as if he had got all the world to himself."

At that moment a tunnelling-sergeant came in, and reported that the Bosche was much nearer. The listener could distinctly hear talking through the 'phone.

An officer immediately got up and went out with the sergeant, one of the speakers meanwhile suggesting that Brother Bosche was certainly going to visit realms of higher kultur than he had hitherto known.

Then came a close scrutinising of maps, showing shafts in the making and mines ready for " blowing "; of sharp orders to the tunnelling-sergeants and fatigue parties to bring charges from the magazine. The whole thing was fascinating in the extreme. A new branch of His Majesty's Service, and one of the most dangerous. To be on duty in a listening-post thirty feet underground—in a narrow tunnel, scarcely daring to breathe, listening to German miners making a counter-mine, and gradually picking their way nearer and nearer, until at last you can hear their conversation—would try the nerves of the strongest of men.

I went out, and made my way towards the well-known Quarries. Noting several interesting scenes of our Scottish battalions at work, I filmed them. A most pathetic touch was added to the scene, for a neat little graveyard occupied the right-hand corner, and about one hundred small crosses were there.

I was not allowed to remain very long. The Bosche sent over several aerial torpedoes, which exploded with terrific force and split up the ground as if a 12-inch H.E. shell had been at work. Naturally every one rushed to obtain as much cover as possible. I crossed to the other side of the Quarry, and entered a small tunnel, which led into a winding maze of narrow communication trenches.

"Be careful, sir," called a sentry. "Bosche is only thirty yards away, and they are plugging this corner pretty thoroughly; they're fairly whizzing through the sandbags, as if they warn't there, sir. They caught my Captain this morning, clean through the head. I was a-talking to him, sir, at the time; the finest gentleman that ever lived; and the swine killed him. I'll get six of them for him, sir." The look in his eyes and the tone of his voice told me he

IN THE MAIN STREET OF CONTALMAISON THE DAY OF ITS CAPTURE

LAUNCHING A SMOKE BARRAGE AT THE BATTLE OF ST. ELOI

A NIGHT ATTACK

was in earnest. I passed on, keeping as low as possible.

The crater, when I reached it, proved to be one of an enormous size. It must have been quite 150 feet across. The place had been converted into a miniature fort. I noticed how spongy the ground was. When walking it seemed as if one was treading upon rubber. I casually enquired of an officer the cause of it. " Dead bodies," said he ; " the ground here is literally choked with them ; we dare not touch it with a spade ; the condition is awful. There are thousands of them for yards down, and when a shell tears away any section of our parapets the sight is too ghastly for words."

At that moment a man yelled out " cover," and, looking up, I saw several Bosche rifle grenades falling. Shouting to my orderly to take cover with the camera, he disappeared into what I thought was a dug-out but which I afterwards discovered was an incline shaft to a mine. He made a running dive, and slid down about four yards before he pulled himself up. Luckily he went first, the camera butting up against him. He told us afterwards he thought he was really going to the lower regions.

I dived under a sandbag emplacement, when the grenades went off with a splitting crash, and after allowing a few seconds for the pieces to drop, looked out. A tragic sight met my gaze. The officer with whom I had been speaking a few moments before had, unfortunately, been too late in taking cover. One of the grenades had struck him on the head, and killed him on the spot. Within a few moments some Red Cross men reverently covered the body with a mackintosh sheet and bore it away. One more cross would be added to the little graveyard in the Quarry.

Shortly after I met an officer of the Mining Section. He was just going down into the gallery to listen to

Bosche working a counter-mine. Did I care to accompany him? " Don't speak above a whisper," he said.

He disappeared through a hole about three feet square. I followed, clinging to the muddy sides like a limpet, half sliding, half crawling, in the impenetrable darkness. We went on, seemingly for a great distance; in reality it was only about fifteen yards. Then we came to a level gallery, and in the distance, by the aid of a glow-lamp, I could see my companion crouching down, with a warning finger upon his lips to assure silence. The other side of him was a man of the tunnelling section, who had been at his post listening. The silence was uncanny after the din outside. In a few moments I heard a queer, muffled tap—tap—tap, coming through the earth on the left. I crept closer to my companion, and with my mouth close to his ear enquired whether that was the Bosche working.

" Yes," he said, " but listen with this," giving me an instrument very similar to a doctor's stethoscope.

I put it to my ear and rested the other end upon a ledge of mud. The effect was like some one speaking through a telephone. I could distinctly hear the impact of the pickaxe wielded by the Bosche upon the clay and chalk, and the falling of the debris.

I turned to him with a smile. " Brother Bosche will shortly have a rise in life ? "

" Yes," said he, " I think we shall ' blow ' first. It's going to be a race, though."

Final orders were given to the man in charge, then we crawled up again into the din of the crashing shells. I was more at home in these conditions. Down below the silence was too uncanny for me. When I reached our dug-out once more a message was waiting for me to return to H.Q., as important things were in prospect the following morning.

A NIGHT ATTACK

The message was urgent. Mines were to be blown at an early hour. I therefore decided that the best thing to do was to go into the trenches and stay the night, and so be prepared for anything that might happen. Little did I dream what the next forty-eight hours were going to bring. It's a good thing sometimes we don't know what the future has in store for us. The stoutest heart might fail under the conditions created by the abnormal atmosphere of a modern battlefield.

I prepared to depart at 8 p.m., and bidding adieu to my friends, I started off in the car. The guns were crashing out continuously. Several times I pulled the car up to shelter under some ruins. Then for a few minutes there was a lull, and directing my chauffeur to go ahead at top speed we reached our destination safely. I had barely entered this scene of desolation when Bosche shells came hurtling overhead and fell with a deafening explosion a short distance away. Here I had my first taste of gas from the German weeping shells. The air was suddenly saturated with an extraordinarily sweet smell. For the first few moments I quite enjoyed it. Then my eyes began to water freely, and pain badly. Realising at once that I was being " gassed," I bade the driver rush through the village, and as far beyond as possible.

His eyes, poor fellow, were in the same state. The car rolled and pitched its way through, smashing into shell-holes, bounding over fallen masonry, scraping by within a hair's-breadth of a recently smashed lorry. On and on, like a drunken thing. Still the air was thick with the foul gas. My eyes were burning; at last it was quite impossible to keep them open. But I had to get through, and so with a final effort looked ahead, and to my great relief found we were beyond the village, and the air smelt cleaner. I told the driver to pull up, and with a final roll the car landed its front wheels into a ditch.

For two hours afterwards I was to all intents and purposes blind. My eyes were burning, aching and weeping. The pain at last subsided, and collecting the apparatus we trudged off along the communication trench to the front line. Threading our way through seemed much more difficult than previously. The sides of the trenches had been blown in by shells a few minutes before, and this necessitated climbing over innumerable mounds of rubble; but working parties were quickly on the scene clearing a way through. At last I reached the dug-out previously referred to, and believe me, I was very thankful. The officer there seemed rather surprised to see me.

"Hullo!" he said. "What news? Anything doing?"

"Yes," I replied. "H.Q. says they are 'blowing' in the early morning, so I decided to come along to-night and fix up a good position for the camera, not desiring to attract the too earnest attentions of a Bosche sniper."

"Whose mine are they blowing?" said he. "I suppose I shall hear any moment." Just then a message came through on the 'phone. He picked up the receiver and listened intently. An earnest conversation was taking place. I could gather from the remarks that H.Q. was speaking. In a few minutes he replaced the receiver, and turning to me, said: "D shaft is going to blow; time, 7.15 a.m."

Soon after I turned in. Rolling myself in a blanket, I lay down on a trestle-bed in the corner, and in doing so disturbed a couple of rats, almost as large as rabbits, which had taken up their temporary quarters there. Apparently there were plenty of them, for several times I felt the brutes drop on my blanket from holes and crannies in the chalk. Needless to say, I could not sleep a wink, tired out as I was, and as I lay there, twenty feet underground, I could hear the rumble and roar of the shells crashing their way through our parapets, tearing, killing and maiming our brave lads, who throughout all these horrors held this section of our line like a wall of steel.

I had been lying there for about half an hour. Then I got up and climbed out of the incline into the open trench. I worked my way towards the firing trench; bullets from Bosche machine-guns and snipers were flattening themselves against the parapet. Several times I had to squeeze myself close to the muddy sides to allow stretcher-bearers to pass with their grim burdens; some for the corner of the Quarry, some for good old " Blighty."

I stayed for a while alongside a sentry.

" Any news ? " I asked.

" No, sir," said he, " but I feel as if something is going to happen."

" Come," said I, with a laugh, " this is not the time for dreaming."

" No, sir, I'm not dreaming, but I feel something—something that I can't explain."

" Well, cheer up," I said. " Good night."

" Good night, sir ! "

And as I wended my way along I could hear him softly whistling to himself the refrain of an old song.

At last I came upon the section opposite which our mine was going up in the morning, and cautiously looking over the parapet I surveyed the ground in front. There were several sandbags that required shifting. If they remained it would be necessary to place the camera higher above the top than was safe or wise. Carefully pulling myself up, I lay along the top of the parapet and pushed them aside. Several star-shells were fired whilst I was so engaged, and I dare not stir—I scarcely dared breathe—for fear the slightest movement would draw a stream of bullets in my direction.

Undoubtedly this was the only place from which to film the mine successfully. So marking the spot I slid down into the trench again, and retraced my steps to the dug-out. I found the officer I had previously seen enjoying a lovely, steaming tin of tea, and it wasn't many minutes before I was keeping him company. We sat chatting and smoking for a considerable time.

"Is everything ready?" I asked.

"Yes," he said. "There is over three thousand pounds of it there" (mentioning an explosive). "Brother Bosche will enjoy it."

"Let me see your map," I said, "and I'll point out the spot where I'm working. It's about eighty yards away from Bosche. If we work out the exact degree by the map of the 'blow,' I can obtain the right direction by prismatic compass, and a few minutes before 'time' lift the camera up and cover the spot direct. It'll save exposing myself unnecessarily above the parapet to obtain the right point of view." The point of view was accordingly settled. It was 124° from the spot chosen for the "blow."

We had been so busy over our maps that we had not noticed how quiet everything had become. Hardly a gun sounded; the silence was uncanny. Save for the scurrying of the rats and the drip—drip—drip of water, the silence was like that of the grave.

"What's wrong?" I asked.

"Bosche is up to no good when he drops silent so soon," he said. The words of the sentry recurred to me. "I've a feeling, sir, that I cannot describe." I was beginning to feel the same.

At length my companion broke the silence.

"As Bosche seems to be going easy, and our

A NIGHT ATTACK

artillery has shut up shop, let's lie down," and with that he threw himself on the bed. I sat on the box, which served as a table, smoking.

Half an hour went by. Things were livening up a bit. We began to hum a tune or two from the latest revue. Suddenly we were brought to our feet by a crashing sound that was absolutely indescribable in its intensity. I rushed up the incline into the trench. What a sight! The whole of our front for the distance of a mile was one frightful inferno of fire. The concentration of artillery fire was terrific! Scores of star-shells shot into the air at the same moment, lighting the ground up like day, showing up the smoking, blazing mass more vividly than ever. Hundreds of shells, large and small, were bursting over our trenches simultaneously; our guns were replying on the German front with redoubled fury; the air was alive with whirling masses of metal. The noise was indescribable. The explosions seemed to petrify one.

I made my way as near the front line as possible. A number of Scots rushed by me with a load of hand grenades. The trenches were packed with men rushing up to the fight. I asked an officer who raced by, breathlessly, if Bosche was getting through.

"Yes," he yelled; "they are trying to get through in part of my section. They have smashed our communication trenches so much that I have got to take my men round on the right flank. It's hell there!"

It was impossible to get through. The place was choked with men, many of them badly wounded; some of them, I'm afraid, destined as tenants of the little cemetery near by.

The awful nightmare continued. Men were coming and going. Reserves were being rushed forward; more bombs were being sent up. The Bosche artillery quietened down a bit, but only, as

I found out immediately afterwards, to allow their bombers to attack. I could see the flash of hundreds of bombs, each one possibly tearing the life out of some of our brave boys. Nothing in the world could have withstood such a concentrated artillery fire as the Germans put upon that five hundred yards of ground. It was torn and torn again, riven to shreds. It was like the vomiting of a volcano, a mass of earth soddened with the blood of the heroes who had tried to hold it.

The Germans came on, bombing their way across to what was left of our trench. They dug themselves in. Then with a whirl and a crash, our guns spoke again. Our boys, who had been waiting like dogs on a leash, sprang to the attack. Briton met Bosche. The battle swayed first this way then that. Our men drove the Germans out twice during the night, and held on to a section commanding the flank of the original position. Towards four o'clock the fighting ceased. Daylight was breaking. The wounded were still being passed to the rear.

I stopped and spoke to an officer. "How have you got on?" I asked.

"We occupy the left flank trench, and command the position. But, what a fight; it was worse than Loos." Then suddenly, "What are *you* doing here?"

"I am taking kinema pictures!" I said.

The look of amazement on his face was eloquent of his thoughts.

"Doing *what?*" he asked.

"I am taking kinema pictures," I repeated.

"Well I'm damned," were his exact words. "I never thought you fellows existed. I've always thought war pictures were fakes, but—well—now I know different," and giving me a hearty shake of the hand he went on his way.

Time was now drawing near for my work to begin.

A NIGHT ATTACK

Taking the camera to the selected point in the front line, which, luckily, was just on the left of the fighting area, I took my bearings by the aid of a compass. Fixing up a tripod in such close quarters was very difficult. I stretched an empty sandbag on a piece of wire, cut a hole in it and hung it on the front of the camera in such a position that the lens projected through the hole. The sandbag stretched far enough on either side to shelter my hands, especially the right one, which operated the machine.

I was now ready. I had to risk the attentions of the snipers; it was unavoidable. Little by little I raised the camera. It was now high enough up, and ramming some sand against the tripod legs, I waited.

Had the Bosche seen it?

Three more minutes, then the mine. One minute went by; no shots! Another minute went by. A bullet flew over my head. Immediately afterwards another buried itself in the parapet, then another. Surely they would hit it! Heavens how that last minute dragged! To be absolutely sure of getting the mine from the very beginning, I decided to start exposing a minute before time. It had to be done; reaching up, I started to expose. Another and another bullet flew by.

Then the thing happened which I had been dreading. The Bosche opened a machine-gun on me.

At that moment there was a violent convulsion of the ground, and with a tremendous explosion the mine went up. It seemed as if the whole earth in front of us had been lifted bodily hundreds of feet in the air. Showers of bombs exploded, showing that it had been well under the German position. Then with a mighty roar the earth and debris fell back upon itself, forming a crater about 150 feet across. Would our men rush the crater and occupy it ? On that chance, I kept turning the handle. The smoke subsided ; nothing else happened.

The show was over. No, not quite ; for as I hurriedly took down the camera, I evidently put my head up a little too high. There was a crack, and a shriek near my head, and my service cap was whisked off. The whole thing happened like a flash of lightning. I dropped into the bottom of the trench and picked up my cap. There, through the soft part of it, just above the peak, were two holes where a bullet had passed through. One inch nearer and it would have been through my head.

Can you realise what my thoughts were at that precise moment ?

CHAPTER IX

FOURTEEN THOUSAND FEET ABOVE THE GERMAN LINES

The First Kinematograph Film Taken of the Western Front—And How I Took It Whilst Travelling Through the Air at Eighty Miles an Hour—Under Shell-fire—Over Ypres—A Thrilling Experience—And a Narrow Escape—A Five Thousand Foot Dive Through Space.

"I FEEL confident I can manage it, and that the result will be both instructive and unique, and provided the weather is clear and I get as small a dose of 'Bosche' as possible, there is no reason why it shouldn't be successful."

"Of course, I am quite aware of the atmospheric difficulties. The fact that it is so thick and misty is entirely due to the heavy body of moisture in the ground—but if I start off early in the morning I may just escape it."

This conversation took place in the office of a certain British aerodrome in France between the Flight Commander and myself. We had been going into the pros and cons of an aerial expedition over the German lines. I was anxious to film the whole line from an aeroplane.

"Well," said he, "what about the height? I think I had better call in the Captain," and pressing a bell an orderly quickly appeared and was sent off to inform the Captain that his presence was required.

"I say," said the Flight Commander, "this is Malins, the War Office Kinematographer." He then explained my mission and requirements.

"Now," he said, after all preliminaries had been

discussed, " the question is about the height. What is a tolerably safe height over ' Bosche ' ? "

"About 8,000 feet, I should say, though of course if we go well over his lines it will be necessary to rise higher. There are too many ' Archibalds ' about to dodge any lower."

"Well," I replied, " I'll start taking my scenes when we arrive at the coast-line. We can then follow it along and turn off inland towards Ypres. I should very much like to film that place from above, then follow down the lines, passing over St. Eloi, Plœgsteert, Armentières, Neuve Chapelle, Richebourg, Festubert, Givenchy, Loos, Hohenzollern Redoubt, and on to Arras. I am of course entirely in your hands. I do not want to jeopardise the trip, nor wish you to run any unnecessary risks, you understand, but I should like to get as low as possible, and so obtain more detail. It will be the first kinematograph film ever taken of the Western Front."

"Well," said the Flight Commander, rising, " you have full permission. You can have the use of a BE 2C machine, with Captain ——. Do what you like, but take care. Don't be rash. Good luck to you. I shall be as anxious as you to see the result."

In the Captain's company I left the office, and together we went round to make arrangements regarding the means of fixing my camera.

The machine was the usual type of passenger-carrying aero, numbered BE 2C, a very stable and reliable machine, but according to the Captain, not very fast. Speed in this case was not an absolute necessity, unless a Fokker favoured us with his attentions.

I went aboard to find the best means of fixing and operating my camera. I decided to use my debrie, not the aeroscope. The latter had jambed a day or

IN THE TRENCHES AT THE FAMOUS AND DEADLY HOHENZOLLERN REDOUBT, AFTER A GERMAN ATTACK. SHORTLY AFTER THIS WAS TAKEN I WAS SHOT THROUGH MY SERVICE CAP BY A GERMAN SNIPER

two previous, and I had not had an opportunity of repairing it. The observer's seat was in the front, and just above, on the main struts, was a cross-tube of metal. On each end was an upright socket, for the purpose of dropping into it a Lewis gun. The pilot also had the same in front of him.

I suggested that a metal fixing, which would fit the socket, and a tilting arrangement, so that it would be possible to raise or lower the camera to any angle, would suit admirably, and on the other side, in case of attack, a Lewis gun could be fitted.

"It's well to be prepared for emergencies," said the Captain. "It's quite possible we shall be attacked."

"Well," I said, "I will have a good shot at him if he does turn up. And who knows—I may be able to get a picture of the Hun machine falling. By Jove, what a thrill it would provide!"

Instructions were given to the excellent mechanics employed in the R.F.C., and within an hour or so the metal tilting-top was made and fixed on the plane.

"You will have to wrap up well," said the Captain. "It's jolly cold up there. It looks rather misty, and that will make it all the worse. Now then, all aboard."

Up I scrambled, or rather wriggled, between a network of wire stays, and taking my seat the camera was handed to me. I fastened it on one side of the gun-mounting and fixed a Lewis gun on the other, making sure I had spare boxes of film ready, and spare drums of ammunition. I then fastened the broad web belt round my waist, and fixed on my goggles.

I was ready for the ascent.

My companion was in his seat, and the machine was wheeled into position for starting. The mechanics were turning the propeller round to suck the gas into the many cylinders, to facilitate easier starting.

"All ready," shouted the Captain. "Right away, contact, let her go." And with a jerk the motor started.

The whirl of the huge blades developed into a deafening roar. The machine vibrated horribly. I clung to my camera, holding it tight to the socket. I knew that once in the air the shake would be reduced to a minimum. Faster and faster whirled the propeller as the Captain opened the throttle. How sweet and perfect was the hum of the giant motor. Not the slightest sound of a misfire. Being an ardent motorist, I could tell that the engine was in perfect tune. The Captain leaned over and shouted to me through the roar to fasten the telephone receiver against my ear under my leather cap.

"That," said he, pointing to a mouthpiece attached to a small rubber tube, " is the transmitter. If you want to give me any instructions shout into that. I shall hear you. All fit ? " he asked.

I nodded my head. He took his seat, and opened the throttle. The engine leapt into new life. The roar was deafening. The whirring blades flung the air back into my face, cutting it as if with a whip. He dropped his arm. The men drew away the chocks from the wheels, and amid shouts of "Good luck!" from the officers present, the machine sprang forward like a greyhound, bounding over the grass, until at last it rose like a gigantic bird into the air.

The earth gradually drew away. Higher and higher we rose, and began to circle round and round to gain height.

"We will get up to three thousand feet before we strike towards the coast," he shouted through the telephone.

The vibration, now we were in the air, was barely

perceptible, at any rate it was not sufficient to affect the taking of my scenes. In case any moisture collected on my lens, I had brought a soft silk pad, to wipe it with occasionally. Higher, still higher, we rose.

"What's the height now?" I asked.

"Very nearly three thousand feet," he said. "We are now going towards the coast. That's Dunkirk over there."

I peered ahead. The port, with its shipping, was clearly discernible. Over the sea hung a dense mist, looking for all the world like a snowfield. Here and there, in clear patches, the sun gleamed upon the water, throwing back its dazzling reflections.

As soon as we reached the coast-line, I shouted: "Proceed well along this side, so that I can obtain an oblique view. It looks much better than directly above the object. What's our speed?"

"Sixty miles," he said. "I shall keep it up until we reach the German lines."

He turned sharp to the right. We are now following the coast-line towards Ostend. How beautiful the sand dunes looked from above. The heavy billows of sea-mist gave it a somewhat mystic appearance. How cold it was. I huddled down close into my seat, my head only above the fuselage. Keeping my eye upon the wonderful panorama unfolding itself out beneath me, I glanced at my camera and tested the socket. Yes, it was quite firm.

"We are nearing the lines now," my companion shouted. "Can you see them on your right? That's the Belgium area. Our section, as you know, begins just before Ypres. Will this height suit you? Shall I follow the trenches directly overhead or a little to one side?"

"Keep this side, I'll begin taking now." Kneeling up in my seat, I directed my camera downwards and started filming our lines and the German position stretching away in the distance.

We were nearing Ypres, that shell-battered city of Flanders. White balls of smoke here and there were bursting among the ruins, showing that the Huns were still shelling it. What a frightful state the earth was in. For miles and miles around it had the appearance of a sieve, with hundreds of thousands of shell-holes, and like a beautiful green ribbon, winding away as far as the eye could see, was that wonderful yet terrible strip of ground between the lines, known as " No Man's Land."

We were now running into a bank of white fleecy clouds, which enveloped us in its folds, blotting the whole earth from view. I held my handkerchief over the lens of the camera to keep the moisture from settling upon it. After a time several breaks appeared in the clouds beneath, and the earth looked wonderful. It seemed miles—many miles—away. Rivers looked like silver streaks, and houses mere specks upon the landscape. Here and there a puff of white smoke told of a bursting shell. But for that occasional, somewhat unpleasant reminder, I might have been thousands of miles away from the greatest war in history.

Who could imagine anything more wonderful, more fantastic ? I had dreamed of such things, I had read of them ; I even remembered having read, years ago, some of the wonderful stories in *Grimm's Fairy Tales*. To my childish mind, they seemed very wonderful indeed. There were fairies, goblins, mysterious figures, castles which floated in the air, wonderful lands which shifted in a night, at the touch of a magic wand or the sound of a magic word. Things which fired my youthful imagination and set me longing to share in their adventures. But never in my wildest dreams did I think I should live to do the same thing, to go where I listed ; to fly like a bird, high above the clouds. It was like an adventure in fairyland to take this weird and wonderful creation of men, called an aeroplane, through the home of the skylark.

Boom! Boom! I was suddenly brought back to—no, not to earth, but to—things more material.

Looking down, I could discern several balls of smoke, which I immediately recognised as shrapnel shells, or "Archibalds," that had been fired at us by the Germans. They were well below. I looked round at the Captain. He was smiling through his goggles, and humorously jerked his thumb in the direction of the bursting "Archies."

"Too high, eh?" I shouted. But I had forgotten that in the fearful hum of the rushing air and whirling motors my voice would not carry. It was literally cut off as it left my lips. I picked up the 'phone and shouted through it.

"Yes, they are pretty safe where they are," he said drily. Then a few more burst underneath us.

By this time we were well out of the cloud bank. The atmosphere was much clearer. I knelt up again on my seat and began to expose, and continued turning the handle while we passed over St. Eloi and Hill 60. On certain sections I could see that a considerable "strafe" was going on. Fritz seemed to be having a very trying time. Near Messines my film suddenly ran out. I had to reload. This was anything but an easy operation. I unscrewed my camera from the gun socket, and in doing so had a near escape from doing a head-dive to earth. Like an idiot, I had unfastened my waist-strap, and in reaching over the fuselage my camera nearly overbalanced, the aeroplane contributing to this result by making a sudden dive in order to avoid an "Archibald."

For a second or two I had clear visions of flying through space on wings other than those of an aeroplane. But fortunately I had the steel crossbar to cling to, and this saved me.

Getting back to my seat, I asked the pilot to circle round the spot for a few minutes. While changing my spool, I settled down in the bottom of the car and reloaded my camera, eight thousand feet above the earth. This operation occupied about ten minutes, and when I had finished I gingerly raised myself on the seat and refixed the camera in its socket.

"Right away," I shouted. "Is it possible to go any lower?"

"It's very risky," he said, "but if you like I will try. Hold tight, it's a dive."

I held tight. The nose of the machine tilted forward until it seemed as if it was absolutely standing on end. The earth rushed up to meet us. For the moment it seemed as if the aeroplane was out of control, but with a graceful glide, which brought us level, we continued our journey at a height of three thousand feet.

"Get what you want quickly," he shouted. "We can't stay here long."

I began to expose again. By now we were over line after line of trenches. At times we were well over the Bosche lines. I continued to film the scenes.

First came Plœgsteert, Fromelles, and Aubers Ridge. Then we crossed to Neuve Chapelle, Festubert, La Bassée and Loos. Town after town, village after village, were passed over, all of them in ruins. From above the trenches, like a splash of white chalk dropped into the middle of a patch of brown earth. The long winding trenches cut out of the chalk twisted and wound along valley and dale like a serpent. Looking down upon it all, it seemed so very insignificant. Man? What was he? His works looked so small that it seemed one could, with a sweep of the foot, crush him out of existence. How small he was, yet how great; how powerful, yet how weak! We were now over La Bassée.

"We shall have to rise," shouted my companion. "Look up there." I looked up, and thousands of feet above us was a small speck.

"Bosche plane," said he. "Hold tight!" And I did.

CHAPTER X

FILMING THE EARTH FROM THE CLOUDS

Chasing an " Enemy " Aeroplane at a Height of 13,500 Feet—And What Came of It—A Dramatic Adventure in which the Pilot Played a Big Part—I Get a Nasty Shock—But am Reassured—A Freezing Experience—Filming the Earth as we Dived Almost Perpendicularly—A Picture that would Defy the Most Ardent Futurist to Paint.

"IS that gun ready?" asked my companion, twisting round in his seat. I nodded. "Right-o! I'm going to get up higher. We are absolutely lost down here."

I fixed on a drum of cartridges, and with a butt in my hand was ready for any emergency. Higher and higher we rose. The mist was becoming more and more dense. Photographing was impossible. The cold seemed to chill one's bones. I could tell by the increasing vibration we were going " all out," in order to get above the enemy machine, which seemed to be drawing closer and closer. I looked at the pilot. He had his eyes fixed upon the Bosche.

" What are we now ? "

" Eight thousand," he said. " That chap must be at least thirteen thousand up. Do you notice whether he is coming nearer ? "

I told him it seemed to me as if he was doing so.

Up and up we went. Colder and colder it grew. My face was frozen. To breathe, I had to turn my head sideways to avoid the direct rush of air from the whirling propeller. I could just discern the ground through the mist. I looked around for the Bosche. He seemed further away. I shouted to the pilot. He looked round.

" I'm going to chase it," he said. And away he went. But the faster we moved the faster went the other machine. At last we discovered the reason. In fact, I believe we both discovered it at precisely the same moment. *The plane was one of our own!* I looked at the Captain. He smiled at me, and I'm positive he felt disappointed at the discovery.

" What's the height ? " I enquired.

" About thirteen thousand feet," he said. " Shall we go higher ? We may get above the mist."

" Try a little more," I replied. " But I don't think it will be possible to film any more scenes to-day ; the fog is much too heavy."

The whole machine was wet with moisture. It seemed as if we should never rise above it. I had never before known it so thick. My companion asked if we should return. With reluctance I agreed, then, turning round face to the sun, we rushed away.

The mist did not seem to change. Mile after mile we encountered the same impenetrable blanket of clammy moisture. I was huddling as tight as possible to the bottom of the seat, taking advantage of the least bit of cover from the biting, rushing swirl of icy-cold air. Mile after mile ; it seemed hours up there in the solitude. I watched the regular dancing up and down of the valves on top of the engine. I was thinking of a tune that would fit to the regular beat of the tappets.

I shouted through the 'phone.

No answer.

He must be too cold to speak, I thought. For myself, I did not know whether I had jaws or not. The lashing, biting wind did not affect my face now. I could feel nothing. Once I tried to pinch my cheek ; it was lifeless. It might have been clay. My jaw was practically set stiff. I could only just articulate.

I tried again to attract my companion's attention. Still no answer.

I was wondering whether anything had happened to him, when something did happen which very nearly petrified me. I felt a clutch on my shoulder. Quickly turning my head, I was horrified to see him standing on his seat and leaning over my shoulder.

"Get off the telephone tube, you idiot. You are sitting on it," he shouted. "We can't speak to one another."

"Telephone be damned!" I managed to shout. "Get back to your seat. Don't play monkey-tricks up here."

If you can imagine yourself fourteen thousand feet above the earth, sitting in an aeroplane, and the pilot letting go all his controls, as he stands on his feet shouting in your ear, you will be able to realise, but only to a very slight extent, what my feelings were at this precise moment.

He returned to his seat. He was smiling. I fumbled about underneath and found the tube. Putting it to my mouth, I asked him what he meant by it.

"That's all right, my dear chap," he said, "there's no need to get alarmed. The old bus will go along merrily on its own."

"I'll believe all you say. In fact I'll believe anything you like to tell me, but I'd much rather you sit in your seat and control the machine," I replied.

He chuckled, apparently enjoying the joke to the full, but during the remainder of the journey I made sure I was not sitting on the speaking tube.

The mist was gradually clearing now. The sun shone gloriously, the clouds, a long way beneath us, looked more substantial; through the gaps in their fleecy whiteness the earth appeared. It seemed a long time since I had seen it. We were again coming to the edge of a cloud bank. The atmosphere beyond was exceedingly clear.

"We are nearly home," said my companion. "Are you going to take any more scenes?"

"Yes," I said, "I suppose you'll spiral down?"

"Right-ho!"

"I'll take a film showing the earth revolving. It'll look very quaint on the screen."

"Here goes then. We are going to dive down to about six thousand feet, so hold on tight to your strap."

The engines almost stopped. Suddenly we seemed to be falling earthwards. Down—down—down! We were diving as nearly perpendicular as it is possible to be. Sharp pains shot through my head. It was getting worse. The pain was horrible. The right side of my face and head seemed as if a hundred pin-points were being driven into it. I clutched my face in agony; then I realised the cause. Coming down from such a height, at so terrific a speed, the different pressure of the atmosphere affected the blood pressure on the head.

Suddenly the downward rush was stopped. The plane was brought to an even keel.

"I'm going to spiral now," said the pilot. "Ready?"

"Right away," I said, and knelt again in my seat. The plane suddenly seemed to swerve. Then it slanted at a most terrifying angle, and began to descend rapidly towards the earth in a spiral form. I filmed the scene on the journey. To say the earth looked extraordinary would be putting it very mildly. The ground below seemed to rush up and mix with the clouds. First the earth seemed to be over one's head, then the clouds. I am sure the most ardent futurist artist would find it utterly impossible to do justice to such a scene. Round and round we went. Now one side, now the other. How I held to my camera-handle goodness only knows. Half the time, I am sure, I turned it mechanically.

Suddenly we came to an even keel. The earth seemed within jumping distance. The nose dipped again, the propeller whirled. Within a few seconds we were bounding along on the grassy space of the aerodrome, and finally coming to rest we were surrounded by the mechanics, who quickly brought the machine to a standstill.

"By the way," I said to the pilot, as we went off to tea, "how long were we up there altogether?"

"Two hours," he replied.

Two hours! Great Scott! It seemed days!

CHAPTER XI

PREPARING FOR THE "BIG PUSH"

The Threshold of Tremendous Happenings—General ——'s Speech to His Men on the Eve of Battle—Choosing My Position for Filming the " Big Push "—Under Shell-fire—A Race of Shrieking Devils—Fritz's Way of " Making Love "—I Visit the " White City "—And On the Way have Another Experience of Gas Shells.

THE time for which England has been preparing during these past two awful years is here. We are now on the threshold of tremendous happenings. The Great Offensive is about to begin. What will be the result ?

We see the wonderful organisation of our vast armies, and we know the firm and resolute methods of our General Staff—as I have seen and known them during the war—would leave nothing to be desired. As a machine, it is the most wonderful that was ever created.

My position as Official Kinematographer has afforded me unique opportunities to gain knowledge of the whole system required to wage the most terrible war that has ever been known to mankind. I have not let these opportunities slip by.

The great day was coming ; there was a mysterious something which affected every one at G.H.Q. There was no definite news to hand ; nobody, with the exception of those directly concerned, knew when and where the blow was to be struck. Some thought on the northern part of our line, others the centre ; others, again, the south. In the home, in the streets, in the cafés and gardens, the one topic of conversation was—the coming Great Offensive.

I was told by a colonel that my chance to make history was coming. That was all. But those few words conveyed an enormous lot to me. Later in the day I was told by a captain to proceed to the front line, to choose a suitable position wherein to fix up my camera. Our section facing Gouerment was suggested to me as the place where there was likely to be the most excitement, and I immediately set out for that section. During the journey I was held up by a large body of our men, who turned out afterwards to be the London Scottish. They were formed up in a square, and in the centre was a general, with his staff officers, addressing the men. His words thrilled the hearts of every one who heard them:

"Gentlemen of the London Scottish: Within the next few days you will take part in the greatest battle in the history of the world. To you has been entrusted the taking and holding of Gouerment. . . . England is looking to you to free the world from slavery and militarism that is epitomized in the German nation and German Kultur. . . . Gentlemen, I know you will not fail, and from the bottom of my heart I wish you the best of luck."

I waited until the address was finished, and then proceeded to a certain place, striking out on the left and trudging through innumerable communication trenches, at times up to my knees in mud and water. Eventually I reached an eminence facing the village of Gouerment. It was in a valley. The German trenches ran parallel with my position, and on the right I could discern the long green ribbon of grass termed "No Man's Land," stretching as far as the eye could see. The whole front of the German lines was being shelled by our heavy guns; the place was a spitting mass of smoke and flame. Salvo after salvo was being poured from our guns.

"What an inspiring sight," I said to an officer

IN A SHELL HOLE IN "NO MAN'S LAND" FILMING OUR HEAVY BOMBARDMENT OF THE GERMAN LINES. I GOT INTO THIS POSITION DURING THE NIGHT PREVIOUS. IT WAS HERE THAT I EARNED THE SOUBRIQUET "MALINS OF NO MAN'S LAND"

PREPARING FOR THE "BIG PUSH" 123

standing by my side, " and these shells were made by the women of England."

"Well," he said, "you see Gommecourt; that's all coming down in a day or two. Every gun, large and small, will concentrate its fire on it, and level it to the ground. That's your picture."

"In that case," I replied, "I shall want to be much nearer our front line. I must get within five hundred yards of it. What a sight! What a film it will be!"

I stood watching the bombardment for some time, then fixing my camera position, I returned. Divisional H.Q. told me I should be informed in ample time when the attack was to be made.

That afternoon I returned to G.H.Q., but the best laid schemes of mice and men aft gang agley. I was told that night to prepare immediately to proceed to the H.Q. of a certain Division, with instructions to attach myself to them for the next week; all particulars would be given to me in the morning.

I received my instructions next morning. I was to proceed to the Division, report myself, and I should receive all the information and assistance I required. With parting wishes for the best of luck, and "don't come back wounded," I left H.Q., and proceeded by car to the Company H.Q., where I was received with every courtesy by General ——.

He told me the best thing to do was to go to Divisional H.Q. and see the General. He had been informed of my arrival, and the final details could be arranged with him, such as the best points of vantage for fixing up my camera. Accordingly I hurried off to Divisional H.Q. and met the General. On being ushered into his room, I found him sitting at a table with a large scale map of a certain section of our line before him. He looked the very incarnation of indomitable will, this General of the incomparable —— Division.

I quickly explained my mission, and told him I should like to go to the front trenches to choose my position.

"Certainly," he said, "that is a very wise plan, but if you will look here I will show you the spot which, in my opinion, will make an ideal place. This is the German position. This, of course, is Beaumont Hamel, which is our objective. This is as far as we are going; it will be a pivot from which the whole front south of us will radiate. We are going to give the village an intense bombardment this afternoon, at 4 o'clock; perhaps you would like to obtain that?"

"Yes, sir," I replied, "it is most necessary to my story. What guns are you using?"

"Everything, from trench mortars to 15-inch howitzers. We are going to literally raze it to the ground. It is one of the strongest German redoubts, and it's not going to be an easy job to occupy it; but we achieved the impossible at Gallipoli, and with God's help we will win here. There is a spot here in our firing trench called 'Jacob's Ladder,'" and pointing to the map, he showed it me.

"That certainly looks a most excellent point, sir," I said. "What is the distance from Bosche lines?"

"About 150 yards. They 'strafe' it considerably, from what I am told; but, of course, you will have to take your chance, the same as all my other officers."

"That is unavoidable, sir. The nature of my work does not permit me to be in very comfortable places, if I am to get the best results."

"Right," he said, "if you will report to Brigade H.Q. the Brigade Major will give you what orderlies you require, and you had better draw rations with

PREPARING FOR THE "BIG PUSH"

them while you are there. He has instructions to give you every assistance."

"Oh, by the way, sir, what time does the mine go up?"

"Ten minutes to zero," he replied. "You quite understand, don't you? Major —— will give you zero time to-morrow night."

After lunching with the General I started off for Brigade H.Q. The weather was vile. It had been raining practically without break for several days, and was doing its best to upset everything and give us as much trouble as possible.

What an enormous number of munition waggons and lorries I passed on the road ; miles and miles of them, all making for the front line. "Ye gods!" I thought, "Bosche is certainly going to get it."

I reached my destination about 2.30. What a "strafe" there was going on! The concussion of what I afterwards found out was our 15-inch howitzers was terrible. The very road seemed to shake, and when I opened the door of the temporary Brigade H.Q., one gun which went off close by shook the building to such an extent that I really thought for the moment a shell had struck the house.

"Captain ——, I presume?" said I, addressing an officer seated at a long table making out reports and giving them over to waiting dispatch riders. The room was a hive of industry.

"Gad, sir," he said, "are you the kinema man? I am pleased to see you. Take a seat, and tell me what you want. You are the last person I expected to see out here. But, seriously, are you really going to film ' The Day ' ? "

"Yes," I replied.

"Where do you propose to take it?"

"General —— suggested ' Jacob's Ladder.' "

"What ? " came a startled chorus from about half a dozen other officers. "Take photos from

'Jacob's Ladder,'" they repeated in tones of amazement. "Good Lord! it's an absolute death-trap. Bosche strafes it every day, and it's always covered by snipers."

"Well," I said, "it certainly seems by the map to be an ideal place to get the mine going up and the advance over ' No Man's Land.' "

"Granted, but—well!—it's your shoot. Will you let us introduce the doctor? You'll need him."

"Gentlemen," I said, with mock gravity, "I assure you it would be most difficult for me to receive a more cordial welcome." This remark caused some laughter. Turning to the Captain, I said: " Will you give me an orderly? One who knows the trenches, as I wish to go there this afternoon to film the 'strafe' at 4 o'clock. I shall stay down there for the next few days, to be on the spot for ' The Day,' and ready for anything that follows."

"Certainly," he said. "Have you got a trench map? What about blankets and grub?"

"I have my blanket and some provisions, but if I can draw some bully and biscuits, I shall manage quite well."

Having secured supplies and filled my knapsack, I strapped it on my shoulder, fixed the camera-case on my back and, handing the tripod to another man, started off. I had hardly got more than two hundred yards when the Captain ran up to me and said that he had just had a 'phone message from D.H.Q., saying that the General was going to address the men on the following day, before proceeding to battle. Would I like to film the scene? It would take place about 10 a.m. Naturally, I was delighted at the prospect of such a picture, and agreed to be on the field at the time mentioned. Then with a final adieu we parted.

The weather was still vile. A nasty, drizzly mist

hung over everything. The appearance of the whole country was much like it is on a bad November day at home. Everything was clammy and cold. The roads were covered to a depth of several inches with slimy, clayey mud. Loads of munitions were passing up to the Front. On all sides were guns, large and small. The place bristled with them, and they were so cunningly hidden that one might pass within six feet of them without being aware of their existence. But you could not get away from the sounds. The horrible dinning continued, from the sharp rat-tat-tat-tat of the French 75mm., of which we had several batteries in close proximity, and from the bark of the 18-pounders to the crunching roar of the 15-inch howitzer. The air was literally humming with shells. It seemed like a race of shrieking devils, each trying to catch up with the one in front before it reached its objective.

Salvo after salvo ; crash after crash ; and in the rare moments of stillness, in this nerve-shattering prelude to the Great Push, I could hear the sweet warblings of a lark, as it rose higher and higher in the murky, misty sky.

At one place I had to pass through a narrow lane, and on either side were hidden batteries, sending round upon round into the German trenches, always under keen observation from enemy-spotting balloons and aeroplanes. The recent shell-holes in the roadway made me pause before proceeding further. I noticed a sergeant of the Lancashire Fusiliers at the entrance to a thickly sand-bagged shelter, and asked him if there was another way to the section of the front line I sought.

"No, sir," he said, "that is the only way ; but it's mighty unhealthy just now. The Hun is crumpling it with his 5·9-inch H.E., and making a tidy mess of the road. But he don't hit our guns, sir. He just improves their appearance by making a nice little frill of earth around them, he does, and—look out, sir; come in here.

"Here she comes!"

With a murderous shriek and horrible splitting roar a German shell burst on the roadway about fifty yards away.

"That is Fritz's way of making love, sir," he said, with a chuckle; which remark admirably reflects the marvellous morale of our men.

"Have they been shelling the avenues much?" I asked, referring to the various communication trenches leading to the front line.

"Yes, sir. Nos. 1, 2 and 3 are being severely crumped. I would suggest No. 5, sir; it's as clear as any of them. I should advise you to get along this lane as fast as possible. I have been here some time, so I know Fritz's little ways."

He saluted, and like a mole disappeared into his dug-out as I moved away.

I told my man to keep about ten yards behind me, so that in the event of a shell bursting near by one or the other of us would have a chance of clearing.

"Now," I said, "let it go at a double. Come on," and with head well forward I raced up the road.

Altogether, with my camera, I was carrying about seventy pounds in weight, so you can guess it was no easy matter. There was about another 150 yards to go, when I heard the ominous shriek of a German shell.

"Down in the ditch," I yelled. "Lie flat," and suiting the action to the word, I flung myself down in the mud and water near a fallen tree. Crash came the shell, and it exploded with a deafening roar more on the side of the road than the previous one, and near enough to shower mud and water all over me as I lay there.

"Now then," I yelled to my man, "double-up before they range the next one," and jumping up

PREPARING FOR THE "BIG PUSH"

we raced away. Not before I had got well clear, and near the old railway station, did I stay and rest. While there several shells crashed in and around the road we had just left. I was glad I was safely through.

With the exception of the usual heavy shelling, getting down to the front trench was quite uneventful. My objective was a place called " The White City," so called because it is cut out of the chalk-bank of our position facing Beaumont Hamel. Getting there through the communication trenches was as difficult as in the winter. In places the mud and water reached my knees, and when you had come to the end of your journey you were as much like dirty plaster-cast as anything possibly could be.

After three-quarters of an hour's trudging and splashing I reached " The White City," and turned down a trench called " Tenderloin Street." About one hundred yards on my right, at the junction of " King Street" and "St. Helena Street," my guide pointed me out the Brigade dug-out. Depositing my camera and outfit close to some sandbags I went inside and introduced myself. Four officers were present.

" By Jove ! " said one, " you are welcome. Have a drink. Here's a cigarette."

" Here you are," said another, " have a match. Now tell us all the news from home. My word, we haven't heard a blessed thing for days. Have you really come to photograph ' The Day ' ? "

" Yes," I replied. " But I have come this afternoon to look round, and to film the ' strafe ' at Beaumont Hamel. You know the trenches round here : where can I see the village to the best advantage ? "

" Well," said one, " there are several places, but Bosche is ' hating ' us rather this afternoon, and the firing trench is anything but healthy. He's been properly dosing us with 'whizz-bangs,' but you know he *will* have his bit of fun. You see, when Fritz starts we let off a few 'flying pigs' in return, which undoubtedly disturbs his peace of mind."

"By my map, a spot called 'Lanwick Street' seems likely," I said. "It's bang opposite the village, and they are putting the 15-inch on the eastern corner. If you will be good enough to guide me, I will have a look now; it will take me some time to fix up my camera in reasonable safety."

"You won't find much safety there," he replied. "We have practically to rebuild the parapet every night, but only for a few more days, thank Heaven! Anyway, come along."

We proceeded by way of "King Street" to "Lanwick Street," and several times we had to fall flat in the trench bottom to escape being hit by shells. They seemed at times to burst almost overhead. The "whizz-bangs" which Fritz puts over are rather little beggars; you have no time to dodge them. They come with a "phut" and a bang that for sheer speed knocks spots off a flash of lightning. One only thinks to duck when the beastly thing has gone off.

"Lanwick Street" was the usual sort of trench. At one end was an artillery observation officer, correcting the range of his guns.

"Go easy, won't you?" he said to me. "Bosche has an idea we use this corner for something rather important. If he sees your camera we shall certainly receive his attention. For Heaven's sake, keep your head down."

"Right-o!" I said. "Lend me your periscope; I will have a look at the ground first through that."

I looked on the village, or rather the late site of it. It was absolutely flattened out, with the exception of a few remaining stumps of trees, which used to be a beautiful wood, near which the village nestled.

PREPARING FOR THE "BIG PUSH"

"That's been done by our guns in five days; some mess, eh?"

"My word, yes. Now about this afternoon's bombardment; they are working on the left-hand corner."

I chose a spot for working and fixing up my tripod, and waited until 4.30 p.m.

In the meantime, with the aid of a stick, I gradually pushed away several sandbags which interfered with my view on the parapet. To do this it was necessary to raise myself head and shoulders above the top and, with one arm pushed forward, I worked the bags clear. I felt much better when that job was done.

"You're lucky," said the A.O. "I had one of my periscopes hit clean by a bullet this morning. Fritz must be having a nap, or he would have had you for a cert."

"Anyway," I replied, "it gives me a comparatively clear view now."

Time was drawing near. I prepared my camera by clothing it in an old piece of sacking, and gently raising it on to the tripod I screwed it tight. Then gradually raising my head to the view-finder, I covered the section which was going to be "strafed," and wrapping my hand in a khaki handkerchief, waited.

Our guns were simply pouring shells on the Bosche. The first of the 15-inch came over and exploded with a deafening roar. The sight was stupefying.

I began to expose my film, swinging the camera first on one side then the other. Shell after shell came roaring over; one dropped on the remaining walls of a château, and when the smoke had cleared there was absolutely nothing left. How in the world anything could live in such a maelstrom of explosive it is difficult to conceive.

I continued to expose my film at intervals until

about 6 o'clock, and twice I had to snatch my camera down hastily and take shelter, for the "whizz-bangs" came smashing too close for safety.

I was just taking down my camera when several shells exploded in the trenches about fifteen yards behind us. Then a man came running into our traverse: "Shure, sor," he said, "and it's gas-shells the dirty swine are sending over. My eyes seem to be burning out." His eyes were undoubtedly bad. Tears were pouring down his cheeks, and he was trying to ease the pain by binding his handkerchief over them. Then I smelt the gas, and having had a previous dose at Vernilles, and not wishing for further acquaintance with it, I bade my man rush as quickly as possible back to "The White City."

I got back to H.Q. dug-out just in time for tea. I told the officers present of my success in filming the "strafe," and I learned that it was the first time Fritz had put tear-shells over them. "We must certainly prepare our goggles," they said.

"Have you seen 'Jacob's Ladder'?" enquired one of the officers.

"No," I replied, "I shall wait until dusk. It will then be safer to move about."

We sat smoking and talking about the prospects of the "Big Push," and at last we all lapsed into silence, which was broken by the arrival of a lieutenant. The Captain looked up from his bench. "Hullo, what's up? Any news?"

"Oh, no; nothing much, sir," said he, "but H.Q. wishes me to go out for a raid to-night. They want a Bosche to talk to; there are a few things they want to know. We haven't brought one in for several nights now. They asked me to go out again; I said, if there was one to be had my Company would bring him along."

GEOFFREY H. MALINS, O.B.E., OFFICIAL KINEMATOGRAPHER TO THE WAR OFFICE

PREPARING FOR THE "BIG PUSH"

"Right-o!" said the Captain. "Who are you taking?"

"—— for one, and a few men—the same lot that have been across with me before. H.Q. specially want to know the actual results of the heavy 'strafe.' They are going to cease fire to-night, between twelve and one. I want to find out where their machine guns are fixed up——" And so the conversation went on.

At that moment another officer came in, and I got him to show me round "Jacob's Ladder." We went through "King Street" again, and followed the trench until we arrived at the place. The formation of this point was extraordinary.

A stranger coming upon it for the first time would undoubtedly get a slight shock for, upon turning into a traverse, you come abruptly upon an open space, as if the trench had been sliced off, leaving an opening from which you could look down upon our front line trenches, not only upon them but well in front of them.

I was on the bank of a small valley; leading down from this position were about twenty-five steps, hence the name "Jacob's Ladder." Our parapet still followed down, like the handrail of a staircase, only of course much higher.

The position from a photographic point of view was admirable, and I doubt whether on any other part of our front such a suitable point could be found. "Jove!" I said, "this is the ideal place. I will definitely decide upon it."

"If you look carefully over here you will see the Bosche line quite plainly. They are about seventy yards away, and at that point we are going to put a barrage of fire on their second line with our Stokes guns. We are going to do that from 'Sunken Road,' midway in 'No Man's Land.' Can you see it there?"

"Yes," I replied; "splendid. As soon as I have

got the mine exploding, and our men going over the parapet and across 'No Man's Land,' I can immediately—if all's well—swing my camera on to the barrage and film that. This is a wonderful position."

"It rests entirely with Fritz now. If he does not crump this place you will be all right, but they are sure to plaster our front trench as soon as they see us go over."

"Well, I must risk that," I said.

And we turned and retraced our steps to the "White City," where I bade my companion good night, and returned to film the scene of the General's speech to his men the following morning.

CHAPTER XII

FILMING UNDER FIRE

The General's Speech to the Fusiliers Before Going Into Action—Filming the 15-inch Howitzers—A Miniature Earthquake—" The Day " is Postponed—Keeping Within " The Limits "—A Surprise Meeting in the Trenches—A Reminder of Other Days—I Get Into a Tight Corner—And Have An Unpleasantly Hot Experience—I Interview a Trench Mortar—Have a Lively Quarter of an Hour—And Then Get Off.

RAIN, rain, rain. It was like a dull, dismal December night. Owing to the tramping of hundreds of feet up and down the trenches, they became like a quagmire. We slipped and slid, clutching to the sticky, clay walls, and floundering up to our knees in holes, and, to make matters worse, Bosche, who knew that this was the time we brought up fresh munitions, crumped the Fifth Avenue as hard as he could. One or two shells crashed into the trench on the way up, and I had to pass over two working parties (by the aid of a candle-light, screened) searching for, and placing the remains of their comrades in sacks.

Good God! it's a hellish game; and the terror of war gripped one's heartstrings that night. The momentary flash of the exploding shells lighted up the faces of the men with ghastly vividness, some grinding out curses then groping blindly on. I was glad when the journey was ended, and I turned into a dug-out in the village to rest for the night.

Next morning a misty, drizzly pall still hung over everything. I wondered how in the world our men were going to attack under such conditions, and to-morrow was " The Day." I pitied them with all my heart and soul. And then I thought of myself, and my own particular job. I couldn't possibly " take " in such disgusting weather. The result would be an absolute failure. I controlled my feelings, and hoped for the best.

The time arrived for the General's speech. Reaching the field, I found all the men mustered up. The General had just arrived. I started to film the scenes as they presented themselves to me. Jove! The speech was the most impressive that I had ever heard. I will give it as it was spoken, as near as I can. I do not think that it has been published before :

" Officers and men of the West Riding Field Company, R.E., and — Battalion, Royal Fusiliers :

" I hoped yesterday to be able to come and wish you good luck, on the first anniversary of the engagement in Gully Ravine, there the Royal Fusiliers took the Turkish fifth line of trenches. Owing to the rain, however, and to the discomfort to which you would have been placed, I postponed my visit until to-day.

" I want to tell you something of the situation as it now stands. You are probably aware that we are now taking part in the greatest battle ever fought by British troops. Not only is it of far more importance than any fight since Waterloo, but the numbers engaged far exceed any assembly of troops in former days. The strength of this army,—the Fourth Army—under General Sir H. S. Rawlinson, is —— times as large as the force of British troops at Mons, when we first came out a year and a half ago.

" The importance of winning a great victory is so great that nothing has been left undone to ensure success. But the higher Commanders know—and I know—that all the best arrangements in the world cannot win battles. Battles are won by infantry, and it is to the battalions like yourself that we look to gain a great victory, equal to the great victory which the Russians have obtained this month.

" The Germans are shut in all round. On their northern flank they are shut in by the British Navy, on the eastern flank pressed back by the Russians, on the southern flank the Italians are advancing, and this week, on the western flank, certain Divisions of the French and many Divisions of the British are determined to break their line and drive them back to their own country.

"Officers and men of the —— Battalion, the Royal Fusiliers : You are very fortunate in having this opportunity to add to the high honours already gained by your distinguished regiment. Not only, however, are you fighting for your battalion and your regiment, you are fighting to maintain against the Germans the same high reputation which you have won for the —— Division on the Gallipoli Peninsula. More than that, you are fighting for your country, and also you are fighting for Christianity and Humanity. You are fighting for truth and justice against oppression. We are fighting for our liberty against slavery.

"It is now thirty-three years since I was first associated with the Royal Fusiliers, the regiment I have looked up to during all my service as a pattern of smartness and efficiency. I have served with you in Gibraltar, Egypt, and many stations in India ; also at Aldershot, and on the Gallipoli Peninsula during the past year. There is no regiment in the service in which I have had a higher confidence, and I hope next week to be able to assemble you again and to congratulate you on the great victory that you are going to win for me, as commanding this Division, and for your country."

The faces of the men shone with a new light. It seemed as if they had seen a sight which other mortals were not allowed to look upon. As upright as poplars, chests well forward and heads thrown back, their souls seemed to speak out of their inflexible determination to win. They marched away, going to that stretch of land from which many have never returned—giving their lives for freedom and the honour of England.

I turned and gave a parting wave of the hand to a group of officers standing by.

"See you to-night," I said, "at the 'White City.' We will drink to the health of 'The Day,'" and with a parting laugh I moved away.

I found out through H.Q. that some of our 15-inch howitzers were in the vicinity, so I decided to film them without delay, to work them into the story of the battle. I discovered their position on my map. I reached the battery. The state of the ground was indescribable. It was more like a "sea of mud," and standing in the middle of this morass was the giant gun, for all the world like a horrible frog squatting on its haunches. Each time it breathed it belched out flame and smoke with the most unearthly crash that could possibly be produced, and with each breath there flew with it a mass of metal and high explosive weighing fourteen hundred pounds, scattering death and destruction for hundreds of yards round the point of impact in the German defences, so that our boys might find it easier to force their way through.

I filmed the firing several times, from various points of view, and when standing only about fifteen yards away the concussion shook the ground like a miniature earthquake. On one occasion, indeed, it lifted my camera and tripod in the air, driving it crashing into my chest. I had unknowingly placed myself in the danger zone which forms a semi-circle on either side of the muzzle when fired, the force being at times so great as to tear trees up by the roots and send them crashing to the ground.

The prospects for "The Day" were certainly bad. As one burly Lancashire lad said to me: "the Devil was looking after his own; but we are going to beat them, sir." That was the spirit of all the men I met there.

I went direct to B.H.Q. to get a full supply of film stock before going to the front line. I wished to get there early, to have a final look round and a discussion with the officers.

A man I knew was there, looking for all the world like a man down and out. He had a face as long as a fiddle, and several other officers were looking just as glum. "You're a cheerful lot," I said. "What's up? Anything wrong?"

"Yes, rather," they replied, "the —— day is postponed for forty-eight hours."

BOMBARDING THE GERMAN TRENCHES AT THE OPENING BATTLE OF THE GREAT SOMME FIGHT, JULY 1ST, 1916

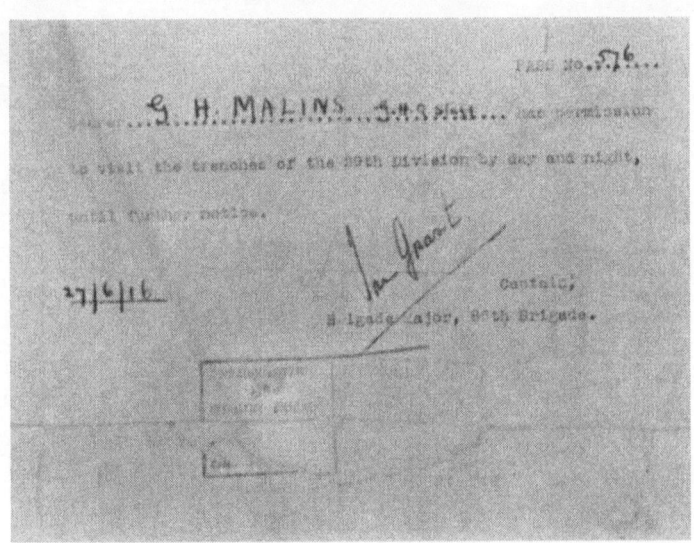

MY OFFICIAL PASS TO THE FRONT LINE TO FILM THE BATTLE OF THE SOMME, JULY 1ST, 1916

" Great Scott ! Why ? " I asked.

" The weather," he answered laconically. " It's quite impossible for our chaps to go over the top in such sticky stuff. They wouldn't stand an earthly. As I said before, it's doing its best to upset the whole affair. I know the men will be awfully disappointed. We can hardly hold them back now—but there, I suppose the Commander-in-Chief knows best. Undoubtedly it's a wise decision. The weather may break—God knows it couldn't be worse ! "

At that moment the Brigade-General came in. He was looking quite bright.

" I hear ' The Day ' has been postponed, sir," I said. " Is that official ? "

" Yes," he said. " If the weather improves ever such a little it will pay us for waiting, and of course it will suit you much better ? "

" Rather," I replied. " It also gives me more time to film the preliminary scenes. I shall, however, keep to my programme, and go to the trenches this afternoon."

I packed all my apparatus together, put some bully and biscuits in my bag, and started off once more for the trenches. I admit that on the journey thoughts crept into my mind, and I wondered whether I should return. Outwardly I was merry and bright, but inwardly—well, I admit I felt a bit nervous. And yet, I had an instinctive feeling that all would be well, that I need not worry. Such is the complex mystery of the human mind, battling within itself against its own knowledge, its own decisions, its own instincts. And yet there is a predominating force which seems to shuffle itself out of the midst of that chaotic state of mind, and holds itself up as a beacon-light, saying " Follow me, believe in me, let me guide you, all will be well." And it is the man who allows himself to be guided by that mysterious something, which for the want of a better name we may call "instinct," who benefits, both spiritually and materially, by it.

The usual big gun duel was proceeding with its usual intensity, but we were putting over about fifty shells to the Huns' one. "Crump" fell both ahead and behind me, compelling me, as before, to fall flat upon the ground. I reached the "Fifth Avenue." The trench was full of men taking down munitions. The news of the postponement had by some means reached them; they also were looking rather glum.

Ye Gods, I thought, it's very nearly worth while to risk walking along the top. In places there was quite two feet of mud and water to wallow through.

"Fritz is crumping down the bottom of the Avenue, sir," said a Tommy to me; "just caught several of our lads—dirty blighters: right in the trench, sir."

"Thanks," I replied.

Thinking there might be an opportunity of getting some scenes of shell-bursts, I hurried on as fast as conditions would permit. With men coming up, and myself and others going down, with full packs on, it was most difficult to squeeze past each other. At times it was impossible, so climbing up on to the parapet, I crawled into another traverse further along.

Just then another shell burst lower down, but well away from the trench, hurting no one. I eventually reached the "White City" without mishap, and was greeted enthusiastically by the officers present.

"What's the programme now?"

"I am waiting for the final kick-off," I said. "Are you going to give me a good show? And don't forget," I said, "hold back some of your bayonet-work on Fritz until I get there with my machine."

"But you're not coming after us with that affair, are you?"

"Yes, certainly; bet your life I shan't be far behind. As soon as you get into Bosche trenches I shall be there; so don't forget—get there."

From the corner some one shouted: "Tell brother Fritz if he gets out of 'the limits,' won't you?" This remark caused much laughter.

"Where have you heard that term used?" I enquired. "'Limits' is a technical term."

"Yes, I heard it used once, a year or two ago. I was staying at a small place called Stevning, near Brighton. A Film Company was taking scenes in the village and on the downs. They had about two hundred horsemen and an immense crowd, and were rehearsing a scene for what I was told was a representation of the Battle of Worcester. It was some fight. The camera man was continually shouting out to them to keep in 'the limits' (I assumed he meant the angle of view). As I say, it was some fight. Everything went well until a section of the men, who were supposed to run away, got a few genuine knocks on the head and, wishing to get their own back, they continued fighting. It was the funniest thing in the world. Of course the camera was stopped, and the scene retaken."

"That's extraordinary," I replied. "Do you know that I was the chap who filmed that scene? it was for a film play called 'King Charles.' It's very peculiar how one meets. I remember that incident quite well."

I again filmed various scenes of the Germans "strafing" our lines. Our guns, as usual, were crashing out. They were pouring concentrated fire on the Hawthorn Redoubt, a stronghold of the Germans, and thinking it would yield an excellent picture, I made my way to a point of vantage, whence I could get an unobstructed field of view. There was only one place, and that was a point directly opposite. To get there it was necessary to cross a sunken road about twenty-five feet wide. But it was under continual fire from German machine guns, and being broad daylight it was absolutely asking for trouble, thick and unadulterated, to attempt to cross it. I was advised not to do so, and I admit I ought to have taken the advice. Anyway, the opportunity of getting such a fine scene of a barrage of fire was too strong, and for once my cautionary instincts were at fault.

To reach the sunken road was comparatively easy. You had only to walk along our front line trench, and fall down flat on the ground when a German shell burst near you, then proceed. I reached the junction where the road ran across at right angles, and from the shelter of our parapet the road looked the quietest place on earth. It appeared easy enough to me to jump up quickly, run across and drop on the further side in our trench.

"Ridiculously easy! I'm going across," I said to my man. "When I'm over I'll throw a cord across for you to tie my tripod on to; then I'll pull it across. It will save you attempting it."

I tied the camera on my shoulders, so as to have my arms quite free. I was now ready. The firing was renewed with redoubled vigour. Shells I could see were falling on the Hun lines like hailstones. "Jove!" I said to myself, "I shall miss it. Here goes."

Clambering up to the road level, I sprawled out flat and lay perfectly still for a few seconds, with my heart jumping like a steam engine. Nothing happened. I gradually drew up my leg, dug the toe of my boot in the ground, and pushed myself forward bit by bit. So far, so good: I was half-way across. I was congratulating myself on my easy task. "What in the world am I lying here for?" I asked myself; "why shouldn't I run the remaining distance?" And suiting the action to the word, I got up—and found trouble! I had barely raised myself to my hands and knees when, with a rattle and a rush, a stream of bullets came swishing by, some striking the ground on my left, about nine feet away.

I took the whole situation in in a flash. To lie there was almost certain death; to stand up was worse; to go back was as bad as going forward. What happened afterwards I don't know. I could hear the bullets whizzing by my head with an ugly hiss. The next moment, with a jump and a spring, I landed head first in the trench on the opposite side. For the moment I did not know whether I was hit or not. I unstrapped my camera, to see if it had caught any bullets, but, thank Heaven, they had cleared it. Some of our men were standing looking aghast at me, and wondering what the devil it was that had made such a sudden dive into their midst. The look on their faces was just too funny for words; I had to roar with laughter, and, realising that I was safe, they also joined in.

But I was not out of the wood yet, for brother Fritz immediately turned " whizz-bangs " on to us. " Phut-bang," " phut-bang," they came. Every one scampered for cover. Needless to say, I did so too. Five minutes went by. All the time these souvenirs dropped around us, but luckily none of them got any direct hits on our trench.

I thought I would wait another five minutes, to see if Bosche would cease fire. But not he. He was rather cross about my crossing the road safely.

Time went by. Still the firing continued. I decided to risk throwing the cord and pulling over my tripod. Keeping low, I yelled to my man: he, like a sage, had also taken cover, but hearing my shouts came out.

" The rope is coming," I yelled. " Tug it as a signal, when you have it."

" Right," came the reply.

Three times I threw it before I received the welcome tug at the other end. Then a voice shouted: "Pull away, sir."

I pulled. I had to do it gently, otherwise the broken nature of the ground might damage the head. At last it was safely over, but Bosche had seen something moving across; then he turned his typewriter on again. More bullets flew by, but with the exception of one which struck the metal revolving top and sliced out a piece as evenly as if it had been done by machine, no harm was caused.

I bade one of the men shoulder my tripod. We rushed up the trench as fast as possible, and I thanked Heaven for my escape. When I reached the section where I judged it best to fit up my camera, I gently peeped over the parapet. What a sight. Never in my life had I seen such a hurricane of fire. It was inconceivable that any living thing could exist anywhere near it. The shells were coming over so fast and furious that it seemed as if they must be touching each other on their journey through the air.

To get my camera up was the work of a few seconds. I had no time to put any covering material over it. The risk had to be run, the picture was worth it. Up went my camera well above the parapet and, quickly sighting my object, I started to expose. Swinging the machine first one way then the other, I turned the handle continuously. Pieces of shell were flying and ripping past close overhead. They seemed to get nearer every time. Whether they were splinters from the bursting shells or bullets from machine guns I could not tell, but it got so hot at last that I judged it wise to take cover. I had exposed sufficient film for my purpose, so quickly unscrewing the camera, my man taking the tripod, I hurried into a dug-out for cover. "Jove!"

I thought, mopping the perspiration from my head, " quite near enough to be healthy ! "

Although the men were all taking cover, they were as happy as crickets over this " strafe." There is nothing a Tommy likes more than to see our artillery plastering Bosche trenches into " Potsdam."

" Well, what's the next move ? " I was asked.

" Trench Mortars," I said. " Both ' Flying Pigs ' and ' Plum Puddings ' ought to make topping scenes."

" Yes," the Captain said. " They are in action this afternoon, and I am in charge of H.T.M. I'll give you a good show. I have only one pit available, as Fritz dropped a ' crump ' in the other yesterday, and blew the whole show to smithereens. My sergeant was sitting smoking at the time, and when she blew up it lifted him clean out of the trench, without even so much as scratching him. He turned round to me, and cursed Bosche for spoiling his smoke. He's promised to get his own back on ' Brother Fritz.' Bet your life he will too."

He had hardly ceased speaking, when our dug-out shook as if a mine had gone up close by. I tumbled out, followed by the others. Lumps of earth fell on our heads ; I certainly thought the roof was coming in on us. Getting into the trench, the bombardment was still going strong, and looking on my left I saw a dense cloud of smoke in our own firing trench.

" What in the world's up ? " I enquired of a man close by.

" Dunno, sir," he said. " I believe it's a Bosche mine. It made enough fuss to be one, yet it seems in such an extraordinary position."

" How about getting round to have a look at it ? " I said to ——.

" Right-o," he said ; " but you know we can't

L

cross the road there. I think if we back well down, about one hundred yards, we may nip across into No. 2 Avenue. That'll bring us out near 'Jacob's Ladder.'"

"Lead on," I said. "I wish I had known. I came in across the road there," pointing down our firing trench.

"You've got more pluck than I have," he said. "You can congratulate yourself that you are alive. Anyway, come on."

Eventually I reached "Jacob's Ladder," and asked an officer what had happened.

"I don't know," he said; "but whatever it was, it's smashed our front trench for about eighty yards: it's absolutely impassable."

Another officer came running up at that moment. "I say," he said, "there's a scene up there for you. A trench mortar gun had a premature burst, and exploded all the munition in the pit; blew the whole lot—men and all—to pieces. It's made a crater thirty yards across. It's a beastly wreck. Can't use that section of the front line. And to make matters worse, Fritz is pumping over tear-shells. Everybody is tickled to death with the fumes."

"Don't cheer me up, will you?" I remarked. "I'm going to film the trench mortar this afternoon, both the H.T.M. and the 2-inch Gee. I can thank my lucky stars I didn't decide to do them earlier. Anyway, here goes; the light is getting rather poor."

The officer with whom I was talking kindly offered to guide me to the spot. Crumps were still falling, and so was the rain. "We'll go through 'Lanwick Street,' then bear to the left, and don't forget to keep your head down."

There are two things I detest more than anything else in the trenches: they are "whizz-bangs"

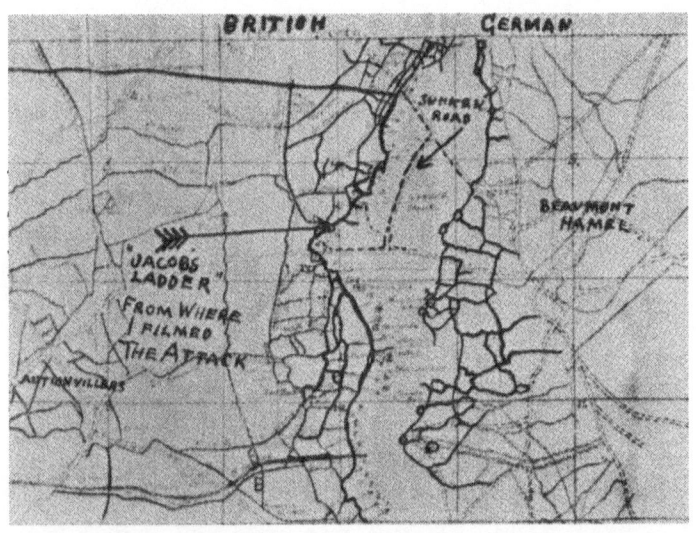

THE PLAN OF ATTACK AT BEAUMONT HAMEL. JULY 1ST, 1916

OVER THE TOP OF BEAUMONT HAMEL. JULY 1ST, 1916

and rats. The latter got mixed up in my feet as I was walking through the trench, and one, more impudent than the rest, when I crouched down to avoid a burst, jumped on to my back and sprang away into the mud.

"We will turn back and go by way of 'White City,' then up King Street. It may be cooler there." It certainly was not healthy in this neighbourhood.

Turning back, I bade my man follow close behind. Entering the main trench, I hurried along, and was quite near the King Street turning when a Hun "crump" came tearing overhead. I yelled out to my man to take cover, and crushed into the entrance of a dug-out myself. In doing so, I upset a canteen of tea over a bucket-fire which one of our lads was preparing to drink. His remarks were drowned in the explosion of the shell, which landed barely twenty-five feet away.

"Now then," I called to my man, "run for it into King Street," and I got there just in time to crouch down and escape another "crump" which came hurtling over. In a flash I knew it was coming very near: I crouched lower. It burst with a sickening sound. It seemed just overhead. Dirt and rubble poured over me as I lay there. I rushed to the corner to see where it had struck. It had landed only twelve feet from the dug-out entrance which I had left only a few seconds before, and it had killed the two men whom I had crushed against, and for the loss of whose tea I was responsible.

It was not the time or place to hang about, so I hurried to the trench-mortar pit to finish my scenes whilst daylight lasted.

I met the officer in charge of the T.M.

"Keep your head down," he shouted, as I turned round a traverse. "Our parapet has been practically wiped out, and there is a sniper in the far corner of the village. He has been dropping his pellets into my show all day, and Fritz has been splashing me with his 'Minnies' to try and find my gun, but he will never get it. Just look at the mess around."

I was looking. It would have beaten the finest Indian scout to try and distinguish the trench from the débris and honeycomb of shell-holes.

"Where the deuce is your outfit?" I said, looking round.

"You follow me, but don't show an inch of head above. Look out." Phut-bang came a pip-squeak. It struck and burst about five yards in front of us. "Brother Fritz is confoundedly inconsiderate," he said. "He seems to want all the earth to himself. Come on; we'll get there this time, and run for it."

After clambering, crawling, running and jumping, we reached a hole in the ground, into which the head and shoulders of a man were just disappearing.

"This is my abode of love," said my guide. "How do you like it?"

I looked down, and at the depth of about twelve feet was a trench mortar. The hole itself was, of course, boarded round with timber, and was about seven feet square. There was a gallery leading back under our parapet for the distance of about eighty feet, and in this were stored the bombs. The men also sheltered there.

I let myself down with my camera and threaded by the numerous "plum puddings" lying there: I fixed my camera up and awaited the order for the men to commence firing.

"Are you ready?" came a voice from above.

"Right, sir," replied the sergeant. I began exposing my film.

"Fire!" the T.M. officer shouted down.

Fire they did, and the concussion nearly knocked me head over heels. I was quite unprepared for such a backblast. Before they fired again, I got a man to hold down the front leg of my tripod. The gun was recharged ; the order to fire was given, the lanyard was pulled, but no explosion.

"Hullo, another——"

"Misfire," was the polite remark of the sergeant. "Those fuses are giving us more trouble than enough."

Another detonator was put on, everything was ready again. Another tug was given. Again no explosion.

Remembering the happenings of the morning in another pit, when a premature burst occurred, I felt anything but comfortable. Sitting in the middle of about one hundred trench mortar bombs, visions of the whole show going up came to me.

Another detonator was put in. " Fire," came the order. Again it failed.

"Look here, sergeant," I said, "if that bally thing happens again I'm off."

"The blessed thing has never been so bad before, sir. Let's have one more try."

Still another detonator was put in. I began turning the handle of my camera. This time it was successful.

"That's all I want," I said. "I'm off. Hand me up my camera. And with due respect to your gun," I said to the T.M. officer, " you might cease fire until I am about fifty yards away. I don't mind risking Brother Fritz's 'strafe,' but I do object to the possibility of being scattered to the four winds of heaven by our own shells." And with a laugh and good wishes, I left him.

"I say," he called out, " come into my dug-out to-night, will you ? It's just in front of Fifth Avenue. I shall be there in about half an hour ; I have got to give Fritz a few more souvenirs to go on with. There is a little more wire left over there, and the C.O. wants it all 'strafed' away. Do come, won't you ? So long. See you later. Keep your head down."

" Right-o ! " I said, with a laugh. " Physician, heal thyself. A little higher, and you might as well be sitting on the parapet." He turned round sharply, then dropped on his knees.

" Strafe that bally parapet. I forgot all about it. Fire ! " he yelled, and I laughed at the pleasure he was getting out of blowing up Fritz.

I scrambled and slithered back into the recognised trench again, and on my way back filmed the H.T.M., or " Flying Pig," in action. By this time it was getting rather dull, so going to a dug-out, I dropped my apparatus, and had another final look at the position from which I was going to film the great attack in the morning.

CHAPTER XIII

THE DAWN OF JULY FIRST

A Firework Display Heralds the Arrival of " The Day "—How the Boys Spent Their Last Few Hours in the Trenches—Rats as Bedfellows—I Make an Early Start—And Get Through a Mine-shaft into " No Man's Land "—The Great Event Draws Near—Anxious Moments—The Men Fix Bayonets—And Wait the Word of Command to " Go Over the Top."

DARKNESS came, and with it a host of star-shells, or Verey lights, which were shot up high in the air from both the German and our own trenches. They looked for all the world like a huge firework display at the Crystal Palace.

Rain had ceased. The heavens were studded with countless millions of stars. " Great prospects for to-morrow," said one. " I hope it's fine, for the sake of the boys. They are as keen as mustard to go over the top."

As we talked, batch after batch of men came gliding by in their full kit, smoking and chatting. While I was standing there hundreds must have passed me in that narrow trench, quietly going to their allotted positions. Now and again sharp orders were given by their officers.

" How's your section, sergeant ? Are you fitted up ? "

" Yes, sir," came a voice from the blackness.

" Now, lads, come along : get through as quickly as possible. Post your sentries at once, and be sharp."

It was not long before little red fires were gleaming out of the dug-out entrances, and crowds of men were crouching round, heating their canteens of water, some frying pieces of meat, others heating soup, and all the time laughing and carrying on a most animated conversation. From other groups came the subdued humming of favourite songs. Some were cursing and swearing, but with such a bluntness that, if I may say so, it seemed to take all the profanity from the words.

And these men knew they were going " over the top " in the morning. The day which they had dreamed of was about to materialise. They knew that many would not be alive to-morrow night, yet I never saw a sad face nor heard a word of complaint. My feeling whilst watching these men in the glow of the firelight was almost indescribable. I was filled with awe at their behaviour. I reverenced them more than I had ever done before ; and I felt like going down on my knees and thanking God I was an Englishman. No words of mine can fitly describe this wonderful scene. And all the time more men, and still more men, were pouring into the trenches, and munitions of all descriptions were being served out.

The bursting German shells, and the shrieks overhead of the missiles from our own guns, were for the moment forgotten in the immensity of the sights around me. I turned and groped the way back to my shelter and, as I did so, our fire increased in intensity. This was the prelude to the greatest attack ever made in the history of the world, and ere the sun set on the morrow many of these heroes—the Lancashire Fusiliers, Royal Fusiliers, Middlesex, etc.—would be lying dead on the field of battle, their lives sacrificed that civilisation might live.

At last I found a friend, and sitting down to our box-table we had a meal together. Afterwards I wandered out, and entered several other dug-outs,

THE DAWN OF JULY FIRST

where friends were resting. They all seemed anxious for the morning to come. I met the mining officer.

"I say; let me check my watch by yours," I said. "As the mine is going up at 7.20 I shall want to start my machine about half a minute beforehand."

"Right-o!" he said. We then checked watches. I bade him good night, and also the others, and the best of luck.

"Same to you," they cried in general chorus. "I hope to heavens you get through with it, and show them all at home in England how the boys fight. They will then realise what war really means. Good night, old man."

"Good night," I replied, and then found my way back to the shelter. I rolled myself in a blanket, and tried to sleep.

The night was very cold. I lay shivering in my blanket and could not get warm. The guns were continually crashing out. Shells were bursting just outside with appalling regularity. Suddenly they seemed to quieten down, as if by some means the Germans had got to know of our great plans and were preparing for the blow. Presently everything was comparatively quiet, except for the scurrying of countless rats, running and jumping over my body, as if it was the most natural thing in the world. I expect I must have dozed off to sleep, for when I awoke day was breaking, and the din of the gun-fire was terrific. Innumerable worlds seemed to be crashing together, and it sounded as if thousands of peals of thunder had concentrated themselves into one soul-terrifying roar.

An officer looked in at the entrance at that moment.

"Hullo!" he said. "Are you the 'movie-man'?"

"Yes," I said, sitting up. "What's up?"

"Well, I'm hanged; I'm glad I've found you.

Do you know, I asked several Johnnies down the line if you were in the trenches and they laughed at me; asked me if I had been drinking; they thought I was pulling their leg. 'A movie man in the trenches,' they said, in tones of amazement; 'not likely!' I told them that you were here last night, and that you are here to film the attack. Well, anyway, this is what I have come for. The Colonel sent me—you know him—to see if you would film a company of our men in occupation of Sunken Road. They occupied it during the night without a single casualty, by tunnelling for about fifty yards through the parapet, under 'No Man's Land'; then sapped up and into the road. It's a fine piece of work," he said, "and would make a good picture."

"Rather," I said; "I'll come. It will be splendid from the historical point of view. Can you let me have a guide, to show me the quickest and best way?"

"Yes, I will send one of our pioneers; he will guide you," he said. "Let me know how you get on, won't you? And, if possible, when you return call in and see the Colonel. He will be frightfully bucked."

"Right-o!" I said. "By Gad! it's bally cold. My teeth won't hold still. Push that man along, and I'll get off."

"Au revoir," he called out as he left. "See you later."

The guide turned up a few minutes afterwards; he took the tripod, I the camera. I started off and entered King Street, making my way towards the firing trench. I have described in previous chapters what it was like to be under an intense bombardment. I have attempted to analyse my feelings when lying in the trenches with shells bursting directly overhead. I have been in all sorts of places, under heavy shell-fire, but for intensity and near-

IN THE SUNKEN ROAD AT BEAUMONT HAMEL, JUST BEFORE ZERO HOUR, JULY 1ST, 1916. MY EXPERIENCES IN GETTING INTO THIS PLACE AT 6.20 A.M. REMAIN THE MOST VIVID OF ALL.

IN A TRENCH MORTAR TUNNEL, DURING THE BATTLE OF THE SOMME, AT BEAUMONT HAMEL, JULY 1ST, 1916

THE DAWN OF JULY FIRST

ness—nothing—absolutely nothing—compared with the frightful and demoralising nature of the shell-fire which I experienced during that journey.

I had only just reached King Street, when it started on that section. Bosche was fairly plastering the whole trench, and smashing down our parapets in the most methodical manner. Four men passed me, with horrible wounds; another was being carried on the shoulders of his comrades, one arm being blown clean off, leaving flesh and remnants of cloth hanging down in a horrible manner. The shells fell in front, overhead and behind us.

I bent low and rushed through traverse after traverse, halting when a shell burst in the trench itself round the next bend, sending a ghastly blast of flame and choking fumes full in my face. At one point I halted, hardly knowing which way to go; my guide was crouching as low as possible on the ground. The further I went, the worse it got; shrieking, splitting shells seemed to envelop us. I looked back. The same. In front, another burst; the flames swept right into my face. If I had been standing up it would have killed me without a doubt. To go back was as dangerous as to advance, and to stay where I was—well, it was worse, if anything. Truth to tell, I had gone so far now that I did not like turning back; the picture of our men in Sunken Road attracted me like a magnet.

"Go on," I shouted to the guide. "We'll get through somehow. Are you game?"

"Yes, sir," said he.

We ran round the next traverse, and had to scramble over a heap of débris caused by a shell a few moments before.

"Look out, sir! There are some dead men here, and the parapet has practically disappeared. Get down on your stomach and crawl along."

Phut-bang! The shells crashed on the parapet with the rapidity of machine-gun fire.

I went down, and crawled along over the dead bodies of some of our lads killed only a few minutes before. It couldn't be helped. Purgatory, in all its hideous shapes and forms, could not possibly be worse than this journey. It seemed years getting through that hellish fire.

"How much more?" I yelled out.

"We are quite near now, sir; about twenty yards."

"Rush for it, then—rush."

I did, and my guide pulled up quickly at the entrance of what seemed like a mine.

"Incline in here, sir," he said, and disappeared. I followed. Never in all my experience had I welcomed cover as I did at that moment.

"Hold on a bit," I said, "for five minutes' breathing space."

The tunnel was no more than two feet six inches wide and five feet high. Men inside were passing ammunition from one to the other in an endless chain and disappearing into the bowels of the earth.

The shaft took a downward trend. It was only by squeezing past the munition bearers that we were able to proceed at all, and in some places it was impossible for more than one to crush through at a time. By the light of an electric torch, stuck in the mud, I was able to see the men. They were wet with perspiration, steaming, in fact; stripped to the waist; working like Trojans, each doing the work of six men.

The journey seemed endless. I could tell by the position that I was climbing. My guide was still in front, and letting me know of his whereabouts by shouting: "Straight ahead, sir! Mind this hole!"

The latter part of the shaft seemed practically

THE DAWN OF JULY FIRST

upright. I dragged my camera along by the strap attached to the case. It was impossible to carry it.

We were nearing daylight. I could see a gleam only a few feet away. At last we came to the exit. My guide was there.

"Keep down low, sir. This sap is only four feet deep. It's been done during the night, about fifty yards of it. We are in 'No Man's Land' now, and if the Germans had any idea we were here, the place would soon be an inferno."

"Go ahead," I said. It was difficult to imagine we were midway between the Hun lines and our own. It was practically inconceivable. The shell-fire seemed just as bad as ever behind in the trenches, but here it was simply heavenly. The only thing one had to do was to keep as low as possible and wriggle along. The ground sloped downwards. The end of the sap came in sight. My guide was crouching there, and in front of him, about thirty feet away, running at right angles on both sides, was a roadway, overgrown with grass and pitted with shell-holes. The bank immediately in front was lined with the stumps of trees and a rough hedge, and there lined up, crouching as close to the bank as possible, were some of our men. They were the Lancashire Fusiliers, with bayonets fixed, and ready to spring forward.

"Keep low as you run across the road, sir. The Bosche can see right along it; make straight for the other side." With that he ran across, and I followed. Then I set my camera up and filmed the scene. I had to take every precaution in getting my machine in position, keeping it close to the bank, as a false step would have exposed the position to the Bosche, who would have immediately turned on H.E. shrapnel, and might have enfiladed the whole road from either flank.

I filmed the waiting Fusiliers. Some of them

looked happy and gay, others sat with stern, set faces, realising the great task in front of them.

I had finished taking my scenes, and asked an officer if the Colonel was there.

"No, but you may find him in 'White City.' He was there about an hour ago. Great heavens," he said, "who would have believed that a 'movie-man' would be here, the nearest point to Bosche lines on the whole front. You must like your job. Hanged if I envy you. Anyway, hope to see you after the show, if I haven't 'gone West.' Cheero," and with that he left me.

Packing up my camera, I prepared to return. Time was getting on. It was now 6.30 a.m. The attack was timed for 7.20. As I wanted to obtain some scenes of our men taking up their final positions, I told my guide to start.

"Duck as low as possible," I said, "when you cross the road."

"We can't go yet, sir; munitions are being brought through, and, as you know, there isn't room to pass one another."

I waited until the last man had come in from the sap, then, practically on hands and knees, made for the sap mouth.

"Cheer up, boys," I shouted to the men as I parted from them, "best of luck; hope to see you in the village."

"Hope so, sir," came a general chorus in reply.

Again I struggled through the narrow slit, then down the shaft and finally into the tunnel. We groped our way along as best we could. The place was full of men. It was only possible to get my tripod and camera along by passing it from one to another. Then as the men stooped low I stepped over them, eventually reaching the other end—and daylight.

The "strafe" was still on, but not quite so violent.

THE DAWN OF JULY FIRST

Our parapets were in a sorry condition, battered out of all shape.

Returning through King Street, I was just in time to film some of the men fixing bayonets before being sent to their respective stations in the firing trench. The great moment was drawing near. I admit I was feeling a wee bit nervous. The mental and nervous excitement under such conditions was very great. Every one was in a state of suppressed excitement. On the way I passed an officer I knew.

" Are you going over ? " I said.

" Rather," he replied, " the whole lot of us. Some stunt, eh ! "

" Don't forget," I said, " the camera will be on you ; good luck ! "

Bidding my man collect the tripod and camera, I made for the position on Jacob's Ladder. But I was to receive a rude shock. The shelling of the morning had practically blown it all down. But there was sufficient for a clearance all around for my purpose, and sufficient shelter against stray bits of shrapnel. I prepared to put up my camera. Not quite satisfied, I left it about thirty yards away, to view the situation quickly, as there were only twenty minutes to go. Hardly had I left the machine than a " whizz-bang " fell and struck the parapet immediately above the ladder, tumbling the whole lot of sandbags down like a pack of cards.

It was a lucky escape for me. The position was absolutely no use now, and I had to choose another. Time was short. I hastily fixed my camera on the side of the small bank, this side of our firing trench, with my lens pointing towards the Hawthorn Redoubt, where the mine—the largest " blown " on the British Front—was going up. It was loaded with twenty tons of a new explosive of tremendous destructive power, and it had taken seven months to build.

Gee, what an awakening for Bosche!

My camera was now set ready to start exposing. I looked along the trench. The men were ready and waiting the great moment.

One little group was discussing the prospects of a race across " No Man's Land."

" Bet you, Jim, I'll get there first."

" Right-o! How much ? "

" A day's pay," was the reply.

" Take me on, too, will you ? " said another hero.

" Yes. Same terms, eh ? Good enough."

" Say Bill," he called to his pal, " pay up from my cash if I ' go West.' "

" Shut up, fathead; we have to kill Huns, ' strafe ' them."

I turned away to speak to an officer as to the prospects.

" Very good," he said. " I hope they don't plaster our trenches before all the men get out. They are as keen as mustard. Never known them so bright. Look at them now; all smoking."

Our guns were still pounding heavily, and the din and concussion was awful. To hear oneself speak it was absolutely necessary to shout.

" You are in a pretty rocky position," some one said to me. " Fritz will be sure to plaster this front pretty well as soon as our men ' get over.' "

" Can't help it," I said; " my machine must have a clear view. I must take the risk. How's the time going ? "

" It's ' seven-ten ' now," he said.

" I am going to stand by. Cheero; best of luck! "

I left him, and stood by my machine. The minutes dragged on. Still the guns crashed out. The German fire had died down a bit during the last half-hour. I glanced down our trenches. The officers were giving final instructions. Every man was in his place. The first to go over would be the engineers,

THE DAWN OF JULY FIRST

to wire the crater. They were all ready, crouching down, with their implements in their hands.

Time : 7.15 a.m. !

Heavens ! how the minutes dragged. It seemed like a lifetime waiting there. My nerves were strung up to a high pitch ; my heart was thumping like a steam-hammer. I gave a quick glance at an officer close by. He was mopping the perspiration from his brow, and clutching his stick, first in one hand then in the other—quite unconsciously, I am sure. He looked at his watch. Another three minutes went by.

Would nothing ever happen ?

CHAPTER XIV

THE DAY AND THE HOUR

A Mighty Convulsion Signalises the Commencement of Operations—Then Our Boys " Go Over the Top "—A Fine Film Obtained whilst Shells Rained Around Me—My Apparatus is Struck—But, Thank Goodness, the Camera is Safe—Arrival of the Wounded—" Am I in the Picture ? " they ask.

TIME: 7.19 a.m. My hand grasped the handle of the camera. I set my teeth. My whole mind was concentrated upon my work. Another thirty seconds passed. I started turning the handle, two revolutions per second, no more, no less. I noticed how regular I was turning. (My object in exposing half a minute beforehand was to get the mine from the moment it broke ground.) I fixed my eyes on the Redoubt. Any second now. Surely it was time. It seemed to me as if I had been turning for hours. Great heavens! Surely it had not misfired.

Why doesn't it go up?

I looked at my exposure dial. I had used over a thousand feet. The horrible thought flashed through my mind, that my film might run out before the mine blew. Would it go up before I had time to reload? The thought brought beads of perspiration to my forehead. The agony was awful; indescribable. My hand began to shake. Another 250 feet exposed. I had to keep on.

Then it happened.

The ground where I stood gave a mighty convulsion. It rocked and swayed. I gripped hold of my tripod to steady myself. Then, for all the world

THE OPENING OF THE GREAT BATTLE OF THE SOMME, JULY 1ST, 1916.
AT 7.20 A.M. THIS HUGE MINE LOADED WITH 20 TONS OF AMINOL WHICH
TOOK 7 MONTHS TO MAKE, WAS SPRUNG UNDER THE GERMAN TRENCHES
AT BEAUMONT HAMEL.

THE DAY AND THE HOUR 163

like a gigantic sponge, the earth rose in the air to the height of hundreds of feet. Higher and higher it rose, and with a horrible, grinding roar the earth fell back upon itself, leaving in its place a mountain of smoke. From the moment the mine went up my feelings changed. The crisis was over, and from that second I was cold, cool, and calculating. I looked upon all that followed from the purely pictorial point of view, and even felt annoyed if a shell burst outside the range of my camera. Why couldn't Bosche put that shell a little nearer? It would make a better picture. And so my thoughts ran on.

The earth was down. I swung my camera round on to our own parapets. The engineers were swarming over the top, and streaming along the sky-line. Our guns redoubled their fire. The Germans then started H.E. Shrapnel began falling in the midst of our advancing men. I continued to turn the handle of my camera, viewing the whole attack through my view-finder, first swinging one way and then the other.

Then another signal rang out, and from the trenches immediately in front of me, our wonderful troops went over the top. What a picture it was! They went over as one man. I could see while I was exposing, that numbers were shot down before they reached the top of the parapet; others just the other side. They went across the ground in swarms, and marvel upon marvels, still smoking cigarettes. One man actually stopped in the middle of "No Man's Land" to light up again.

The Germans had by now realised that the great attack had come. Shrapnel poured into our trenches with the object of keeping our supports from coming up. They had even got their "crumps" and high-explosive shrapnel into the middle of our boys before they were half-way across "No Man's Land." But still they kept on. At that moment my spool ran out. I hurriedly loaded up again, and putting the first priceless spool in my case, I gave it to my man in a dug-out to take care of, impressing upon him that he must not leave it under any circumstances. If anything unforeseen happened he was to take it back to Headquarters.

I rushed back to my machine again. Shells were exploding quite close to me. At least I was told so afterwards by an officer. But I was so occupied with my work that I was quite unconscious of their proximity. I began filming once more. The first lot of men, or rather the remainder of them, had disappeared in the haze and smoke, punctured by bursting shells. What was happening in the German lines I did not know. Other men were coming up and going over the top. The German machine-gun fire was not quite so deadly now, but our men suffered badly from shell-fire. On several occasions I noticed men run and take temporary cover in the shell-holes, but their ranks were being terribly thinned.

Still more went over, and still a stream of men were making for the mine crater; they then disappeared in the smoke. The noise was terrific. It was as if the earth were lifting bodily, and crashing against some immovable object. The very heavens seemed to be falling. Thousands of things were happening at the same moment. The mind could not begin to grasp the barest margin of it.

The German shells were crashing all round me. Dirt was being flung in my face, cutting it like whipcord. My only thought was whether any of it had struck my lens and made it dirty, for this would have spoiled my film. I gave a quick glance at it. It was quite all right.

Fearful fighting was taking place in the German trenches. The heavy rattle of machine-guns, the terrible din of exploding bombs, could be heard above the pandemonium. Our men had ceased to flow from our trenches. I crept to the top of the parapet, and looked towards the left of the village of Beaumont Hamel. Our guns were bursting on the other side of the village, but I could distinguish nothing else as to how things were going.

I asked an officer who was standing close by.

"God knows," he replied. "Everything over there is so mixed up. The General said this was the hardest part of the line to get through, and my word it seems like it, to look at our poor lads."

I could see them strewn all over the ground, swept down by the accursed machine-gun fire.

A quick succession of shell-bursts attracted my attention. Back to my camera position. Another lot of our men were going over the top. I began exposing, keeping them in my camera view all the time, as they were crossing, by revolving my tripod head.

Shell after shell crashed in the middle of them, leaving ghastly gaps, but other men quickly filled them up, passing through the smoke, and over the bodies of their comrades, as if there were no such thing as a shell in all the world. Another spool ran out, making the fourth since the attack started. I gave it in charge of my man, with the same instructions as before. I loaded again, and had just started exposing. Something attracted my attention on the extreme left. What it was I don't know. I ceased turning, but still holding the handle, I veered round the front of my camera. The next moment, with a shriek and a flash, a shell fell and exploded before I had time to take shelter. It was only a few feet away. What happened after I hardly know. There was the grinding crash of a bursting shell; something struck my tripod, the whole thing, camera and all, was flung against me. I clutched it and staggered back, holding it in my arms. I dragged it into a shrapnel-proof shelter, sat down and looked for the damage. A piece of the shell had struck the tripod and cut the legs clean in half, on one side, carrying about six inches of it away. The camera, thank heaven, was untouched.

Calling my man, we hastily found some pieces of wood, old telephone wire and string, and within an hour had improvised legs, rigid enough to continue taking scenes.

I again set up my camera. Our gun-fire was still terrible, but the Germans had shortened their range and were evidently putting a barrage on our men, who had presumably reached the enemy's front trenches. Nobody knew anything definitely. Wounded men began to arrive. There was a rush for news.

"How are things going?" we asked.

"We have taken their first and second line," said one.

An officer passed on a stretcher.

"How are things going?"

"God knows," he said. "I believe we have got through their first line and part of the village, but don't know whether we shall be able to hold out; we have been thinned shockingly."

"Have you been successful?" he asked me.

"Yes, I've got the whole of the attack."

"Good man," he said.

First one rumour then another came through. There was nothing definite. The fighting over there was furious. I filmed various scenes of our wounded coming in over the parapet; then through the trenches. Lines of them were awaiting attention.

Scenes crowded upon me. Wounded and more wounded; men who a few hours before had leaped over the parapet full of life and vigour were now dribbling back. Some of them shattered and broken for life. But it was one of the most glorious charges ever made in the history of the world. These men had done their bit.

"Hullo," I said to one passing through on a stretcher, "got a 'blighty'?"

"Yes, sir," he said; "rather sure Blighty for me."

"And for me too," said another lad lying with him waiting attention, "I shan't be able to play footer any more. Look!" I followed the direction of his finger, and could see through the rough bandages that his foot had been taken completely off. Yet he was still cheerful, and smoking.

A great many asked me as they came through: "Was I in the picture, sir?" I had to say "yes" to them all, which pleased them immensely.

Still no definite news. The heavy firing continued. I noticed several of our wounded men lying in shell-holes in "No Man's Land." They were calling for assistance. Every time a Red Cross man attempted to get near them, a hidden German machine-gun fired. Several were killed whilst trying to bring in the wounded. The cries of one poor fellow attracted the attention of a trench-mortar man. He asked for a volunteer to go with him, and bring the poor fellow in. A man stepped forward, and together they climbed the parapet, and threaded their way through the barbed wire very slowly. Nearer and nearer they crept. We stood watching with bated breath. Would they reach him? Yes. At last! Then hastily binding up the injured man's wounds they picked him up between them, and with a run made for our parapet. The swine of a German blazed away at them with his machine-gun. But marvellous to relate neither of them were touched.

I filmed the rescue from the start to the finish, until they passed me in the trench, a mass of perspiration. Upon the back of one was the unconscious man he had rescued, but twenty minutes after these two had gone through hell to rescue him, the poor fellow died.

During the day those two men rescued twenty men in this fashion under heavy fire.

THE ROLL CALL OF THE SEAFORTHS AT "WHITE CITY," BEAUMONT HAMEL, JULY 1ST, 1916

FAGGED OUT IN THE "WHITE CITY" AFTER WE RETIRED TO OUR TRENCHES, JULY 1ST, 1916. SOME OF THE INCOMPARABLE 29TH DIVISION

CHAPTER XV

ROLL-CALL AFTER THE FIGHT

A Glorious Band of Wounded Heroes Stagger Into Line and Answer the Call—I Visit a Stricken Friend in a Dug-out—On the Way to La Boisselle I Get Lost in the Trenches—And Whilst Filming Unexpectedly Come Upon the German Line—I Have a Narrow Squeak of Being Crumped—But Get Away Safely—And later Commandeer a Couple of German Prisoners to Act as Porters.

THE day wore on. The success of the fighting swayed first this way, then that. The casualties mounted higher and higher. Men were coming back into our trenches maimed and broken; they all had different tales to tell. I passed along talking to and cheering our wonderful men as much as I could. And the Germans, to add to this ghastly whirlpool of horror, threw shell after shell into the dressing station, killing and wounding afresh the gallant lads who had gone " over the top " that morning. They seemed to know of this place and played upon it with a gloating, fiendish glee worthy only of unspeakable savages.

As I was passing one group of wounded, I ran against my doctor friend of the night before.

" Busy day for you ? " I said.

" My word, yes," he replied. " They are coming faster than I can attend to them. I am just off to see P——. He's caught it badly."

" Serious ? " I asked.

" Yes, rather; in the back. He's in the dug-out."

And the doctor rushed away. I followed him. P—— was lying there on a stretcher looking ghastly. The doctor was bending over him. Poor old chap.

Only that morning he had hooked me out to film the sunken road scenes as full of life and hope as anyone could conceive. Now he was on his back, a broken wreck. In the trenches there were hundreds of cases as bad, or even worse, but they did not affect me. There were far too many for the mind to fully grasp their meaning. But down here in this dark dug-out, twenty feet below the earth, the sombre surroundings only illuminated by a guttering candle in a bottle, I was far more affected. It was natural though, for one always feels things more when some one one knows is concerned.

P—— was the first to speak.

"Hullo, old man," he said in a husky, low voice. "You've pulled through?"

"Yes," I replied. "But 'touchwood'! I'm so sorry. Anyway, you're all right for 'Blighty,'" and to cheer him up I continued in a bantering strain: "You knew how to manage it, eh? Jolly artful, you know." His face lighted up with a wan smile.

"Yes, Malins, rather a long 'Blighty,' I'm afraid."

Two stretcher-bearers came in at that moment to take him away. With difficulty they got him out of the trench, and grasping his hand I bade him good-bye.

"I'm glad you got our boys, Malins. I do so want to see that film," were his last words.

"I'll show it to you when I get back to England," I called after him, and then he disappeared.

The fighting was now beginning to die down. The remnants of four regiments were coming in. Each section was accumulating in spaces on their own. I realised that the roll-call was about to take place. I filmed them as they staggered forward and dropped down utterly worn out, body and soul. By an almost superhuman effort many of them staggered to their feet again, and formed themselves into an irregular line.

ROLL-CALL AFTER THE FIGHT

In one little space there were just two thin lines—all that was left of a glorious regiment (barely one hundred men). I filmed the scene as it unfolded itself. The sergeant stood there with note-book resting on the end of his rifle, repeatedly putting his pencil through names that were missing. This picture was one of the most wonderful, the most impressive that can be conceived. It ought to be painted and hung in all the picture galleries of the world, in all the schools and public buildings, and our children should be taught to regard it as the standard of man's self-sacrifice.

I stayed in the trenches until the following day, filming scene after scene of our wounded. I learned that nothing more was to be attempted until later, when fresh divisions were to be brought up. Knowing this I decided to leave this section of the trenches. But the ghastly scenes of which I was witness will always remain a hideous nightmare in my memory, though I thank God I had been spared to film such tremendous scenes of supreme heroism and sacrifice in the cause of freedom.

I got safely back through the trenches to ——, where Brigade H.Q. told me of an urgent message from G.H.Q. I was to report as soon as possible. On my way I called on General ——, who was delighted to hear I had successfully filmed the attack, the record of which would show the world how gloriously our men had fought.

Reaching advanced G.H.Q. I reported myself. All were pleased to see me safe and sound, and to hear of my success. I was told that lively things were happening at La Boisselle. I heard also how successful our troops had been in other parts of the line. Fricourt and Mametz and a dozen other villages had fallen to our victorious troops. This news put new life into me. At La Boisselle they said we had pushed through, and fighting was still going on. I decided to leave for that district right away.

Passing through Albert, I halted the car at the top of Becourt Wood. From this point I had to walk. In the distance I could see hundreds of shells bursting, and guns were thundering out. I gave one camera to my orderly and another had the tripod. Taking the second camera myself, I started off. We threaded our way through the wood and out into the trenches. Shells were falling close by, but by hugging the parapet we got along fairly well.

The communication trench seemed interminable.

"Where the deuce am I?" I asked an officer in passing. "I want to get to our front trenches."

"You want to go the other way. This trench leads back to ——."

This was anything but cheering news. I had been walking for about an hour, always seeming to just miss the right turning. Truth to tell I had failed to provide myself with a trench map, and it was my first time in this section. The bursting shells were filling up the trenches, and I was becoming absolutely fogged. So, in sheer desperation—for the bombardment was getting more intense and I was afraid of losing pictures—I climbed on to the parapet to look round. What a scene of desolation. The first thing I saw was a dead German. That didn't help to cheer me up overmuch. Making a slight detour I stopped to fix the Hun front line if possible. Our own I could see. But no matter where I looked the Bosche line was apparently non-existent. Yet our shells were smashing into the ground, which seemed to be absolutely empty.

I set up my camera and started to expose. While doing so I happened to glance down, for I must explain that I was on a slight mound. Which was the most surprised—the Bosche or myself—I do not know, for less than a hundred yards away was the

German line. I stopped turning. Immediately I did so bullets came singing unpleasantly past my head. I dropped flat on the ground, which luckily for me was slightly protected by a ridge of earth. I dragged the camera down on top of me and, lying flat, the bullets whizzed by overhead. The Bosche must have thought he had got me, for in a few moments fire ceased. I wriggled towards the trench and dropped like a log into the bottom, dragging my camera after me. One of my men had followed, and seeing me drop, did the same. He came tumbling head first into the trench.

"That was a near squeak, sir," he said. "Yes, come on, they will probably start shelling us. Cut through here. I noticed some German prisoners coming this way. I must get them. Where's the other man? Keep him close up."

Reaching a trench through which the German prisoners were being led, I hurriedly fixed my camera and filmed them shambling in, holding their hands up, their nerves completely shattered by the intensity of our terrific bombardment. Some were covered with wounds, others were carrying our wounded Tommies in on stretchers. It was an extraordinary sight. Ten minutes before these men were doing their utmost to kill each other. Now, friend and foe were doing their best to help each other. Shells were dropping close by. One fell in the midst of a group of prisoners and, bursting, killed fourteen and wounded eleven. The others were marched on.

Whether I had been spotted or not, I do not know, but German shells were crumping unpleasantly near. I was just thinking of moving when another burst so close that it made me quickly decide. I looked round for my men. One was there; the other was missing.

"Get into a dug-out," I yelled. "Where is L——?"

"Don't know, sir," he said.

He dived into a dug-out at the first shell which burst near. At that moment another "crump" crashed down and exploded with a crunching roar, throwing a large quantity of earth all around me. One after another came over in quick succession.

"Where the devil is that fellow?" I said to ——. "He's got my aeroscope. When brother Fritz has smoothed down this little 'strafe' I will try and find him."

"He was in that section, sir, where Bosche crossed."

For over half an hour the crumping continued, then it practically ceased. The Bosche evidently thought he had distributed us to the four winds of heaven. I emerged from my shelter and hurriedly ran along the trench to find my man. He was nowhere to be found. Several dug-outs had been smashed in, and in one place the water in the trench was deep red with blood, and wading through this was anything but pleasant. At that moment a telephone man came up.

"Can you tell me, sir, if there is a machine-gun position hereabouts? I have been sent to run a wire." I was just replying when a crump came hurtling over.

"Duck," I yelled, and duck we did. I tried to cover the whole of my body under my steel helmet, and crouching low on the ground, the crump burst just on the parapet above, showering huge lumps of dirt which clattered upon us.

"You had better get out of this," I said, and suiting the action to the word I attempted to run, when another crump burst, this time in the traverse close behind. Well, which of us ran the fastest for cover I don't know, but I was a good second!

The non-appearance of my other man worried me. He was nowhere to be found. It occurred to me that as he did not find me on emerging from his dug-out, and as it was coming on to rain, he had returned to the car thinking he might find me there. Packing up my camera, therefore, I started off, passing more prisoners on the way. I promptly collared two of them to carry my tripod and camera, and as we proceeded I could not restrain a smile at the sight of two German prisoners hurrying along with my outfit, and a grinning Tommy with his inevitable cigarette between his lips, and a bayonet at the ready, coming up behind. It was too funny for words.

When I reached the car my lost man was not there. I enquired of several battle-police and stretcher-bearers if they had seen a man of his description wandering about, and carrying a leather case, but nobody had seen him. After having a sandwich, I decided to go again to the front line to find him. I could not leave him there. I must find out something definite. On my way down I made further enquiries, but without result. I searched around those trenches until I was soaked to the skin and fagged out, but not a trace of him could I discover; not even my camera or pieces of it. The only thing that could have happened, I thought, was that he had got into a dug-out, and the entrance had been blown in by heavy shell-fire.

Retracing my steps I examined several smashed dug-outs. It was impossible to even attempt to lift the rubble. With gloomy thoughts I returned again to the car, and on my journey back left instructions with various men to report anything found to the town major at ——. I stayed the night in the vicinity in the hope of receiving news; but not a scrap came through. Again next day, and the next, I hunted the trenches, unsuccessfully, and finally I came to the conclusion that he had been killed and decided to post him as missing. I had arrived at this decision whilst resting on the grass at the top of Becourt Wood and was making a meal of bully and biscuits when, looking up, I saw what I took to be an apparition of my missing man walking along the road and carrying a black case. I could scarcely believe my eyes.

"Where the devil have you been?" I asked. "I was just on my way back to post you as missing. What has happened?"

"Well, sir, it was like this. When that shell burst I dived into a dug-out, and was quite all right. Then another shell burst and struck the entrance, smashing it in. I have been all this time trying to get out. Then I lost my way and—well, sir, here I am. But your camera case is spoilt." So ended his adventure.

Thinking that the films I had obtained of the Somme fighting should be given to the public as quickly as possible, I suggested to G.H.Q.—and they fully agreed—that I should return to England without delay. So packing up my belongings I returned to London next day.

Little time was lost in developing and printing the pictures, and the Military authorities, recognising what a splendid record they presented of "The Great Push," had copies prepared without delay for exhibition throughout the length and breadth of the land; in our Dependencies over seas, and in neutral countries. They were handled with wonderful celerity by Mr. Will Jury, a member of the War Office Committee, and put out through the business organisation over which he so ably presides. It is sufficient here to record the deep and abiding impression created by the appearance of the films on the screen. People crowded the theatres to see the pictures; thousands were turned away; and it has been estimated that the number of those who have seen these Official War Films must run into many millions.

THE GERMANS MAKE A BIG COUNTER ATTACK AT LA BOISSELLE AND OVILLERS. JULY 3RD AND 4TH, 1916

MEN OF SCOTLAND RUSHING A MINE CRATER AT THE DEADLY "HOHENZOLLERN REDOUBT"

The Somme Film has proved a mighty instrument in the service of recruiting; the newspapers still talk of its astounding realism, and it is generally admitted that the great kinematograph picture has done much to help the people of the British Empire to realise the wonderful spirit of our men in the face of almost insuperable difficulties; the splendid way in which our great citizen army has been organised; the vastness of the military machine we have created during the last two and a half years; and the immensity of the task which still faces us.

His Majesty the King has declared that "the public should see these pictures"; and Mr. Lloyd George, after witnessing a display of the film, sent forth the following thrilling message to the nation: "Be up and doing! See that this picture, which is in itself an epic of self-sacrifice and gallantry, reaches every one. Herald the deeds of our brave men to the ends of the earth. This is *your* duty."

A thrilling message truly, and I am proud indeed to think that I have been permitted to play my part in the taking and making of this wonderful film.

CHAPTER XVI

EDITING A BATTLE FILM

The Process Described in Detail—Developing the Negative—Its Projection on the Screen—Cutting—Titling—Joining—Printing the Positive—Building Up the Story—It is Submitted to the Military Censors at General Headquarters—And After Being Cut and Approved by Them—Is Ready for Public Exhibition.

IN view of the immense and widespread interest aroused by the appearance of the Somme Film, it may perhaps be permissible to depart for a spell from the narration of my story, in order to explain briefly, for the benefit of those interested, how such a picture is prepared, and the various processes through which it must necessarily pass before it is ready for public exhibition.

The process is technically known as " editing," and it must be admitted that this part of the work more nearly approaches the art of the newspaper editor than any other I know. Indeed, I am not sure that the functions of the film editor—at least in the case of a picture such as the Somme Film—do not call for a greater exercise of discretion, diplomacy and tact ; for so many interests have to be taken into account ; so much has to be left out, for so much is at stake.

Time and thought is doubly intensified in editing or cutting up the film in all its various scenes and assembling them in their right order with suitable sub-titles. Immediately films arrive in London they are sent by the War Office to the works, and there in a long dark-room, with many compartments, the film is wound upon wooden frames, about

EDITING A BATTLE FILM 179

three feet by four feet. Each section as it is unwound from the roll is numbered by a perforated machine, to save the unnecessary handling that would otherwise be caused if one had to wade through all the small sections to join in the original lengths in which they are received.

The frames are then taken into the developing-room, where they are placed in tanks of developing mixture, warmed to a temperature of about sixty-five degrees. It is there that the technique of a developing expert asserts itself; he can either make or mar a film. During development the picture is carefully rinsed, and eventually it is ready for fixing. It is taken out, washed in a bath of pure water, and then dropped into an acid fixing bath and there allowed to remain until fixation is complete, usually a matter of about fifteen minutes.

The films are then taken to the washing-room, where they are placed in huge tanks, taking from fifty to one hundred frames, and each one holding one hundred and twenty feet of films. Jets of water run continually over them, and in an hour they are taken out and sent to the drying-room, where the film is rewound whilst wet upon very large drums, about thirty feet long and seven feet in diameter. An electric motor is then started, and the drum revolves at an ever-increasing speed. Drum after drum is loaded in the same way, until the whole of the film is in position and the whirling continues until the negative is perfectly dry.

Cleanliness in every possible respect is absolutely essential during the process of development, until the film is dry once more. The most minute speck of dust or foreign matter might adhere to the wet emulsion permanently disfiguring it. Therefore to avoid this the utmost care must be maintained throughout, and the negative is now ready to be projected on the screen for the first time in order to see that it is technically perfect in quality, and to decide upon the possibilities of a big feature film, or a series of short ones.

For simplicity's sake we will assume that we are dealing with a subject such as the Battle of the Somme, approximately five thousand feet in length. As the film is projected, notes are taken of each scene in strict rotation. The negative, as in the ordinary process of photography, is quite the reverse to the film shown in the picture theatre. The black portions of the picture as we see it on the screen are white, and all whites are black. It therefore calls for a highly trained eye to be able to follow the film.

Only now do I find out whether the scenes I have taken live up to my expectations. Sometimes yes —sometimes no. One great drawback is that the sounds are not there! When the projection is finished the whole of the negative is taken to the cutting and joining-room. I take every reel, and each scene is cut out separately and titled by means of a label fastened to the section by an elastic band.

So the process goes on until I have the whole of the film cut up and registered. I often go through each scene again separately and closely scrutinise it, cutting out all blemishes, black stops, uninteresting sections of the scene, and many other faults which unavoidably present themselves. Before going further I should say that the film is " taken " in lengths of four hundred feet, and they are always kept at that length and in a separate tin box. Even when they are cut up the sections go back into the same tin. Each box is taken in turn and numbered one, two, three, four, five, six, and so on. Number one contains ten sections, representing ten scenes. Each is labelled and every title is copied on a sheet of foolscap, and each section numbered and credited to box one. The process continues in this way until the whole negative is registered.

Meantime I am mentally building up my film story. In story form it must grip the interest of the general public, and yet I have to keep to strict military correctness. I think of my main title. That in itself is a great thing. It has to epitomise the story of the whole film. It has to be short and it must " hold." The title once decided upon, the first reel must deal with preparatory action. I then take the lists prepared as described and call for my sections. For instance, number twenty section, box fourteen; number twelve section, box six; and so on, gradually building up the first reel. The sub-titles must be appealing and concise, and in phraseology that can be easily understood by all.

Eventually reel number one is finished. All the sections are joined together, with spaces marked for the titles. The same process continues with the other reels. Number two must finish their story so far as preparatory action goes. You are then ready for the thrill, and the harder you can hit that thrill into reels three and four the greater the ultimate success of the film. Reel five finishes the story. But after seeing a battle film through full of suffering and agony, as it unavoidably must be to be genuine, you must not leave the public with a bitter taste in their mouth at the end. The film takes you to the grave, but it must not leave you there; it shows you death in all its grim nakedness; but after that it is essential that you should be restored to a sense of cheerfulness and joy. That joy comes of the knowledge that in all this whirlpool of horrors our lads continue to smile the smile of victory. Therefore the film must finish with a touch of happiness to send you home from the picture theatre with a light heart—or at least as light a heart as circumstances permit.

The film is now edited, and it goes into the printer's hands. A positive print is made from it on film stock, and after the printing the copies are returned to the dark-room and the process of developing is gone through again, as in the case of a negative.

The print is then dried and joined up in its right order, and so divided that it makes five reels. The titles by this time have been corrected from the military point of view by the War Office, and are printed for insertion in their appropriate position. The length of reading matter controls the length of the title to be printed. In some instances it will take ten seconds to read a title. Ten feet of film is therefore necessary for insertion between the scenes to explain them. In other cases three feet of titling suffices.

The film is then shown to the War Office officials, and once they have approved it, it is packed in a safe and sent to General Headquarters in France. Here it is again projected in a specially constructed theatre, before the chief censor and his staff, and it may happen that certain incidents or sections are deleted in view of their possible value to the enemy. These excisions are carefully marked and upon the return of the film to London those sections are taken out and kept for future reference. The film is now ready for public exhibition.

CHAPTER XVII

THE HORRORS OF TRONES WOOD

Three Times I Try and Fail to Reach this Stronghold of the Dead—Which Has Been Described as " Hell on Earth "—At a Dressing Station Under Fire—Smoking Two Cigarettes at a Time to Keep Off the Flies—Some Amusing Trench Conversations by Men who had Lost Their Way—I Turn in for the Night—And Have a Dead Bosche for Company.

I HAVE just come from England after seeing the Somme Film well on its way to the public. It has caused a great sensation. I really thought that some of the dead scenes would offend the British public. And yet why should they? It is only a very mild touch of what is happening day after day, week after week, on the bloody plains of France and Belgium. Bloody? Yes, inevitably so. There never was such dearly bought land since creation. The earth in the Somme district has been soaked with the blood of men. Sit out on a field a mile or two from our front line any morning early, when the mist is just rising. Sit out there on the ground which our boys have fought for and won. The place reeks with the horrible stench of countless decaying bodies, and every minute adds to their number.

But the British public did not object to these realistic scenes in the film. They realised that it was their duty to see for themselves. They had been told by the press; they had been told by Parliament; they had been told by lecturers what was happening, but to no purpose. They must be shown; they must see with their own eyes. And the kinematograph camera performed this service. Has it justified itself? I put that question to all who have seen the film. What effect did it have upon you? Did you realise till you saw it what this vast battle-front was like? Did you realise what our Army was doing; how our wonderful soldiers—your husbands, your sons, your brothers— were driving the Huns back; how they were going to their death with a laugh upon their faces and a cigarette between their lips, fighting and dying like true Britons? That those who came back wounded and broken still had that smile?

Yes: the truth has at last dawned upon you. With that knowledge new resolutions were born within you; resolutions that bade you never to slack for an instant in your endeavour to bring success to our arms.

Trones Wood! That name had been drummed into my ears for days. It seemed to have a fascination for me. I asked several men to describe the place.

"Quite impossible, sir; there baint anything like it on earth, and if hell is at all like it then I have been there. It's dead; just dead—dead— dead! And the smell—awful."

"Is Fritz strafing there much?"

"Yes, sir, he's at it all day: there's not room for a cat to hide in, so why Fritz is dropping his souvenirs there heaven knows; I don't."

From the description the place seemed rather satisfactory from a scenic point of view, so I made up my mind to try and film it, as I wanted scenes of heavy bombardment which I could get if Fritz was concentrating upon the wood, for the Hun is a tolerably safe person to deal with if he has a target to fire at; he is so methodical.

Going up by my car as far as the top of Camoy Valley, I left it there near a dressing station.

FILMING THE KING DURING HIS VISIT TO FRANCE IN 1916. HE IS ACCOMPANIED BY PRESIDENT POINCARIE, SIR DOUGLAS HAIG, GENERAL JOFFRE AND GENERAL FOCH

THE HORRORS OF TRONES WOOD

"Strafing!" I was out for "strafing," and by all appearances I was likely to get it hot and strong before long. I had only just stopped when a shell came hurtling overhead, falling about one hundred and fifty yards behind the dressing station. I went over to a doctor who was tending some wounded men—our own and Germans.

"Has Fritz been sending you these souvenirs very often?" I enquired.

The doctor rose, and mopping his forehead, grinned and replied: "Yes; the blighter won't let us alone. Why doesn't he play cricket? He must know this is Red Cross. That sign there," pointing to a large Red Cross lying on the ground, "is large enough to be seen by the men in Mars. Only this morning he put one bang through the roof of our dug-out, rewounding a lot of our chaps lying there. By the way, are you leaving your car there?"

"Yes," I replied.

"Well, you had better say good-bye to it; several of our ambulances have been strafed there."

"Well," I said, "can't be helped; it must take its chance. I'm going to take a few scenes of you at work. Where did these Bosches come from?"

"This morning, from Guillemont; our boys had a bit of a stunt on and landed a few of the beggars."

I filmed various incidents showing the treatment of wounded prisoners. They received the same careful attention as our own men; whatever they asked for they had. Several padres were kneeling down beside our boys, taking down messages to be sent to their relatives.

Stretcher after stretcher with its human freight of Briton and Hun was deposited on the ground. Immediately doctors and orderlies were upon their knees tending to their wants with a gentleness that was wonderful. While I was there several shells fell and exploded only a short distance away.

I left the dressing station and paused upon a mound near a tree stump, the top of which had been carefully split off by shell-fire. I stood looking in the direction of Trones. The Bosches were "strafing" it pretty thoroughly. Away across at Montaubon village the same thing was happening. They were fairly watering the place with H.E. and shrapnel. Our guns were rattling out as well, and I am glad to say that it sounded to me as though ours were at least ten to their one.

Well, the scenes had to be obtained. I admit the job looked anything but pleasant. "Well, here goes!" I said, and putting on a cigarette, I trudged off with my apparatus across the open, making a bee-line midway between Montaubon and Bernafay Wood. I gave both places a wide berth, thereby steering clear of possible Bosche shells. How hot it was. Perspiration was literally pouring from me. I kept on over the ground captured from the Germans. The smell in places was almost unbearable. I puffed away at my cigarette, thereby reducing the stench to a minimum.

Several shells came whizzing overhead in the direction of the dressing station I had just left. With a grinding crash they exploded. "Shrapnel, woolly bears," I said under my breath. They seemed to burst right on top of them too. I thought of all those poor wounded Tommies lying helpless on their stretchers. Another—then another—came hurtling over. The splitting crash of the burst can only be appreciated by those who have been in close proximity to a German H.E. Woolly Bear exploding. It gives one rather a sickening sensation. Another came over. This time it burst nearer. "Gee! they're dropping the range." I hastily grabbed my tripod and hurried off at a tan-

THE HORRORS OF TRONES WOOD 187

gent. Proceeding for a distance of about five hundred yards I turned off again and made tracks for my original point.

In front, at a distance of about seven hundred yards, one of our forward field batteries of 18-pounders opened fire. I at first thought they were French 75 mm. owing to the extreme rapidity of fire. From my position I could not see the guns, but stretching across the country a rough line of brown earth was thrown up, which I afterwards found out was one of the old German lines. The guns were cunningly concealed in the trench. Thinking that it would make rather a good scene I decided to film it in action.

I may add that I have previously been rather wary about having much to do with forward artillery positions. On three previous occasions I have been badly "strafed" by brother Fritz. He has the uncommonly irritating habit of putting his whizz-bangs much too near to be pleasant, with the result that I have more than once been compelled to take my camera and self off to the more congenial quarters of a dug-out, from which place, you will agree, one cannot obtain very interesting pictures.

Reaching the batteries I unlimbered myself of my gear and approaching the C.O. in charge told him who I was and what I wanted. He was quite pleased to see me and said that he was just about to give Fritz a good dose of "iron rations," firing in salvos. Quickly fixing up my camera I filmed the scenes from various points of view. The men were stripped to the waist, jumping out the shells as fast as they could be handled. While I was filming the scene brother Fritz replied with whizz-bangs thick and fast. They are perfect devils, and it is practically impossible to hear them coming until they burst. I turned my machine round upon the spot near which they were dropping. Several times they got within the range of my camera, and I continued to turn upon them until two came much too close, so thinking discretion the better part of valour, I hastily disappeared into the doubtful shelter of a broken-down Hun trench. Then they came over, several smothering me in dust as they exploded close by. Having obtained all the pictures I required I thanked the C.O. and went on my way.

My clothes were absolutely saturated with perspiration as I shambled away towards the top end of Bernafay Wood. I looked back at the battery. Bosche was still " strafing." I vowed I would never go near any forward guns again ; but good resolutions are made to be broken, and my lust for pictures is too strong within me.

Moving was now difficult. The weight of my camera outfit seemed to be getting heavier. I could only get along at a very slow pace. The strap around my chest seemed to squeeze the very breath out of my lungs. But worse was to come. The Huns began shelling the section with shrapnel in a searching manner, and several times I collapsed into a shell-hole, in the hope of obtaining a little cover. But there is very little shelter from shrapnel. On several occasions I felt like throwing away my steel helmet ; the weight seemed abnormal ; but prudence warned me and I clung to it.

The fire was now too bad to proceed in the open. If there were any trenches or ditches I availed myself of their protection. The heat in the trenches was terrific, and to add to the horrors of the stench and heat there were millions of flies. Filthy brutes ! They seemed to cling to one like leeches, and, my arms being full, I could not keep them off my face. Several times I almost decided to turn back, asking myself if it was worth while. But when I

THE HORRORS OF TRONES WOOD

looked at Trones Wood in the distance, and the heavy shells bursting all round, I gritted my teeth and decided to push on.

Thinking that more smoke might help to keep off the flies I lighted two cigarettes and puffed away at them, one in each corner of my mouth. I'm sure I must have looked a most extraordinary specimen of humanity at this moment. Loaded with kit, perspiring like a bull; my steel helmet cocked on one side of my head; puffing away like a chimney at two cigarettes, and millions of flies buzzing all around me. Picture me if you can.

I was proceeding like an automaton along the trench when suddenly I came upon an officer who, I afterwards found out, was going up to fix his next gun positions. He was sitting on a sandbag swearing like Hades, and trying to disperse the clouds of flies which were settling upon him. He looked up as I approached, then suddenly burst into a peal of laughter. I stood still and grinned, not daring to open my mouth to laugh for fear of losing my cigarettes. Then I dropped my tripod and leaned against the trench side to rest. His laughter suddenly developed into a coughing and spluttering, spitting and swearing, which in itself was strong enough to drive all the flies in existence away.

"Bust the things!" he spluttered. "I got a mouthful of them! They might have just come off some dirty Bosche. Got a drink on you?"

"Yes," I said, and handed him my water-bottle.

He rinsed out his mouth.

"I do believe it's worth risking shrapnel rather than tolerate these vile things!" he remarked. "But excuse my laughter; you did look funny coming along there."

"Yes, I expect I did," I said, still puffing away at my cigarettes. "I'd smoke a dozen at once if I could. Anything to keep the flies away."

"Well," he said, "I'm stumped. Have you one to spare?"

I handed him my case. He lighted up and both of us, puffing as hard as we could, made quite a healthy volume of smoke. From above it must have looked as if a small fire was raging.

We had sat there alternately puffing and chatting and killing flies by the hundreds for about ten minutes. I told him I wanted to get some scenes of Trones. He politely told me I ought to have brought my keeper out with me, but as he was going in that direction he would help me on the way to being killed by carrying my tripod.

We started off. The shelling was getting unpleasantly near. Phoot-bang! We both ducked, my head getting a nasty knock against the tripod top. For the moment I thought I had been struck by the whizz-bang. Presently we reached a junction in the trench, and as my friend's road lay in an opposite direction we parted, and I trudged on alone.

I was brought to a standstill by a mound of earth which completely blocked the way. By all appearances the shell that had caused it could have only come over a few minutes before, for a thin wisp of smoke was still curling up from the débris. "Well," I thought, placing my kit on the ground, "it's got to be done; so over I go." Here the air was completely free from flies. Evidently the gas from the bursting shell had choked them off for a time. Jove! I was glad. It was like heaven; and my tongue was beginning to burn rather badly through fiercely smoking two cigarettes at once.

Cautiously I crept up to the top of the parapet! What a sight! Shells were falling thick and fast over Trones and towards Baentin-le-Grand. I must film this, Bosche or no Bosche! So hastily fixing up my tripod, I fastened on the camera and began

THE HORRORS OF TRONES WOOD

exposing. "Excellent," I thought; "I've got it." Another shell came along. This time it was evidently a 5·9, and was right in the centre of my view, about one hundred and fifty yards away! Another one. Rotten! Just out of my limits. Phut-bang! Phut-bang! I grabbed my camera and fell with it on the opposite side of the mound. I let it lie there, and dashing back into the other section of trench grabbed my bags and returned. Whizz-bangs followed; whizz-bangs in front and behind! I crouched as low as possible and replacing the camera in its case hung it over my back and, still bending low, hurried away dragging my tripod behind me.

The trench was blocked by a batch of men returning. They were crouching down for cover. The officer in charge asked me what in the world I was doing.

"Thunder," he said, "if I knew the 'movie' man had been here I would have gone the other way. You've evidently drawn fire by that contraption of yours. Where are you going?"

"To Trones Wood," I said.

The look of blank amazement on his face was amusing.

"My dear chap," he said, "are you serious?"

"Well," I replied, "I had intended going there till a moment ago, but the strafing seems to get worse."

Shrapnel was now bursting overhead, a piece hitting one of the men close by.

"Where's he hit?" enquired the officer. The poor fellow was lying down.

"In the shoulder, sir," one of the others shouted back. "Seems rather bad."

"Two of you bring him through and get ahead to the dressing station as quickly as possible. Keep your heads down." Then turning to me the officer said: "Look here, I've just come from the Wood, and, by gad, it's fair hell there! The place is a charnel-house. It's literally choked with corpses; heaps of them; and we dare not bring them in. We've tried even at night, but the shelling prevents us. The place reeks. And the flies! They're awful. It's more than flesh and blood can stand! To put your head up means certain death and—well, you see what your camera did here. You can imagine what it would be like over there, can't you?"

"Yes, I see, but of course if I had known any men were about I wouldn't have put my machine up. I know there is always the possibility of drawing fire. It has happened quite a number of times to me!"

"If you respect your life don't go any further. The shell-fire is impossible, and the sight over there is too ghastly for words."

So I decided to relinquish my visit for the time being.

A call was made to proceed. "Half a minute," I said, "the trench had been blown in about fifty yards down, wouldn't it be better to clear it away rather than take these men over the top?"

The officer decided that it was. The men worked away with a will, and quickly replaced the earth in the hollow of the trench wall from which it had been blown.

Again we trudged on. The flies were beginning to annoy us once more. I put on a couple of cigarettes. All the men had ransacked odds and ends from their pockets, and the result was a line of men smoking as hard as they could, and enveloped in a haze of bluish white smoke. But the flies refused to budge. Smoke had no effect on them, and I'm inclined to think that nothing short of a 5·9 would do the trick. Not until we were out in the open were we free from them.

On two further occasions I tried to enter Trones

Wood, and both times the conditions were if anything worse. The merest sign of a camera put up over a parapet would have instantly brought a host of shells clattering round; therefore, on the third try, I decided to abandon the trip until a later date. But those attempts will always remain in my memory as a ghastly nightmare. The essence of death and destruction, and all that it means, was horribly visible everywhere.

I have been there since. I reached the place just before the final cleansing, and brother Fritz, just to let us know that he existed, and that he had a spite against us, persisted in flinging his shrapnel around, thereby keeping me well on the run. He did not give me the slightest chance to get pictures, nor to meditate on the surroundings; in fact the only meditation I indulged in was to wonder whether the next shrapnel bullet would strike my helmet plumb on the top or glance off the rim. Then thinking of George Grave's remark, I called Fritz a " nasty person," with a few extra additions culled from the " trench dictionary."

Being a fine night I decided to stay in the vicinity. An officer of a pioneer battalion kindly offered me a share of his dug-out—one of Fritz's cast-offs. I gladly accepted, and over a cup—or rather a tin—of tea, we exchanged views on various subjects. About ten o'clock I went above to terra firma and watched the shells bursting over the German lines. Myriads of star-shells or Verey lights shot high in the sky, lighting up the whole country-side like day. The sight was wonderful, and silhouetted against the flashes I could see countless bodies of men tramping on their way like silent phantoms.

Here and there I watched a shell burst. I could see and hear that it had dropped into a section of those men, adding to the number of that great army of heroes who had already " gone West." But into those gaps, through which the blasting shells had torn their way, stepped other men. A sharp word of command was rapped out, then on again to take up their battle position, leaving the dead behind to be reverently buried on the morrow. The wounded were brought away by the stretcher-bearers, and as one lot passed me I heard a voice from the darkness murmur, " Bill, it's a blighty."

I wandered on in the direction of our line. Near a junction of by-roads I heard some funny remarks passed by ration parties trying to find the way to their sections. To pick one's way in the dark over strange ground littered with débris is not an easy task. The exact language I heard would hardly bear repeating.

One party had evidently bumped into another. " D—— and —— who are you? Cawn't yer see, mate, I'm taking up company rations? Blimy, but 'ow the 'ell I am going to find the way—blowed if I know. Do you know where —— Company is? I'm taking up sandbags. Lost me —— way. 'Ave yer passed a dead 'orse? I knowed I passed it coming up. Good night, mate."

Both men went off into the darkness, swearing like troopers. Another man came up. He was whistling a homely song, but it came to an abrupt conclusion, for he evidently stumbled over some obstacle. Compliments began to fly, and he told the Bosche in plain language what he thought of him for leaving it there. His remarks were too pointed for expression in cold print.

The next to come along was an engineering officer. He could faintly discern me in the darkness.

" Hullo," he said. " Are you the —— ? "

" No," I replied. " I'm sorry I can't help you. I haven't the least idea where they are. What's wrong ? "

" I have to run out some wires to-night, but

THE HORRORS OF TRONES WOOD

bothered if I know where they are. Missed my way near the wood. Some silly ass sent me wrong."

"Well," I said, "most of the troops I have seen have gone in that direction," pointing the way. He disappeared.

Apparently he was held up a minute or two later by some one else, for in the distance I heard a voice, "Do you know where —— Company is, sir?"

"No, I don't," in a rather irritated tone. "I can't find my own blooming way."

This sort of thing went on for over an hour; first one then another. Whether all of them eventually found their various points Heaven only knows!

I had wandered so far, owing to my interest in other people, that I had some difficulty in retracing my steps to the dug-out. Eventually I arrive there about one o'clock. I had been given up for lost.

I told —— of my experiences.

"That kind of thing happens practically every night. They manage to find their way somehow. Come along; let's turn in. Look out for your head as you crawl through. Don't mind the rats. Cover your head well up. They won't touch your face then."

I crawled in on to my bed. Then I noticed a peculiar and decidedly unpleasant smell.

"Have you got any corpses here?" I asked him.

"Yes, I believe so," he said. "You see the other entrance has been blown in. It's the other end of your bed, and I believe some Bosches were buried in the débris. Never mind, stick it; they won't bite."

"Pleasant dreams," I mumbled as I drew my blanket well around my face; in a few minutes the presence of dead Bosche ceased to trouble me. I slept.

CHAPTER XVIII

FILMING AT POZIÈRES AND CONTALMAISON

Looking for " Thrills "—And How I Got Them—I Pass Through " Sausage Valley," on the Way to Pozières—You May and you Might—What a Tommy Found in a German Dug-out—How Fritz Got " Some of His Own " Back—Taking Pictures in What Was Once Pozières—" Proofs Ready To-morrow."

THINGS, from my point of view, were slackening down. Plenty of preparatory action was taking place, and here and there small local engagements, but the fact that they were local made it very difficult for me to get to hear of them. None of the Corps Commanders knew exactly when or where the nibble would develop, or, if they did know, they were naturally chary of giving me the information. On occasions too when I did know I had not sufficient time to make my arrangements, I had to be content with scenes which unfolded themselves after the action had taken place.

This was getting rather monotonous. The aftermath of one attack was to all intents and purposes an exact replica of the previous one, except that the surroundings were different. There was the return of the attackers ; the bringing in of prisoners, the wounded, the dead ; and to vary these scenes to make my pictures generally interesting required a lot of thought and a careful choice of view point.

In the course of the " push," which began in July, there were hundreds, I might almost say thousands, of incidents that to the eye were of enthralling interest, but to have filmed them with the idea of conveying that interest on the screen would have been so much wasted effort. Even the kinematograph has its limitations.

Over my head all the time, like a huge sword, hung the thought of British public opinion, and the opinion of neutral countries. They would accept nothing unless there was great excitement in it; unless the pictures contained such "thrills" as they had never seen before, and had never dreamed possible. Once I had secured that thrill I could then—and only then—take the preparatory scenes, depicting the ordinary life and action of the men and the organisation which are necessary to run the war. Such scenes—interesting as they undoubtedly are—without that "thrill" would have fallen flat, would have been of no use, from the exhibition point of view, and I had always to bear that fact in mind.

I have spent many sleepless nights wondering how and where I was to obtain that magnetic thrill, that minute incident, probably only ten per cent of which would carry the remaining ninety per cent to success. One that would positively satisfy the public.

I had been filming a lot of stuff lately, but when I looked through my list, excellent as the scenes were—many of which I would probably never be able to get again—they struck me as lacking "thrill." That was what I required. So I set out to get it.

The Australians had just captured Pozières, and hearing that the Bosche were continually "strafing" it I decided to make for that quarter with the object of getting a good bombardment. If possible, I would also get into the village itself where there ought to be some very good pictures, for the capture had only taken place two days previously.

Pozières then it should be. Leaving my base early in the morning I made my way through Becourt Wood and beyond, up "Sausage Valley"—why that name I don't know. The whole area was crowded with men of the Australian division.

As there was no road I took my car over the grass, or rather all that was left of it. The place was covered with shell-holes. Driving between, and more often than not into them, was rather a tiresome job, but it saved several miles of tramping with heavy stuff. "Sausage Valley" during this period was anything but healthy. I was warned about it as I left an Australian battery where I had stayed to make a few enquiries. A major told me the place was "strafed" every day, and I soon found that this was so when I arrived. Several "crumps" fell in the wood behind me, and two on the hillside among some horses, killing several. If I saw one dead horse I must have seen dozens; they were all over the place. But every one was much too busy to bury them at the moment. The stench was decidedly unpleasant, and the flies buzzed around in swarms. I soon had a couple of cigarettes alight. What a boon they were at times.

After much dodging and twisting I halted the car close to a forward dressing station. While I was there several shells dropped unpleasantly near, and I could not restrain my admiration for the medical staff who tended the wounded, quite oblivious of the dangers by which they were surrounded in so exposed a position. I obtained several very interesting scenes of the wounded arriving.

I waited awhile to watch the Bosche shelling before going over the ridge to Pozières. I could then tell the sections he "strafed" most. I would be able to avoid them as much as possible. I watched for fully an hour; the variation in his target was barely perceptible. On one or two occasions he "swept" the ridge. I decided to make a start after the next dose.

Strapping the camera on my back, my man

POZIERES AND CONTALMAISON 199

taking the tripod, we started off. There was a light railway running towards Contalmaison. I followed this until I got near the spot brother Fritz was aiming at, hugging a trench at the side of a by-road. The bank was lined with funk-holes, which came in very useful during the journey, and I had to seek their shelter several times, but the nearest shell fell at a junction between that road and a communication trench. Just this side lay a very much dead horse. The shell came over. Down I went flat on my stomach. My man dived into a hole. The shell exploded, and the next thing I remember was a feeling as if a ton of bricks had fallen on top of me. I managed to struggle up and make quickly for the trench, my man following; and you may be quite sure I took care that I was well out of line of the next before I eased up. Beyond a few scratches on the camera-case and a torn coat, I was quite sound.

I was told of a Hun battery of 77 mm. guns on the left-hand side of the valley leading to Pozières, so I decided to make for that spot. I enquired of a man as to the whereabouts of them.

"Well, sir," he said, "you may come to them if you keep straight on, but I shouldn't advise you to do so as you have to cross the open. Bosche has a pretty sharp eye on anyone there; he knows the lay of the battery and he just plasters it. You *might* get round at 'Dead Man's Corner,' on the Contalmaison Road. It's pretty bad there, but I think it's the best place to try, and once you are round the corner you *may* be all right."

"Well, which way do I take?"

"Down this way, then turn to your left at the corner; the battery is about two hundred yards along on the hill-side."

"But, man alive," I said, "they're strafing it like blazes. Look!"

They were, too, and 8-inch shells were dropping wholesale.

"No, I think I will take the risk and run over the open. Are there any dug-outs at the battery?"

"Yes, sir, jolly good ones; forty feet deep; regular beauties. Evidently made up their minds to stay the winter. Electric light, libraries, and beds with real spring mattresses. My, sir, but they were comfortable. And what do you think I found there, sir?"

"Heaven knows," I replied.

"Well, sir, several ladies' fringe nets and hair-pins."

"The devil you did. Well, Fritz knows how to make himself cosy."

With that remark we parted, Tommy having a broad grin on his face.

"You will see the place where you get out of this ditch, sir," he called out; "a shell has blown it in; strike off on your left straight ahead. You'll see them in front of you."

The shelling was getting very unpleasant, and I had to keep low in the trench the whole of the time. At length we reached the point where we had to get over the top.

"Well, come on, let's chance it," I said to my man. I saw the battery in the distance before getting over.

Up we went and bending low raced for the spot. On the way I passed several dead bodies, all Bosche, and numbers of pieces blown to bits by our shell fire. A whizz-bang came over whilst we were crossing. Down we went into a shell-hole. Another, and another came over. Murderous little brutes they were too. Seven of them. Then they ceased. We immediately jumped up again and reached our objective. Then getting under cover of some twisted ironwork, which once formed the roofing

POZIERES AND CONTALMAISON

of the emplacement, I took breath. "Anyway," I thought, "here I am."

In a few minutes I had a look round. What an excellent view of Pozières, about eight hundred yards away on my left. On the right was Contalmaison, which had only been taken a short time previously. The Bosches were shelling the place pretty frequently. I set up the camera and waited. Away on the opposite hill shells were falling thickly. I started filming them and got some interesting bursts, both high explosive and H.E. shrapnel.

Now for Pozières. The enemy must have been putting 9-inch and 12-inch stuff in there, for they were sending up huge clouds of smoke and débris. I secured some excellent scenes. First Pozières, then Contalmaison. My camera was first on one then on the other. For a change Bosche whizz-banged the battery. I could see now why he was so anxious to crump it, for lying all around me in their carriers, were hundreds of gas shells. I was in fact standing on them. They were all unused, and if Fritz got a good one home, well good-bye to everything.

One time I thought I would seek the shelter of a dug-out, but the fire swept away in the opposite direction. By careful manœuvring I managed to film the German guns there. Every one of the four was quite smashed up. An excellent example of artillery fire, and by the date upon them they were of the latest pattern.

In all there were three batteries in that small area, making twelve guns. But out of the twelve sufficient parts were found intact to make one good one, so that Fritz would get "some of his own" back in a way that he least expected; for there were thousands of rounds of ammunition found in the dug-outs beneath the gun pits.

How to get into Pozières was the next problem. I had, while filming, been making mental notes as to the section which Fritz did not "strafe," and that place, by all that's wonderful, was the actual thing he was undoubtedly trying for—the road.

By hugging the bank-side, along which here and there I could spot a few funk-holes, I managed to get into the chalk-pit. Here I filmed various scenes, but Bosche, as usual, kept me on the jump with his shrapnel, forcing me to take hurried shelter from time to time.

There is one thing I shall always thank Fritz for, and that is his dug-outs. If he only knew how useful they had been to me on many occasions I am sure he would feel flattered.

From the chalk-pit to Pozières was no great distance. The ground was littered with every description of equipment, just as it had been left by the flying Huns, and dead bodies were everywhere. The place looked a veritable shambles. Believe me, I went along that road very gingerly, picking my way between the shell bursts. Just before I reached the place the firing suddenly ceased. The deadly silence was uncanny in the extreme; in fact I seemed to fear it more than the bombardment. It seemed to me too quiet to be healthy. What was Bosche up to? There must be some reason for it. I took cover in a shallow trench at the roadside. Along the bottom were lying several dead Bosches, and a short distance away fragments of human remains were strewn around.

The place was desolate in the extreme. The village was absolutely non-existent. There was not a vestige of buildings remaining, with one exception, and that was a place called by the Germans "Gibraltar," a reinforced concrete emplacement he had used for machine-guns. The few trees that had survived the terrible blasting were just stumps, no more.

Fritz's sudden silence seemed uncanny, but taking

advantage of his spell of inactivity I hastily rigged up the camera and began exposing. In a few minutes I had taken sufficient, and packing up I hurried down the road as fast as I could.

I reached the chalk-pit safely and then, cutting across direct to the gun pits, I took up my original position and awaited Fritz's good pleasure to send a few more crump to provide me with scenes. But not a shell came over.

Before leaving this section I thought I would film Contalmaison, a name immortalised by such fighting as has rarely been equalled even in this great war. To get there it was necessary to go to "Dead Man's Corner." The road was pitted with shell-holes, and dead horses lay about on both sides. Boche was still uncannily quiet. I was beginning to think I should just manage to get my scenes before he interfered with me. But no! Either he had finished his lunch or had some more ammunition, for he started again. One came over and burst in the village in front of me, with a noise like the crashing of ten thousand bottles. I took shelter behind a smashed-up limber, and waited to see where the next would fall. It burst a little further away. Good enough, I thought. Here goes before he alters his range.

Jumping up I ran and scrambled on to the ruins of a house, and took some fine panoramic views of the village, first from one position then from another. Some of the scenes included a few of our men in possession. Altogether a most interesting series, including as it did both Pozières and Contalmaison. It was the first time they had been filmed since their capture.

At that moment I heard another crump coming over. It seemed to be unpleasantly near, so I made a running dive for a dug-out entrance, from which poked the grinning face of an officer.

"Look out," I yelled.

Crash came the crump.

"Near enough anyhow," I said, as a piece flew shrieking past close overhead.

"Are you the 'movie' man? I'm pleased to meet you," he said. "Did you get me in that last scene?"

"Yes," I said. "Proofs ready to-morrow." And with a laugh I hurried down the road.

CHAPTER XIX

ALONG THE WESTERN FRONT WITH THE KING

His Majesty's Arrival at Boulogne—At G.H.Q.—General ——'s Appreciation—The King on the Battlefield of Fricourt—Within Range of the Enemy's Guns—His Majesty's Joke Outside a German Dug-out—His Memento from a Hero's Grave—His Visit to a Casualty Clearing Station—The King and the Puppy—Once in Disgrace—Now a Hospital Mascot.

THAT evening I reported at headquarters. "Well, Malins," said Colonel ——, "I have a special job for you. Will you be on the quay at Boulogne to-morrow morning by twelve o'clock? Captain —— is going down; he will make all arrangements for you there; he will also tell you who it is that's coming. Start at eight o'clock to-morrow morning. It is very important; so don't fail to be there."

Leaving the Colonel I met Captain —— outside. "Who's coming?" I asked.

"Don't know," he said. "Tell you to-morrow."

"Is it the King?" I asked.

"Well," he said, "as a matter of fact it is. He arrives to-morrow. I shall have the full programme in the morning, and will give you a copy."

What a film! My first thought was whether he would visit the battlefield. What scenes I conjured up in my imagination. To see Britain's King on the battlefield with his troops; to see him inspecting the ground; to see him in trenches lately captured from the Germans. My imagination began to run away with me. No, I thought, it will be just the ordinary reviews and reception.

But I was wrong. The scenes that I had pictured to myself I was soon to witness.

On the morrow the Captain, the still picture man and myself, left G.H.Q. for Boulogne. Arriving at the quay I looked around for any signs of preparation, but the whole place was as usual. The Captain called at the A.M.L.O.

"Do you know what time the King is due?" he asked.

The A.M.L.O. in tones of amazement ejaculated a long-drawn-out "What; never heard of his coming."

"Well, he is," said the officer. "He's arriving at midday."

"I was never informed," said the other. "I will ring up the M.L.O." He did so, and after a short time the information came through. "The King will not arrive to-day; he will be here to-morrow at 9 a.m. His sailing was altered at the last moment."

That night I turned in at the Hôtel Folkestone, making arrangements for my car to take me and my apparatus to the quay at 8.30 in the morning.

The morning fortunately was beautifully bright. I sincerely hoped it would continue. What excellent quality it promised in the films. I compared it with the weather during the last visit to France of the late Lord Kitchener; unfortunately it rained all the time.

I arrived at the quay. The French officials were gathered there, and lined up was a guard of honour, formed by the North Staffordshire Regiment. Every man had been through many engagements during the war.

I fixed up the camera. The boat had already drawn up by the quay-side. There was a hushed whisper from several officials standing by: "There he is." I looked and saw the King gaily chatting to the Naval Officer in charge.

HIS MAJESTY THE KING, WITH PRESIDENT POINCARIE, IN FRANCE, 1916. HIS MAJESTY GRACIOUSLY CONSENTED TO POSE FOR ME

I wondered whether His Majesty would like being photographed, therefore I carefully kept my camera under cover of a shelter close by. At that moment the King's equerry came ashore. I asked him what time His Majesty was due to land.

"Another half an hour yet," he said, "the Governor of Boulogne and other French officials are just going aboard to be introduced."

I arranged some wheeled railings in such a manner that the opening was close by my camera, thereby making sure that the King would pass very near me.

The moment arrived. My camera was in position. At that moment the King came down the gangway —he was in Field-Marshal's uniform—followed by his suite, including Lord Stamfordham, Sir Derek Keppel, Lieutenant-Colonel Clive Wigram, and Major Thompson. I started turning as he stepped on the shores of France. He gravely saluted.

Passing close by he reviewed the guard of honour, giving them a word of praise as he went. I filmed him the whole of the time, until he reached his car, bade adieux to the many officers present, and drove away to G.H.Q.

I had made an excellent start. The landing was splendid. Now to follow. The King was going to G.H.Q., breaking his journey to lunch with Sir Douglas Haig on the way. I knew I should have ample time therefore to get well ahead and film the arrival at General Headquarters.

Arriving at G.H.Q. I took up my stand near the entrance to the building. The Prince of Wales and other officers were there. I noticed that the Prince, as soon as he saw me, turned and said something to a friend near by. He evidently remembered my two previous attempts to film him.

His Majesty arrived. The Prince of Wales came to the salute, then His Majesty—not as a king, but as a father—embraced his son. I should have obtained a better view of that incident, but unluckily an officer side-stepped and partly covered the figures from my camera.

I obtained many scenes during the day of His Majesty visiting, in company with General Sir Douglas Haig, various headquarter offices, where he studied in detail the general position of the armies. I noticed that Sir Douglas did not look upon my camera very kindly. He was rather shy of the machine, though latterly he has looked with a more sympathetic eye upon it.

On the second day of the King's visit I started out and proceeded to an appointed place on the main road, where the King's car would join us.

The weather was very dull. It was causing me much concern, for to-day of all days I wanted to obtain an excellent film.

The cars pulled up. We had about fifteen minutes to wait. I fixed up my camera ready to film the meeting with General Sir Henry Rawlinson. While waiting, the General came over to me and began chatting about my work.

"I hear," he said, "that you filmed the attack of the 29th Division at Beaumont Hamel on the 1st July, and have been told of the excellence of the result."

He seemed much impressed by what I told him of the possibilities of the camera.

A patrol signalled the King's arrival. His car drew up; His Majesty alighted and heartily greeted the General. I filmed the scenes as they presented themselves.

All aboard once more—the King leading—we started on our journey for the battlefield of Fricourt.

Having hung about until the last second turning the handle, it was a rush for me to pack, and pick them up again. My car not being one of the best, I had great difficulty in keeping up with the party.

WITH THE KING

The news of the King's arrival and journey to Fricourt seemed to have spread well ahead, for everywhere numbers of troops were strewn along the roadside, and even far behind as I was, I could hear the echoing cheers which resounded over hills and valleys for miles around.

Finally the cars came to a halt at an appointed place near the ruins of the village and once beautiful woods of Fricourt, well within range of the enemies' guns.

The spot where the King alighted was known as the Citadel, a German sandbag fortification of immense strength.

It was arranged in the form of a circle, with underground tunnels and dug-outs of great depth. In various sections of the walls were machine-gun emplacements, and the whole being on the top of the hill, formed a most formidable obstacle to the advance of our troops. I may add that the hill is now known as " King George's Hill."

The King and his party had already alighted when I arrived to set up my camera, and hurrying forward was very difficult work, especially as I had to negotiate twisted masses of enemy barbed wire entanglements. But eventually, after much rushing, and being very nearly breathless, I got ahead, and planted my machine on the parapet of an old German trench and filmed the party as they passed. To keep ahead after filming each incident was very hard work. It meant waiting here and there, jumping trenches, scrambling through entanglements, stumbling into shell-holes, and at times fairly hanging by my eyebrows to the edge of trenches, balancing my camera in a way that one would have deemed almost impossible. But I am gratified to think that I managed to keep up with the King, and I succeeded in recording every incident of interest.

At a point on the hill-top the King halted, and

General —— described the various movements and details of the attack and capture of the village, the King taking a very keen interest in the whole procedure.

I continued turning the handle. I did not allow a single scene to pass. Such a thing had never been known before. Throughout it all the guns, large and small, were crashing out, and the King could see the shells bursting over the German lines quite distinctly.

The guide, who was a lieutenant in the Engineers, suddenly called attention to an old German trench. The Prince of Wales first entered and examined from above the depths of an old dug-out.

With a jump I landed on the other side of the trench and sticking the tripod legs in the mud I filmed the scene in which His Majesty and the Prince of Wales inspected the captured German trenches.

The party halted at the entrance to another dug-out. The guide entered and for some moments did not reappear, the King and the General meanwhile standing and gazing down. Suddenly a voice echoed from the depths :

"Will you come down, sir ?"—this remark to the King.

His Majesty laughed, but did not avail himself of the invitation.

All the party joined in the laughter, and all those who have seen that picture on the screen of His Majesty's visit to his troops, will recall the incident to which I refer. Many of the London papers in their articles, referring to the film, wondered what the joke was that the King so thoroughly enjoyed outside a German dug-out.

The party passed on, but some difficulty was experienced when they tried to get out of the trench again. The King was pulled out by the Prince of

WITH THE KING

Wales, and another officer, but some members of the party experienced a difficulty which provided quite an amusing episode.

At times I had to stop and change spools. Then the party got well ahead, and on several occasions His Majesty, with his usual thoughtfulness and courtesy, hung back and debated on various things in the trenches, in order to allow me time to catch them up again.

His Majesty passed over old mine craters, and stood with his deer-stalking glasses, resting against a tree which had been withered during the fighting, watching the bombardment of Pozières. He made sympathetic enquiries by the side of a lonely grave surmounted by a rough wooden cross, on which the name and number of this hero were roughly inscribed. A shrapnel helmet, with a hole clean through the top, evidently caused by a piece of high-explosive shell, rested upon the mound.

The King stooped and picked up a piece of shell and put it in his pocket.

It was now time for His Majesty's departure. Gathered near his car was a crowd of Tommies, ready to give their King a rousing cheer as he drove away. I filmed the scene, and as the car vanished over the brow of the hill, three more were called for the Prince of Wales.

Hurriedly picking up my kit I chased away after them. On the way masses of Anzacs lined both sides of the road, and the cheers which greeted His Majesty must have been heard miles away. The scene made a most impressive picture for me. At that moment a battalion of Anzacs just out of the trenches at Pozières were passing. The sight was very wonderful, and the King saw with his own eyes some of his brave Colonials returning from their triumph, covered with clay, looking dog-tired but happy.

His Majesty was now going to view some ruins near the front, but unfortunately, owing to burst tyres, I could not keep up with the party, and by the time I got on the move again it would have been impossible for me to reach the place in time to film this scene. Therefore, knowing that he was due at No. 18 C.C.S. or " Casualty Clearing Station," I made hurried tracks for it. A most interesting picture promised to result.

I arrived at the C.C.S. and was met by the C.O. in charge.

"Hullo, Malins," he said, "still about? Always on the go, eh? The last scenes you took here came out well. I saw them in London on the R.A.M.C. film. What do you want now?"

"Well, sir," I said, " I am chasing the King, and some chase too, my word. I lost him this morning when my old bus broke down. But up to the present I have obtained a most excellent record. Topping day yesterday on the battlefield of Fricourt. I wouldn't have missed it for anything."

Half an hour later the royal car drew up. The King and the Prince of Wales alighted, and were conducted around the hospital by the C.O.

I did not miss a single opportunity of filming, from His Majesty's talk to some wounded officers, to his strolling through the long lines of hospital tents and entering them each in turn. At one point my camera was so close to the path along which the King passed, that the Prince of Wales, evidently determined not to run into my range again, quickly slipped away and crossed higher up between the other tents. An officer standing by me remarked with a laugh, " The Prince doesn't seem to like you."

A touching incident took place when the King was on the point of leaving. He stooped down and tenderly picked up a small puppy, and gently caressed and kissed it, then handed it back to the

Colonel. This scene appears in the film, and illustrates His Majesty's affection for dumb animals.

I had just finished turning, when an officer came up to me and said in a low tone : " That's funny."

" What's funny ? " I asked.

" Why that incident. Do you know that dog only came in here yesterday, and he has done so much mischief through playing about, that at last the C.O. determined to get rid of him. But we won't now. I shall put a red, white, and blue ribbon round his neck and call him George. He shall be the hospital's mascot."

Before I had time to reply His Majesty prepared to leave, so running with my camera I planted it in the middle of the road and filmed his departure, amid the cheers of the officers and men of the hospital.

CHAPTER XX

KING AND PRESIDENT MEET

An Historic Gathering—In which King and President, Joffre and Haig Take Part—His Majesty and the Little French Girl—I Am Permitted to Film the King and His Distinguished Guests—A Visit to the King of the Belgians—A Cross-Channel Journey—And Home.

I HEARD that night that the King was going to meet M. Poincaré, the French President, at the house of Sir Douglas Haig, and very possibly General Joffre might be there, as well.
. In the morning there was an excellent light, the sun was blazing; and at 9 a.m. sharp we started off, the royal car leading. By cutting across country I was able to save a considerable distance as I wished to get there first, in order to film the arrival.

The château was a typical French one, not very large, but situated in a charming spot, seemingly miles away from such a thing as war. Everything was as peaceful indeed as if we were at home in the midst of the beautiful Surrey Hills.

Yet in this scene of profound peace the rulers of England and France, with the leading Generals, were meeting to discuss the future policy of the greatest and most bloody war of all time.

I took my stand on a grass patch in a position that commanded views of both the main gates and the entrance to the house. Lining the drive from the main gates were men of Sir Douglas Haig's regiment, the 17th Lancers, standing to attention, their lance points glistening in the sun.

KING AND PRESIDENT MEET

The sentries at the gates came smartly to the salute as the royal car, in which were the King and Sir Douglas Haig, drew up. I started turning as he entered the gates. At that moment a little French girl ran out with a bunch of flowers and presented them to the King, who, smiling, stopped and patted her cheek, passed a remark to Sir Douglas, and then proceeded down the lines of troops, and entered the house, the Prince of Wales following close behind.

Shortly afterwards a signal was given. His Majesty and Sir Douglas came down the steps and reached the gates as the car, bringing M. Poincaré, the French President, and General Joffre, drew up. What a scene it would make.

M. Poincaré came first, and was warmly greeted by the King. He was immediately followed by General Joffre, and an incident then occurred which took " Papa " Joffre unawares. For the moment he was perplexed. The same little French maid ran out with another bunch of flowers and offered them to the General.

" No, no," he said, " not for me, give them to the President."

But the child thought otherwise. She intended that Papa Joffre, the idol of France, should have them. He must have them. But no ; the General, taking the child gently by the arm, led her to where M. Poincaré was speaking to the King and Sir Douglas Haig, and drew their attention to the child. They all smiled, and were greatly amused by the incident. Then the little one gave her flowers to the President, who taking them, stooped and kissed her forehead, and the little one satisfied with her success ran away.

The President, not knowing what to do with the flowers, looked around for an officer to take them to his car, but General Joffre, anticipating the desire, called up his A.D.C. who took them away. The party then moved into the house. General Foch also entered with the Prince of Wales.

After the lunch and conference, word was sent in to Colonel Wigram who endeavoured to persuade the King and M. Poincaré to pose for a short scene on the balcony. Word came back that they would do so.

To fix my camera up on the balcony was the work of only a few seconds.

The King came out through the French window, followed by M. Poincaré. They were both smiling and seemed to be very interested in the coming experience.

" Where do we go ? " said the King.

" Would your Majesty stand over there ? " I said, pointing to one end of the terrace. They stood there side by side, King and President laughing and chatting. While I turned on them, General Joffre came out.

" Come along, Joffre, you stand here," said His Majesty, " and you there," he said laughingly to General Foch. Sir Douglas Haig then came out and stood at the end of the line.

For fully a minute they stood there, making a scene, the like of which I had never dreamed.

King, and President, and Generals, who held in their hands the destiny of the world. I continued turning, until His Majesty, thinking I had enough, withdrew, laughing and chatting by the camera, followed by General Joffre, Sir Douglas Haig, and General Foch.

By this time my spool had run out, so quickly changing I got round to the front of the house to film the royal party leaving.

After they had all gone, I heard that Mr. Lloyd George was on his way up from Paris. How late he was, one officer was saying : " We expected him before this." Hearing that I decided to wait. About

KING AND PRESIDENT MEET

half an hour later, up he came in a great hurry, and I just managed to film him as he left his car and entered the building.

To-day was Sunday. His Majesty attended Divine Service with some of the troops stationed near by, in a small country church perched high up on the hill-side. Quiet and contentment pervaded everything; not even the sound of a gun was heard.

A visit to His Majesty, King Albert of Belgium, was the next item on the programme.

The King and Prince of Wales and their suite entered their respective cars and, amidst the cheers of the civilian populace, we left the village on the hill. The red and gold of the little Royal Standard on the King's car glittered bright in the morning sun.

Away we went. How my old " bus " did go; every ounce was being obtained from it; she fairly rocked and roared on the tails of the high-power machines ahead. I knew the road only too well; many a time in the early part of the war had I traversed it, and passed through these self-same gates.

On we tore to where, in an unostentatious little villa, lived the King and Queen of the Belgians.

By the time I arrived King George had alighted, and the Belgian Guard of Honour was playing the national hymn. I hurried through the villa gates, ignoring the guards stationed there who tried to hinder me. I wanted to film the meeting. But I was too late, for by the time I had my machine on the stand the two Kings had passed along the line of troops, crossed the sand-dunes and entered the villa. I had unfortunately missed the meeting by a few minutes, but I vowed I wouldn't move far away from them during the afternoon. I heard that after lunch King George, assisted by Prince Alexander of Teck, was going to award decorations and medals to Belgian officers, and during the afternoon I obtained many good scenes. The Queen was there, and with her the two Princes and little Princess Josephine. They were all most interested in the proceedings.

I filmed the King visiting a 6-inch Howitzer Battery. I noticed specially how keen he was in enquiring about every little detail. Not a single thing seemed to miss his eye, from the close examination of the gun's breech, to inspecting the dug-outs of the men. He then left, and knowing he was going to inspect the Canadians I hurried off in order to get there ahead.

When I arrived the Canadian Generals and staff were there waiting. Here I met many old friends of the St. Eloi battle and, curiously enough, it was at this very spot that I filmed the scene of the Northumberland Fusiliers, or Fighting Fifth, returning from battle, fagged out, but happy.

General Burstall was there, and as soon as he saw me he came up and said:

"Hullo, Malins, you here? Why I thought you would have been killed long ago."

"No, sir," I said, "I don't think I am much of a corpse, though really Brother Fritz has tried very hard to send me West."

"You must have a charmed life," he said. "Have you come to film our show?"

"Yes," I replied. "The King will be along shortly. Ah! here he comes now."

And down the road, stretching away in the distance, a line of cars came tearing along in our direction. Everybody came to attention. I got ready my camera. The King drew up, and from that moment, until he passed through the camp, lined with thousands of cheering Canadians, I filmed his every movement.

The five days' continuous rush and tear was beginning to tell on me. I was feeling fagged out. But to-morrow His Majesty was sailing again for

HER MAJESTY, THE QUEEN OF THE BELGIANS, TAKING A SNAP OF ME AT WORK WHILE FILMING THE KING

THE PRINCE OF WALES SPEAKING WITH BELGIAN OFFICERS AT LA PANNE, BELGIUM

KING AND PRESIDENT MEET 219

England. That night, through a member of the Headquarter Staff, I enquired of Colonel Wigram if it was at all possible for me to accompany the King on his boat across the Channel. It would make a most excellent finish to my film, I pleaded, and it would show the people at home and neutrals that the British Navy still held the seas secure, and that our King could go on the seas where and when he liked, and to film His Majesty on board, among his naval officers, what a splendid record to hand down to posterity.

Colonel Wigram immediately saw the possibilities of such a finish, and agreed to allow me to accompany them.

Very jubilant, I thanked him and promised to be at the boat by midday.

In my hurry and anxiety to obtain permission I had entirely forgotten to enquire at which port the boat was sailing from—Calais or Boulogne. I rushed back to find Colonel Wigram, but unluckily he had gone. I enquired of the Intelligence officers present, but they did not know.

I therefore decided that the only thing to do was to start off early in the morning and go to Boulogne, and then on to Calais, if the boat was leaving from there.

Early next morning, with my kit, I rushed away to Boulogne, but on my arrival I found out that the King was not leaving from there, but from Calais. Off to Calais I went. How the time was going. Ill luck seemed to dog me on the journey, for with a loud noise the back tyre burst. To take if off and replace it with a new one was done in record time. Then on again. How the old " bus " seemed to limp along.

" How many miles is she doing ? " I asked the chauffeur.

" Nearly fifty to the hour, sir, can't get another

ounce out of her. I shouldn't be surprised if the engine fell out."

"Never mind, let her have it," I yelled.

Down the hills she rocked and swayed like a drunken thing. If there had happened to be anything in the way—well, I don't know what would have happened ; but there would have been " some " mess ! Anyway, nothing did happen, and I arrived at the dock in due course. No, the boat had not gone, but by the appearance of every one there, it was just on the point of moving off. To get on to the quay I had to pass over a swing bridge ; a barrier was across it, and soldiers on duty were posted in order to send all cars round, some distance down, over the next bridge. Knowing that if I went there I should be too late, I yelled out to the man to allow me to pass.

"No, sir," he said. "You must go the other way."

Well, what I said I don't know, but I certainly swore, and this evidently impressed the fellow so much that he removed the barrier and allowed me to pass. I literally tumbled out of the old " bus," and shouting to L—— to bring along my tripod, I rushed to where the boat was lying against the quay.

All the French, British, and Belgian officials were lined up, and the King was shaking hands as a parting adieu. Whether it was right or not I did not stop to think. I swept by and rushed up the gangway as the King turned with a final salute.

So close a shave was it that I barely had time to screw my camera on the stand ere the Prince of Wales saluted the King and went ashore. The gangway was drawn away and, amid salutes from the officers and allied representatives, the boat left the quay. I had filmed it all. Not an incident had passed me.

The King with the Admiral in charge of the ship,

KING AND PRESIDENT MEET

entered the cabin, and only then did I have a moment's respite to realise what a narrow squeak I had had.

We were just leaving the harbour. The sea looked very choppy, and just ahead were seven torpedo boats waiting to escort us across.

I went up on to the top deck, and obtained some very interesting scenes of these boats taking up their positions around. Then the King came up and mounted the bridge. How happy he looked! A King in every sense of the word. Who, if they could see him now, could ever have any doubts as to the issue of the war? I filmed him as he stood on the bridge. In mid-channel the sea was getting rather rough, and to keep my feet, and at the same time prevent the camera from being bowled overboard, was rather a task, and this compelled me at times to call in the help of some blue-jackets standing near by.

At last the white cliffs of old England hove in sight, and to make my film-story complete I filmed the cliffs, with Dover Castle perched high above like the grim watch-dog it is.

And then, as the boat drew into the harbour, I got near the gangway in order to land first and film His Majesty as he came ashore. I managed to do this, and entering the royal special (by which I was permitted to travel) I reached Victoria in due course with what, in my humble judgment, was one of the finest kinematograph records that could possibly be obtained of an altogether memorable and historic journey.

CHAPTER XXI

THE HUSH! HUSH!—A WEIRD AND FEARFUL CREATURE

Something in the Wind—An Urgent Message to Report at Headquarters—And What Came Of It—I Hear for the First Time of the " Hush ! Hush ! "—And Try to Discover What It Is—A Wonderful Night Scene—Dawn Breaks and Reveals a Marvellous Monster—What Is It ?

I HAD been busy in London preparing the film of the King's visit to his troops in France, when I received an urgent message to report immediately at General Headquarters—most important. I reported to Captain ——.

" Can you get away in the morning, Malins ? The boat train leaves early."

" If there is something doing I wouldn't miss it for worlds ! " I replied.

" It's quite evident there is," he said, " or they wouldn't want you so urgently."

" I've only got to get my supply of film stock," I said ; " I'll manage it during the night somehow, and meet you at Charing Cross in the morning."

No, I certainly was not going to miss a fight, for undoubtedly another offensive was about to take place.

That night I managed to get sufficient film stock together. In the morning we proceeded to France. The following morning at General Headquarters I got the news. Reporting to Colonel ——, he told me of the coming attack. " Do you want to get it ? " he said.

" Yes, sir, I do ; and from the first line if possible.

THE FIRST "TANK" THAT WENT INTO ACTION, H.M.L.S. "DAPHNE." SEPT. 15, 1916

I want to improve on the Battle of the Somme film. What time does it come off?"

"I don't know; but if you will call on—mentioning a captain at the Headquarters of one of the corps—he will be able to put you right on the section of the attack." With that information I left, and packing my apparatus left for Headquarters. The captain was there.

"You are the 'movie' man, eh? Come in. Now tell me what you want."

"Where is the attack taking place, and at what time?" I asked.

"Look here," he said, unfolding a map, "this is our objective," pointing to a certain place. "We are going to get up to the yellow line, and I suggest that you go to —— Brigade Headquarters. They are in a wood just below —— Redoubt. I will ring up the General and tell him you are coming. He will give you all the information and assistance you require. They know the ground more intimately than we do back here. You are prepared to stay up there, of course?"

"Of course," I said. "I always carry my blanket with me."

"Well it comes off on the fifteenth, rather early in the morning. The General will give you zero hour."

"Do you know the exact time?" I said. "Do you think it will be too early for me—so far as the light is concerned?" I added hurriedly, with a laugh.

"Well no. I think you will just manage it," he said.

Thanking him I hurried off to Brigade Headquarters. They were in an old German dug-out of huge dimensions. There were three distinct floors or rather corridors, one above the other. The galleries wound in and around the hillside, and the bottom one must have been at the depth of eighty feet. Scottish troops were in the trenches, which were being held as support lines. I entered the dug-out, and around a long table was seated the General and his staff.

"General ——, sir?" I enquired.

"Yes," he said; "come in, will you? You are 'Movies,' aren't you? They have just rung me up. Have some lunch and tell me what you want."

During lunch I explained my mission.

"Well," he said, "I am glad you are giving us a show. There is no need to tell you what the Scottish battalion have accomplished."

Lunch finished, the General with the Brigadier-Major went into details as to the best position from which I could see the show.

"I want, if possible, to get an unobstructed view of the Brigade front."

"' —— Trench,' is the place," he said. "What do you say? you know it."

"I think, sir, that's as good as anywhere, but it's strafed rather badly."

"How far is that from the Bosche front line?"

We measured it on the map. It was eight hundred yards.

"Too far off; I must get much closer," I said. "Isn't there a place in our front trench?"

"There's a machine-gun position in a sap head," said an officer. "I am sure that would suit you, but you'll get strafed. Bosche cannot fail to see you."

"What time is zero hour?" I asked the General.

"At 6.20," he said.

Great Scott, I thought, 6.20 summer time—real time 5.20, and in September only one chance in a million that the sky would be clear enough to get an exposure. Certainly if the mornings were anything like they had been during the last week it would be an absolute impossibility.

THE BATTLEFIELD OF "GINCHY." I WAS HURLED INTO THE TRENCH IN FOREGROUND BY THE BURSTING OF A GERMAN SHELL, AND AWOKE MANY HOURS LATER WITH SHELL SHOCK AND REALISED I HAD BEEN LYING BESIDE A DEAD GERMAN ALL NIGHT. HE HAD BEEN THERE I SHOULD SAY ABOUT THREE WEEKS

RESERVES WATCHING THE ATTACK AT MARTINPUICH, SEPT. 15TH, 1916

THE HUSH! HUSH!

Anyway there was just a chance, and I decided to take it.

Therefore I suggested that I should go up very early in the morning to our front line, getting there about four o'clock. There would just be sufficient light for me to have a look round, that is if Brother Fritz wasn't too inquisitive. I could then fix up the camera and wait.

"What time does the barrage start?" I asked.

"Ten minutes to zero. It's going to be very intense, I can tell you that."

"Well, sir, there is one special point I would like you to clear up for me if possible. What the deuce is the 'Hush! Hush!'?"

At that question every one in the place laughed. "Hush! hush! not so loud," one said, with mock gravity. "You mean the Tanks."

"I am just as wise as ever. Anyway, whether they are called the 'Hush Hushers' or 'Tanks,' what the dickens are they? Every one has been asking me if I have seen the 'Hush! hush!' until I have felt compelled to advise them to take more water with it in future. At first I thought they were suffering from a unique form of shell-shock."

"I haven't seen them," he said. "All I know is that we have two of them going over with our boys. This is their line; they will make straight for the left-hand corner of the village, and cross the trenches on your left about two hundred yards from the point suggested. They are a sort of armoured car arrangement and shells literally glance off them. They will cross trenches, no matter how wide, crawl in and out shell-holes, and through barbed wire, push down trees and . . ."

I turned to the General. "I certainly suggest, sir, that —— should go to hospital; the war is getting on his nerves. He will tell me next that they can fly as well."

The General laughed. But quite seriously he told me it was all true.

"Then I hope I shall be able to get a good film of them," I said, "especially as this will be the first time they have been used."

Finally it was agreed that ——, who was going up to the front line to observe for the division, should act as my guide, and take me up in the morning at three o'clock.

"We shall have to start about that time," he said; "it will be possible to go there for quite a good distance over the top of the ridge. It will save trudging through '—— Trench,' and there's sure to be a lot of troops packed in it. In any case it will take us about three-quarters of an hour."

"And I want at least an hour to look round and find a suitable spot; so three o'clock will suit me very well."

"Hullo!" I said, as I heard the crack of a 5·9 crump burst just outside the dug-out. "Can't Bosche let you alone here?"

"No," he said, "he strafes us sometimes. He put quite a lot in here the other day, and one went clean through our cook-house, but no damage was done, beyond spoiling our lunch. If he anticipates our show in the morning, he will be sure to plaster us."

At night I watched the effect of the flashes from our guns. They were rattling off at quite a good pace. What a gorgeous night! Dotted all round this skeleton of what was once a wood, but now merely a few sticks of charred tree trunks, and in and out as far as the eye could see, were scores of tiny fires. The flames danced up and down like elves, and crowded round the fires were groups of our boys, laughing and chatting as if there was no such thing as war. Now and then the flash of the big howitzers momentarily lighted up the whole landscape. What a scene!

Having seen as much of the war as I have done, and having been practically through the campaign from the very outset, it may surprise you that I had not used myself to such sights. Possibly I ought to have done, but the fact remains that I cannot. These night scenes always appeal to me. Every scene is so different, and looking at everything from the pictorial point of view I wished with all my heart I could have filmed such a wonderful scene. But even had I been able to do so I could not have reproduced the atmosphere, the sound of the guns, the burst of the shells, the glare of the star-shells, the laughter of the men—and some of them were swearing. The impenetrable blackness was accentuated by the dancing flames from the fires. It was a sight to dream about; and almost involuntarily reminded one of a scene from the *Arabian Nights*.

It was now midnight. My guide told me to follow him. " We'll go down below and find a place in which to snatch a little sleep." Down a long flight of stairs we went, along corridors, then down another flight and round more corridors. The passages seemed endless, until at last we came to a halt beside the bunk-like beds fastened on the wall.

" What an extraordinary place; how deep is it ? "

" About sixty feet," said my companion. " The place is like a rabbit warren."

" Well, I'm glad you are with me, for I should never find my way out alone." And I rolled my blanket round me and went to sleep.

I was awakened by my guide. " Come on," he said ; " time we moved off."

I quickly got out of my blanket. Jove, how cold it was! My teeth chattered like castanets.

" It's like an ice-house down here; let's go out

and see if any of the men have any fire left. Might be able to have a little hot tea before we go. I have some biscuits and odds and ends in my satchel."

"Will you let me have a man to help me with my tripod?"

"Certainly, as a matter of fact I arranged for one last night."

Up we went. Along the corridors men were lying about in their blankets, fast asleep. Holding a piece of guttering candle in my hand, and shaking like a leaf with cold, I stepped between the sleeping men; but it was anything but an easy task.

During the journey I missed my companion. By a lucky accident I managed to find an exit, but it was nowhere near the one I entered last night. Ah, here's a fire, and quickly getting the water on the boil, made some tea; then shouldering the camera, and —— helping me, by taking one of the cases, we started off.

It was still very dark, but the sky was quite free from clouds. If only it would keep like that I might just get an exposure.

We proceeded as fast as the innumerable shell-holes and old barbed wire would allow, and made straight for the ruins of ——, then crossing the road we followed the communication trenches along the top.

It was still pitch dark. I looked at my watch. It was 4.30.

The trenches were full of life. Men were pouring in to take up their positions. Bosche put a few shells over near by, but fortunately nobody was touched. He was evidently nervous about something, for on several occasions he sent up star-shells, in batches of six, which lighted up the whole ridge like day, and until they were down again I stood stock still.

Day was breaking in the east. A low-lying mist

OVER THE TOP AT MARTINPUICH, SEPT. 15, 1916. I PHOTOGRAPHED THIS SCENE AT 5.20 IN THE MORNING

TWO MINUTES TO ZERO HOUR AT MARTINPUICH, SEPT. 15TH, 1916, THEN "OVER THE TOP"

THE HUSH! HUSH!

hung over the village. I hoped it would not affect my taking.

We were now in the trenches, and daylight was gradually beginning to appear.

"It's got to light up a lot more if I'm going to be able to film," I said. "But thank heaven the sky is cloudless. That's the one chance."

All at once it seemed as though the sky lightened. Actinic conditions improved considerably, and I was just congratulating myself on my good fortune when——

"What's that, sir?" said the man at my side, who had been peering through a periscope.

Gingerly I raised myself above the parapet and peered in the direction in which his finger pointed.

For a moment I could discern nothing. Then, gradually out of the early morning mist a huge, dark, shapeless object evolved. It was apparently about three hundred yards away. It moved, and judging by the subdued hum and a slight smoke which it emitted—like the breath of an animal—it lived!

I had never seen anything like it before. What was it?

CHAPTER XXII

THE JUGGERNAUT CAR OF BATTLE

A Weird-looking Object Makes Its First Appearance Upon the Battlefield—And Surprises Us Almost as Much as It Surprised Fritz—A Death-dealing Monster that Did the Most Marvellous Things—And Left the Ground Strewn with Corpses—Realism of the Tank Pictures.

WHAT in the world was it? As we stood there peering at the thing, we forgot for the moment that our heads were well above the parapet. We were too fascinated by the movements of the weird-looking object to bother about such a trifle as that! And the Bosche trenches were only two hundred yards away! For the life of me I could not take my eyes off it. The thing—I really don't know how else to describe it—ambled forward, with slow, jerky, uncertain movements. The sight of it was weird enough in all conscience. At one moment its nose disappeared, then with a slide and an upward glide it climbed to the other side of a deep shell crater which lay in its path. I stood amazed and watched its antics. I forgot all about my camera, and my desire to obtain a picture of this weird and terrifying engine of destruction. Like every one else, its unexpected appearance on the scene first surprised and then held me under its strange influence.

So that was the "Hush! hush!"—the Juggernaut Car of Battle. One of the Tanks, the secret of whose appearance, and indeed of whose very existence, had been guarded more carefully than all the treasures of the Indies.

THE JUGGERNAUT CAR OF BATTLE

Truly Bosche was in for a big surprise.

All this time I had scarce taken my eyes off the ugly-looking monster. It waddled, it ambled, it jolted, it rolled, it—well it did everything in turn and nothing long—or wrong. And most remarkable of all, this weird-looking creature with a metal hide performed tricks which almost made one doubt

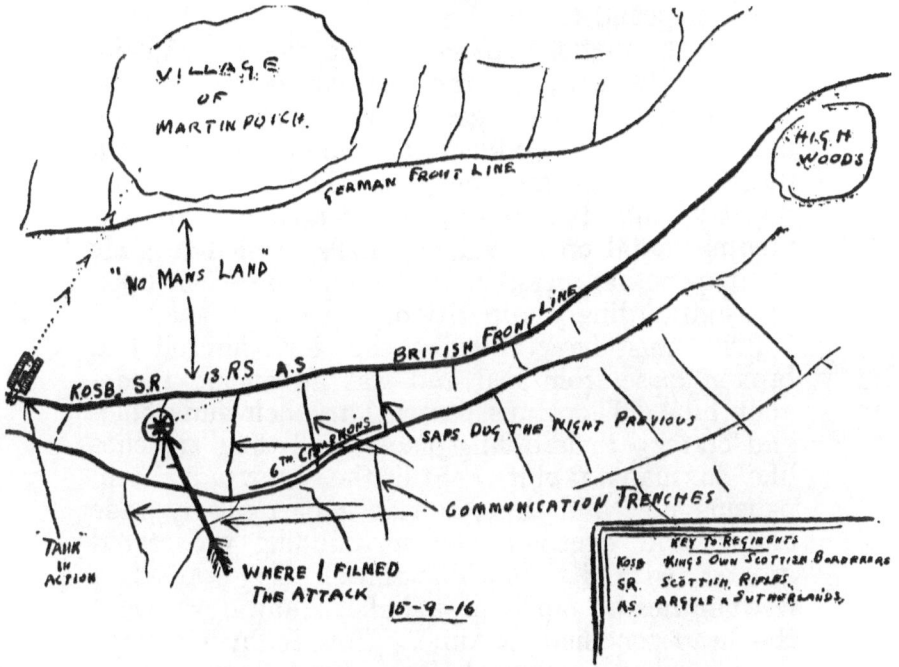

the evidence of one's senses. Big, and ugly, and awkward as it was, clumsy as its movements appeared to be, the thing seemed imbued with life, and possessed of the most uncanny sort of intelligence and understanding. It came to a crater. Down went its nose; a slight dip, and a clinging, crawling motion, and it came up merrily on the other side. And all the time as it slowly advanced, it breathed and belched forth tongues of flame; its nostrils seemed to breathe death and destruction, and the Huns, terrified by its appearance, were mown down like corn falling to the reaper's sickle.

Presently it stopped. The humming ceased. The spell was broken. We looked at one another, and then we laughed. How we laughed! Officers and men were doubled up with mirth as they watched the acrobatic antics of this mechanical marvel—this Wellsian wonder.

Now the metal monster was on the move again. It was advancing on the German position. The Bosche machine-guns got busy and poured a very hail of shells and bullets upon the oncoming death-dealer. It made no difference. The Tank pursued its way, unperturbed by all the racket of the exploding metal on its sides. Shells seemed to glide off it quite harmlessly. Bullets had no effect upon this extraordinary apparition.

Fritz must have thought the devil himself had broken loose from hell and was advancing to devour him. The Huns scurried to their funk-holes and craters, their hiding-places, and their trenches like so many rabbits. Still the Tank advanced, pausing now and then, astride a particularly wide crater, and sweeping the surrounding pit-scarred ground with its machine-guns. Up popped a German head. Zip went a bullet; and down went the head for the last time. How many Germans were crushed in their holes in that first advance goodness only knows.

Presently the monster stopped again. There was a pause. Nothing happened. A minute—two minutes went by. Still nothing happened. The Germans began to regain their courage. Heads popped up all over the place. Enemy troops began to edge nearer and nearer to it, in spite of the hail of bullets from our trenches. Then they began to swarm round the strange creature the like of which they had never seen before. To do them justice, these Germans showed exceptional courage in the face of unknown and altogether exceptional danger.

Mr. Tank meanwhile was not a bit disconcerted by their attentions, and continued to breathe forth flames of fire, which did great havoc in the ranks of the sightseers. But once their curiosity was satisfied the Huns did their level best to damage the brute. They fired at it; they bombarded it; they shelled it; they clambered over it. All to no purpose. Presently that ominous humming, snorting sound reached us again, and the monster began to move away. Where it had stood the ground was strewn with the dead bodies of German soldiers, and I was told afterwards that over three hundred corpses were counted to the credit of the first Tank that ever crossed " No Man's Land."

Meanwhile our boys had been busy. Following in the wake of the Tank, they had cleaned up quite a lot of ground, and all the time, with my camera on them, I had secured a series of fine pictures.

I don't think I ever laughed so heartily at anything as I did on the first day that I saw the Tanks in action, and officers and men all agree that they never saw a funnier sight in all their lives. But whilst they amused us they put the fear of the devil into Fritz, and whole parties of men ran forward, hands up, waving their handkerchiefs, and shouting " Kamerad," and gave themselves up as willing prisoners in our hands.

The Tanks have been one of the big surprises and big successes of the war.

CHAPTER XXIII

WHERE THE VILLAGE OF GUILLEMONT WAS

An Awful Specimen of War Devastation—Preparing for an Advance —Giving the Bosche "Jumps"—Breakfast Under Fire—My Camera Fails Me Just Before the Opening of the Attack—But I Manage to Set it Right and Get Some Fine Pictures—Our Guns "Talk" Like the Crack of a Thousand Thunders—A Wonderful Doctor.

AFTER the battle of Martinpuich the nature of my work brought me in contact with many stirring incidents, which, if put on record here, would be merely repeating to a certain degree many of my previous experiences, therefore I do not intend to bore my readers by doing so.

From one section of our front to the other I was kept continually on the move. On the 25th September an attack was timed for twelve o'clock noon for Morval and Lesboeufs, and the Guards, London Scottish, Norfolks, Suffolks and many other regiments were to take part. The day before I visited our front in that section to obtain preliminary scenes. The London Scottish were preparing to leave to take up their battle positions. From one front to the other I hurried, obtaining scenes of the other regiments on the way up. I stayed during the night with an officer of an 18-pounder battling on the left of Guillemont. The Bosche was "strafing" the place pretty badly. I will not say I slept comfortably, for shells came crashing over much too closely to do so; in fact, I was up all night.

On several occasions I really thought my last minute had come. The noise was deafening, the

THE HIGHLAND BRIGADE GOING OVER THE TOP AT MARTINPUICH. SEPTEMBER 15TH, 1916

glare and flash although beautiful was sickening. Our guns were pouring out a withering fire, and the ground quivered and shook, threatening to tumble the temporary shelter about my ears. One shell, which came very near, burst and the concussion slightly blew in the side of the shelter; it also seemed to momentarily stun me; I crouched down as close to earth as possible. I will admit that I felt a bit "windy," my body was shaking as if with ague; a horrible buzzing sensation was in my head, dizziness was coming over me. I dare not lose control of myself, I thought; with an effort I staggered up and out of the shelter, clutching my head as the pain was terrible. I dropped down into an old German trench and sat in the bottom. In a few minutes my head pains eased down slightly, but my nerves were still shaky. At that moment one of the battery officers came along.

" Hullo ! you got clear then ? " he said.

" Yes, only just, by the appearance of things."

" I saw it drop near by where we left you and felt quite certain it had done you in. Feel all right ? "

" Yes," I said, " with the exception of a thick head. I will get my camera stuff down here. Lend me your torch, will you ? "

I took it out and found my way back to the shelter.

Fritz was now jumping over shrapnel, so, believe me, I did not hang about on my journey. Our guns continued their thundering and fire was literally pouring from their mouths. I got down in the trench, as close as possible, sat on my camera-case and so passed the remainder of the night, thinking—well, many things.

Towards dawn the firing gradually died down until, comparing it with the night, it was quite peaceful. I got out of my trench and sat up on the parapet. My head was still throbbing from the concussion of the night, and having no sleep made me feel in rather a rotten state.

"How's the head, old chap?" asked an officer I knew who came up to me at that moment.

"Better," I replied, "but needs improvement."

"We are just making some tea; come and join us."

"Jove, rather! It may stop this jumping."

A slight mist was hanging over the shell-pocked ground, it was gradually rising, as I had seen it on previous occasions, and the horrible stench from the putrifying dead seemed to rise with it. As far as the eye could see in every direction the ground had been churned up by the fearful shell-fire. The shell-holes met each other like the holes in a sponge. Not a blade of grass or green stuff existed; the place which once marked a wood was now a space with a twisted, tangled mass of barbed wire and, here and there, short wooden stumps, slashed, split, and torn into shreds—the remains of once beautiful trees.

The village of Guillemont literally does not exist, in fact, it is *an absolute impossibility to tell where the fields ended and the village began.* It is one of the most awful specimens of the devastating track of war that exists on the Western Front. The village had been turned by the Bosche into a veritable fortress; trenches and strong points, bristling with machine-guns, commanded every point which gave vantage to the enemy. But, after much bloody fighting, our troops stormed and captured the place and the German losses must have been appalling. Many had been buried, but the work of consolidating the ground won and pressing on the attack does not permit our men thoroughly to cleanse the square miles of ground and bury the bodies and fragments that cover it.

Unknowingly, when I had hurried for cover in the

WHERE GUILLEMONT WAS

trench, the night before I had been within twelve feet of a party of five dead Bosches, and the atmosphere in the early morning was more than I could tolerate, so picking up my camera, etc., I took up fresh quarters.

A snorting, crunching sound struck my ears and looking on my left I observed a Tank ambling forward to take up its position for the coming show. It was emitting clouds of bluish-grey smoke from its exhaust which gave it a rather ghostly appearance in the mist. . . . Now and again as it came to a very deep shell-hole it stopped to poise itself on the rim and then gently tipped its nose downwards, disappearing, to rise like a huge toad on the other side, and then continue its journey.

More troops were coming up in platoon to take up their position in supports, ammunition carriers were taking up fresh supplies of bombs, Red Cross men were making their way forward—not a sound was to be heard from them and the whole place was now a line of silent movement. All the main work and preparation was to finish before the last shadow of night had been chased away by the light of the rising sun, before the setting of which many of the boys would lay down their lives that justice and civilisation might triumph over the false doctrine of blood and iron and barbarism—*German Kultur*.

"Come along, Malins, your cup of tea is ready," shouted an officer.

I left my camera under cover of a fallen tree trunk and crossed to a covered shell-hole which answered to the name of dug-out. Anyway, apart from shrapnel or a direct hit from an H.E., we were comparatively safe, being below ground level. Along the centre was a rough plank on two boxes and grouped either side were several other officers of the battery. We all of us soon forgot about the previous night's efforts of Fritz in a gorgeous repast of *bacon*, fried bread, and tea.

Bosche was now fairly quiet; he was "strafing" the ridge in front with an occasional H.E.; some of our batteries on my right were still at it. It was now quite daylight; our aeroplanes were flitting across the sky, diving low to obtain better observation of the enemy, and incidentally getting "strafed" by his anti-aircraft guns which did not interest them in the least.

"What time is zero-hour?" I asked.

"Twelve-thirty," was the reply. "We start our intense at twelve o'clock, every gun we have in this section is going to fairly give Bosche jumps; in fact he will have to find a ' better 'ole.'"

This remark caused considerable laughter.

"I am going to get my scenes from ' Ginchy Telegraph '; it seems a very likely spot by the map. Shall I get there about eleven o'clock and fix up?"

"Good," said one. "I will lend you an orderly to act as guide if it's any benefit to you."

Thanking him, I gladly accepted the offer.

Breakfast over, I collected my apparatus and stood to watch the sections which Fritz "strafed" the most. By practising this method it has made it possible for me to do my work in comfort on previous occasions. I noticed there were one or two points which he "strafed" methodically, therefore I judged it safe to make direct for my point over the top, then enter a communication trench just on this side of the ridge.

By this time my guide came up, so sharing my apparatus, we started off. The distance to Ginchy Telegraph was about one kilometre. Shrapnel was playing upon both roads leading from Guillemont, H.E. was bursting on my right in Lueze Wood, or " Lousy Wood," as it is called here, also in Delville Wood on my left. After a very tiring tramp over shell-holes and rubble I eventually reached my post. From this point I could see practically the whole of our section between Lesboeufs and Morval, but I immediately found out to my annoyance that the slight breeze would bring all the smoke back towards our lines. The resulting effect would not be serious enough to in any way hinder our operations, but photographically it was disastrous, and even if photographed the effect would not be impressive in the slightest degree, merely a wall of smoke which to the public would appear unintelligible. But in that seemingly useless cloud were falling thousands of shells of all calibres, tearing the earth into dust, the German line into fragments, forming a living and death-dealing curtain of blazing steel behind which our men were advancing.

But adverse wind conditions were not all, for when I had taken the camera out of its case I found that by some means or other the lens mounts had received such a knock as to throw it out of alignment. How it happened I cannot think, for the case was intact, the only possible explanation being that I must have dropped it the night before when I took shelter in the trench and in my dazed condition did not remember doing so.

It was quite impossible to repair it even temporarily in time to obtain the opening attack, so I hurried away and took shelter behind some ruins on the south-west side of the village. It was now close on twelve; our intense bombardment would shortly begin, and I worked feverishly at the repair to the camera, perspiring at every pore.

Suddenly, like the terrific crack of a thousand thunders, our fire on the German position began. Bursting from the mouths of hundreds of British guns it came, the most astonishing, astounding, brain-splitting roar that I had ever heard. In a few moments it reached a crescendo; every one near by was transfixed with awe. Hundreds of shells went shrieking overhead. The air was literally alive with blazing metal.

Imagine, if you can, being in the midst of five hundred drums. At a given moment every drummer beats his drum with ever-increasing force without a fraction of a moment's respite. Add to this the most soul-splitting crash you have ever heard and the sound as of a gale of wind shrieking through the telegraph wires. It will give you a little idea of what it was like under this bombardment. It seemed to numb one's very brain. What it must have been like in the German position is beyond me to conceive. We were certainly giving Fritz a jump.

At last my camera was finished. Looking in the direction of Bouleaux Wood I could see our men still pouring forward over the open. I raced towards them as hard as possible and filmed them going across first one section then the other; Bosche shells were falling near them, knocking a few out but missing most, first one line then the other.

Bosche was dropping large " coal boxes " all along our supports. Two Tanks coming up provided me with several interesting scenes as Fritz was pestering them with his attentions but without injury. I obtained a scene of two heavy " crumps " bursting just behind one of them, but the old Tank still snorted on its way, the infantry advancing close behind in extended formation.

Throughout the remainder of the day I was kept well on the move, filming the many-varying scenes of battle, either whilst they were in progress or immediately afterwards. Prisoners came pouring in from all directions, first a batch of two hundred and then odd stragglers, then further batches. The Guards seemed to have had a rather good bag, as I noticed that most of the Bosches were brought in under care of guardsmen. One Tommy came in the proud possessor of six.

From the immediate fighting ground I made my way towards Trones Wood, upon the outskirts of which the Guards had their dressing station. Many of our men were there, lying about in all directions on stretchers, waiting to be taken away to the Casualty Clearing Station. I filmed many scenes here of our wonderful men suffering their physical torments like the heroes they were. One, in particular, sitting on a box making a cigarette, had a broad smile on his face, though the *whole of his elbow was shot completely away*. Another came in, helped along by two other men; he was a raving lunatic, his eyes ghastly and horrible to look upon, and he was foaming at the mouth, and gibbering wildly.

"Shell-shock," said the doctor, close beside me; "bad case too, poor chap! Here, put him into this ambulance; three men had better go with him to look after him."

"Do you get many cases like that?" I asked the doctor.

"Yes," he said, "quite a few, but not all so bad as that."

Wounded were still pouring in, both ours and German. The Bosche was shelling the ground only a short distance away and I managed to film several of our wounded men being dressed whilst shells were bursting in the near background.

Another man was brought in on a stretcher. I looked closely at him when he was set on the ground. He had been knocked out by shell-fire. A piece of shrapnel was buried in his jaw, another large piece in his head, and, by the bloodstains on his tunic, about his body also.

He was groaning pitiably. The doctor bending down had a look at him, then stood up.

"It's no use," he said, "he's beyond human aid;

R

he cannot last many minutes. Place him over there," he said to the stretcher-bearers. The men gently lifted the poor fellow up, and less than three minutes afterwards one came up to the doctor.

"He's dead, sir."

"Just tell the padre then, will you, and get his disc and name and have his belongings packed up and sent home."

And so the day drifted on. The sun was blazing hot; every man there was working like a demon. Perspiring at every pore, each doctor was doing the work of four; the padre was here, there and everywhere, giving the wounded tea and coffee, and cheering them up by word and deed.

Towards evening there came a lull in the attack. It had been a great success; all our objectives had been gained; the wounded drifted in in lessening numbers.

An elderly doctor in his shirt sleeves had just finished binding up the stump of a man's leg, the lower part of which had been torn away by a piece of shell. He stood up, mopped his forehead, and, after bidding the carriers take the man away, he lay on the ground practically exhausted, dried blood still upon his hands and arms and scissors held loosely in his fingers; he closed his eyes to try and doze.

"That doctor is a marvel," said an officer to me. "He snatches a few moments sleep between his cases. Now watch!"

Another stretcher-party was coming in, and it was set down. An orderly went up to the doctor and lightly touched him on the shoulder.

"Another case, sir," he said.

The doctor opened his eyes and quickly rose to his feet.

The wounded man's head was bound round with an old handkerchief, matted with blood which had dried hard. Warm disinfectant was quickly brought and the doctor proceeded to gently loosen the rough bandage from the head, revealing a nasty head wound, a gash about three inches long and very swollen.

"What do you think of that?" he said, holding out something in his hand to me, "that's from this lad's head."

I looked and saw that it was a piece of his shrapnel helmet about two inches square, it had been driven into the flesh on his head, fortunately without breaking the skull. The wound was quickly dressed and the doctor again lay down to snatch a few more moments' respite.

"This will go on all night," said the padre, "and all day to-morrow. Have a cup of tea at my canteen, will you?"

Having had nothing to eat or drink all day I accepted the invitation. On the opposite side of the wood was a small shack built of old lumber, and every man before he left by ambulance received a cup of tea or coffee and biscuits.

"I find the boys greatly appreciate it," he said.

I joined him in a cup of tea.

"Don't you think it's a good idea?"

"Excellent," I replied, "like heaven to a lost soul."

"Look round here," he said, pointing away in the distance. "Did you ever see such a ghastly travesty of nature, the whole country-side swept clean of every green and living thing, beautiful woods and charming villages blown to the four winds of heaven, and *this* might have been our own beautiful sunny downs, our own charming villages. The British public should go down on its knees every day of the week and thank God for their deliverance."

The sun was now setting, and having obtained all the scenes I required, I decided to make my way back. We were still shelling the German lines very hard, and the Bosche was putting over a few of his H.E. and high shrapnel, but fortunately none came within a hundred yards of us.

I bade adieu to the doctors and the padre.

"I hope we shall see the films in town," they said. "It's a pity you can't introduce the sounds and general atmosphere of a battle like this. Good-bye, best of luck!" they shouted.

I left them and made my way across to the battery to thank the Captain. When I arrived I met one of the subalterns.

"Where's —— ?" I asked.

"I am afraid you won't see him," he replied.

"Why?" half suspecting some bad news.

"Well, he and four others were killed shortly after you left."

I turned slowly away and walked off in the direction of Guillemont.

A hundred yards further on I came upon a scene which afforded some relief to the tragedies of the day. A short bantam-like British Tommy was cursing and swearing volubly at a burly German sitting on the ground rubbing his head and groaning like a bull. Tommy, with a souvenir cigar in his mouth, was telling him in his best cockney English to get a move on.

"What's the matter?" I said.

"Well, sir, it's like this. This 'ere cove is my own prisoner and 'e's been giving me no end of trouble, tried to pinch my gun, sir, 'e did, so I 'it 'im on 'is head, but 'e ain't 'urt, sir, not a bit, are yer, Fritz? Come on." And Fritz, thinking discretion the better part of valour, got up, and Tommy strutted off with his big charge as happy as a peacock.

CHAPTER XXIV

FIGHTING IN A SEA OF MUD

Inspecting a Tank that was *Hors de Combat*—All that was Left of Mouquet Farm—A German Underground Fortress—A Trip in the Bowels of the Earth—A Weird and Wonderful Experience.

AFTER our successful attack and capture of Lesboeufs and Morval on September 25th, 1916, beyond consolidating our gains there was comparatively little done in the way of big offensives until the capture of Mouquet Farm and Thiepval and the capture of Beaumont Hamel—that fortress of fortresses—on November 13th, and I devoted the interval to recording the ground won.

One interesting incident occurred when I filmed Mouquet Farm situate between Pozières and Thiepval. Looking at the Farm from the strategical point of view, I feel quite confident in saying that only British troops could have taken it. It was one of the most wonderful defensive points that could possibly be conceived, and chosen by men who made a special study of such positions. The whole place was thickly planted with machine-guns, so cunningly concealed that it was impossible to observe them until one was practically at the gun's mouth.

To get here it was necessary to go down a long steep glacis, then up another to the farm. The Germans, with their network of underground passages and dug-outs, were able to concentrate at any threatened point with their machine-guns in such a manner that they would have our troops under a continual stream of lead for quite one thousand yards without a vestige of cover. The farm had been shelled by our artillery time after time, until the whole ground for miles round was one huge mass of shell-craters, but the Germans, in their dug-outs forty and fifty feet underground, could not be reached by shell-fire. I will not go into details of how the place was eventually taken by the Midlanders—it will remain an epic of the war.

The weather was now breaking up. Cold winds and rain continually swept over the whole Somme district, invariably accompanied by thick mists. I wanted to obtain a film showing the fearful mud conditions, which we were working hard and fighting in and under. And such mud! You could not put the depth in inches. Nothing so ordinary; it was feet deep. I have known relief battalions take six hours to reach their allotted position in the front line, when, in the dry season, the same journey could be accomplished in an hour; and the energy expended in wading through such a morass can be imagined. Many times I have got stuck in the clayey slime well above my knees and have required the assistance of two, and sometimes three men to help me out. To turn oneself into a lump of mud, all one had to do was to walk down to the front line; you would undoubtedly be taken for a part of the parapet by the time you arrived. I asked a Tommy once what he thought of it.

"Sir," he replied, "there ain't no blooming word to describe it!" And I think he was right.

On one journey, when filming the carrying of munitions by mule-back—as that was the only method by which our advanced field-guns could be supplied—while they were being loaded at a dump near —— Wood, the mud was well above the mules' knees, and, in another instance, it was actually touching their bellies. In such conditions our men were fighting and winning battles, and not once did

I hear of a single instance where it affected the morale of the men. We cursed and swore about it ; who wouldn't ? It retarded our progress ; we wallowed in it, we had to struggle through miles of it nearly up to our knees ; we slept in it or tried to ; we ate in it, it even got unavoidably mixed up with our food ; and sometimes we drank it. And we tolerated it all, month after month. If it was bad for us, we knew it was far worse for the Bosche, for not only had he to live under these conditions, but he was subjected to our hellish bombardment continually without rest or respite.

Thus it was I filmed Mouquet Farm and other scenes in the neighbourhood. I went to Pozières and then struck across country. On my way I passed a Tank which, for the time being, was *hors de combat*. It naturally aroused my interest. I closely inspected it, both inside and out, and, while I stood regarding it, two whizz-bangs came over in quick succession, bursting about thirty feet away. The fact immediately occurred to me that the Tank was under observation by the Bosche and he, knowing the attraction it would have for enquiring natures, kept a gun continually trained upon it. I had just got behind the body of the thing when another shell dropped close by. I did not stop to judge the exact distance. I cursed the mud because it did not allow me to run fast enough, but really I ought to have blessed it. The fact that it was so muddy caused the shell to sink more deeply into the ground before exploding, its effective radius being also more confined.

When I got clear of the Tank, the firing ceased. I mentally vowed that, for the future, temporarily disabled Tanks near the firing-line would not interest me, unless I was sure they were under good cover.

I continued my journey to the farm, but kept

well below the top of the ridge. At one section, to save my dying a sailor's death, duck-boards had been placed over the mud to facilitate easier travelling. It made me feel like going on for ever, after ploughing for hours through mud the consistency of treacle.

Eventually I arrived on the high ground near Mouquet. Many of our field-gun batteries had taken up their position near by : they had turned old shell-holes into gun-pits—occasionally a burst of firing rang out, and Bosche was doing his level best to find them with his 5.9 crump. Here I managed to obtain several very interesting scenes.

The farm, as a farm, did not exist ; a mass of jumbled-up brickwork here and there suggested that once upon a time, say 100 B.C., it might have been. In due time I reached the place. A machine-gun company were in possession, and I found an officer, who offered to show me over the Bosche's underground fortress. I entered a dug-out entrance, the usual type, and switching on my electric torch, proceeded with uncertain steps down into the bowels of the earth. The steps were thick with mud and water ; water also was dripping through all the crevices in the roof, and the offensive smell of dead bodies reached me.

" Have you cleaned this place out ? " I called to my friend in front.

" Yes," he said. His voice sounded very hollow in this noisome, cavernous shaft. And it was cold—heavens how cold ! Ugh !

" There was one gallery section ; where it leads to we cannot find out, but it was blown in by us and evidently quite a few Bosches with it ; anyway, we are not going to disturb it. There is a possibility of the whole gallery collapsing about our ears."

" We are at the bottom now ; be careful, turn sharp to the left."

FIGHTING IN A SEA OF MUD

" Why this place must be at least forty feet deep."

" Yes, about that. This gallery runs along to more exits and a veritable rabbit warren of living compartments. See these bullet-holes in the side here," pointing to the wooden planks lining the gallery. " When our men entered the other end the Bosche here had a machine-gun fixed up and so they played it upon anybody who came near ; lit up only by the gun flashes it must have been a ghastly sight. It must have been the scene of devilish fighting judging by the number of bullet-holes all over the place. There are plenty of bloodstains about, somebody caught it pretty badly."

I followed my guide until eventually we came to a recessed compartment ; it was illuminated by two German candles stuck in bottles, and a rough wooden table with two chairs, evidently looted from the farm when the Bosche arrived.

We made our exit from another shaft and came out at a spot about one hundred yards from the place we had entered.

This will give you some idea of the way the ground was interlaced with subterranean passages, and this, mind you, was only one tunnel of many.

It was quite pleasant to breathe comparatively fresh air again after the foul atmosphere down below.

Bosche was more lively with his shell-fire and they were coming much too near to be pleasant. I fixed up my machine and filmed several very good bursts near some guns. He was evidently shooting blind, or by the map, for they dropped anywhere but near their objectives. Anyway it was his shoot and it was not up to us to correct him.

CHAPTER XXV

THE EVE OF GREAT EVENTS

A Choppy Cross-Channel Trip—I Indulge in a Reverie—And Try to Peer Into the Future—At Headquarters Again—Trying to Cross the River Somme on an Improvised Raft—In Peronne After the German Evacuation—A Specimen of Hunnish "Kultur."

SINCE I left France in December many changes had taken place; tremendous preparations for the next great offensive were in progress. We shall now see the results of all our hard and bloody work, which began on the Somme on July 1st, 1916. I think I can safely say that we have never relaxed our offensive for a single day. Granted the great pressure has not been kept up, but in proportion to the weather conditions the push has been driven home relentlessly and ground won foot by foot, yard by yard, until, in February, 1917, the Germans retired behind their Bapaume defences.

Just how far they are going back one cannot decide. The fact remains that the enemy is falling back, not for strategical reasons, as he is so anxious for his people and neutrals to believe, but because he is forced to by the superiority of our troops and our dominating gun-power. The beginning of the end is at hand, the eve of great events is here; the results of this year's fighting will decide the future peace of the world, the triumph of Christianity over barbarity, of God over the devil.

I received instructions to proceed again to France. "The capture of Bapaume is imminent, you must certainly obtain that," I was told, "and add another to your list of successes." So I left by the midday

THE EVE OF GREAT EVENTS 251

boat-train; the usual crowds were there to see their friends off. A descriptive writer could fill a volume with impressions gathered on the station platform an hour before the train starts. Scenes of pathos and assumed joy; of strong men and women stifling their emotions with a stubbornness that would do justice to the martyrdom of the Early Christians in the arenas of Rome.

I arrived at Folkestone; the weather was very cold and a mist hung over the sea, blotting everything out of view beyond the end of the breakwater. The train drew up alongside and it emptied itself of its human khaki freight, who, with one accord, made their way to the waiting steamboats, painted a dull green-grey. All aboard : quickly and methodically we passed up the gangway, giving up our embarkation tickets at the end and receiving another card to fill up, with personal particulars, as we stepped on board. This card was to be given up upon one's arrival at Boulogne.

Gradually the boat filled with officers and men; kits and cars were hoisted aboard, life-belts were served out; everybody was compelled to put them on in case of an accident.

Everything was aboard ; the three boats were ready to leave ; the two in front, one an old cross-Channel paddle boat, the other one of the later turbine class—but still no sign of leaving.

"What are we waiting for ? " I asked a seaman near by.

"We must wait until we get permission ; the mist is very thick, sir—going to be a cold journey." With that he left. I buttoned my warm great-coat well round my throat, pulled my cap firmly down over my ears and went to the upper deck and peered out into the thickening sea-mist towards the harbour entrance.

I went to the deck-rail and leaned over. Crowds

of sea-gulls cawed and wheeled round, seemingly hung suspended in the air by an invisible wire. The gulls fascinated me ; one second they were in the air motionless on their huge outstretched wings, then suddenly, seeing either the shape of a fish coming to the surface, or a crumb of bread floating, one of the birds would dart down, make a grab with its beak at the object, skim the surface of the water, then gracefully wing its way upwards and join its fellows.

I turned my gaze again seawards : the mist was drawing nearer, threatening to envelop our boats in its embrace. How cold it was ! The upper deck was now full of officers, busily putting on their lifebelts—I had secured mine to my kit-bag, ready to put it on when required. At that moment an officer came up to me.

" Have you a lifebelt ? " he said, " if so would you mind putting it on ? I have to go all round the boat and see that everybody has one."

" Right," I said, and so I donned my life-belt, and passing along the deck stood underneath the Captain's bridge and gazed around. The men in the two boats ahead of us were singing lustily, singing because they were going back to the land of bursting shells and flying death, laughing and singing because they were going again out to fight for the Empire.

As I stood there, gazing into the mist and hearing the continuous roar of the sea beating upon the rocks behind me, a review of the events passed through my mind which have happened to me, and the countless scenes of tragedy and bloodshed, of defeat and victory that I had witnessed since I first crossed over to France in October, 1914. I recalled my arrival in Belgium ; the wonderful rearguard actions of the Belgian troops ; the holding up of the then most perfect (and devilish) fighting machine the world had ever known, by a handful of volunteers. The frightful scenes in the great retreat through

THE EVE OF GREAT EVENTS 253

Belgium lived again ; the final stand along the banks of the Ypres canal ; the opening of the dykes, which saved the northern corner of France ; the countless incidents of fighting I had filmed. Then my three months with the French in the Vosges mountains, the great strain and hardships encountered to obtain the films, and now, after eighteen months with the British army on the Western Front, I was again going back—to what ?

How many had asked themselves that question ! How many had tried as I was doing to peer into the future. They had laid down their lives fighting for the cause of freedom. " But, although buried on an alien soil, that spot shall be for ever called England."

I was quickly recalled to the present by the flashing of a light on the end of the harbour jetty. It was answered by a dull glare seawards ; everybody was looking in that direction ; and then . . .

A sudden clanging of bells, a slipping of ropes from the first boat, a final cheer from the men on the crowded decks, and, with its bow turned outwards from the quay, it nosed its way into the open sea beyond. The second boat quickly followed, and then, with more clanging of bells and curt orders to the helmsman, she slid through the water like a greyhound, and, with shouts of " good luck ! " from the people on the quay, we were quickly swallowed up in the mist ahead.

The boats kept abreast for a considerable time and then, our vessel taking the lead, with a torpedo boat on either side and one ahead, the convoy headed for France.

The journey across was uneventful. It was quite dark when we backed into harbour at Boulogne ; flares were lit and, as the boat drew alongside the quay, the old familiar A.M.O. with his huge megaphone shouted in stentorian tones that all officers and men returning on duty must report to him at his offices, fifty yards down the quay, etc., etc., etc. His oration finished, the gangway was pushed aboard and everybody landed as quickly as possible. *I* had wired from the War Office earlier in the day to G.H.Q., asking them to send a car to meet the boat. Whether *they* had received *my* message in time I did not know—anyway I could not find it, so, that night, I stayed at Boulogne, and the following evening proceeded to G.H.Q. to receive instructions.

Here I collected my apparatus and stood by for instructions. News of our continued pressure on the German line of retreat was penetrating through. First one village, then another fell into our hands. The fall of Peronne was imminent. My instructions were to proceed to Peronne, or rather the nearest point that it was possible to operate from.

I journeyed that night as far as Amiens, and arriving there about midnight, dog tired, went to my previous billet in the Rue l'Amiral Cambet, and turned in. Early next morning I reported to a major of the Intelligence Department, who told me our troops had entered Peronne the previous night. Rather disappointed that I had not been there to obtain the entry, I made tracks for that town.

I took by-roads, thinking that they would be more negotiable than the main ones, and, reaching the outskirts of the village of Biaches, I left the car there and prepared to walk into Peronne. I could see in the distance that the place was still burning; columns of smoke were pouring upwards and splashing the sky with patches of villainous-looking black clouds.

Strapping my camera upon my back, and bidding my man follow with my tripod, I started off down the hill into Biaches. Then the signs of the German retreat began to fully reveal themselves. The ground was absolutely littered with the horrible wastage of war; roads were torn open, leaving great yawning gaps that looked for all the world like huge jagged wounds. On my right lay the Château of La Maisonnette. The ground there was a shambles, for numerous bodies in various stages of putrefaction lay about as they had fallen.

I left this section of blood-soaked earth, and, turning to my left, entered the village, or rather the site of what had once been Biaches. I will not attempt to describe it; my pen is not equal to the task of conveying even the merest idea of the state of the place. It was as if a human skeleton had been torn asunder, bone by bone, and then flung in all directions. Then, look around and say—this was once a man. You could say the same thing of Biaches—this was once a village. I stayed awhile and filmed various scenes, including the huge engineers' dump left by the Germans, but, as the light was getting rather bad, I hurried as fast as possible in the direction of Peronne.

I wandered down the path of duck-boards, over the swamp of the Somme, filthy in appearance, reeking in its stench, and littered with thousands of empty bottles, that showed the character of the drunken orgies to which the Huns had devoted themselves.

I reached the canal bank. Lying alongside was the blackened ribs of a barge. Only the stern was above water and it was still smouldering; even the ladders and foot-bridges were all destroyed; not a single thing that could be of any use whatsoever had been left. I trudged along the canal bank; bridge after bridge I tried, but it was no use, for each one in the centre for about ten or twelve feet was destroyed—and, stretched between the gap, I found a length of wire netting covered over with straw—a cunning trap set for the first one across. Not a bridge was passable—they were all down!

Peronne lay on the other side and there I must

get before the light failed and while the place was still burning; if I had to make a raft of old timber I made up my mind to get there.

Returning to the bank I placed my camera upon the ground and with the help of three men gathered up some rusty tin cylinders, which, earlier in the campaign, had been utilised as floats for rafts.

I had fished out of the river three planks, and laying them at equal distance upon the cylinders, I lashed them together and so made a raft of sorts. With care I might be able to balance myself upon it and so reach the other section of the bridge and then a rope at either end would enable my man and tripod to be pulled across.

The idea was excellent, but I found that my amateur lashing together with the strong current that was running made the whole plan quite impossible, so, after being nearly thrown into the river several times, and one of the floats coming adrift and washing away, and then doing a flying leap to save myself being hurled into the water upon a trestle which collapsed with my weight, I decided to give up the experiment and explore the river bank further down in the hope of getting across. Eventually, after going for about two kilometres, I reached the ruins of the main bridge leading into the town. This, also, was blown up by the retreating Huns, but, by using the blocks of stone and twisted iron girders as " stepping-stones," I reached the other side.

The old gateway and drawbridge across the moat were destroyed ; the huge blocks of masonry were tossed about, were playthings in the hands of the mighty force of high explosives which flung them there. These scenes I carefully filmed, together with several others in the vicinity of the ramparts.

The town was the same as every other I had filmed —burnt and shell-riven. The place as a habitable

LORD KITCHENER'S LAST VISIT TO FRANCE. HE IS VERY INTERESTED IN THE CARE OF THE WOUNDED

THE EVE OF GREAT EVENTS 257

town simply did not exist. German names were everywhere; the names of the streets were altered, even a French washerwoman had put up a notice that "washing was done here," in German.

Street after street I passed through and filmed. Many of the buildings were still burning and at one corner of the Grande Place flames were shooting out of the windows of the three remaining houses in Peronne. I hastily fitted up my camera and filmed the scene. When I had finished it was necessary to run the gauntlet, and pass directly under the burning buildings to get into the square.

Showers of sparks were flying about, pieces of the burning building were being blown in all directions by the strong wind. But I had to get by, so, buttoning up my collar tightly, fastening my steel shrapnel helmet on my head, and tucking the camera under my arm, I made a rush, yelling out to my man to follow with the tripod. As I passed I felt several heavy pieces of something hit my helmet and another blazing piece hit my shoulder and stuck there, making me set up an unearthly yell as the flames caught my ear and singed my hair. But, quickly shooting past, I reached a place of safety, and setting up the camera I obtained some excellent views of the burning buildings.

Standing upon a heap of rubble, which once formed a branch of one of the largest banking concerns in France, I took a panoramic scene of the great square. The smoke clouds curling in and around the skeleton walls appeared for all the world like some loathsome reptile seeming to gloat upon its prey, loath to leave it, until it had made absolutely certain that not a single thing was left to be devoured.

With the exception of the crackling flames and the distant boom of the guns, it was like a city of the dead. The once beautiful church was totally destroyed. In the square was the base of a monument upon which, before the war, stood a memorial to France's glorious dead in the war of 1870. The " kultured " Germans had destroyed the figure and, in its place, had stuck up a dummy stuffed with straw in the uniform of a French Zouave. Could ever a greater insult be shown to France!

Not content with burning the whole town, the Huns had gone to the trouble of displaying a huge signboard on the side of a building in the square on which were these words: "Don't be vexed—just admire!"

Think of it! The devils!

CHAPTER XXVI

AN UNCANNY ADVENTURE

Exploring the Unknown—A Silence That Could be Felt—In the Village of Villers-Carbonel—A Cat and Its Kittens in an Odd Retreat—Brooks' Penchant for " Souvenirs "—The First Troops to Cross the Somme.

LIEUTENANT B——, the official " still " photographer, and I have been companions in a few strange enterprises in the war, but I doubt whether any have equalled in strangeness, and I might say almost uncanny, adventure that which I am about to record. In cold type it would be pardonable for anyone to disbelieve some of the facts set forth, but, as I have proved for myself the perfect application of the well-known saying that " truth is stranger than fiction," I merely relate the facts in simple language exactly as they happened, and leave them to speak for themselves.

It was early morning on March 17th, 1917, when the Germans began their headlong flight towards their Cambrai, St. Quentin, or " Hindenburg " Line. When B—— and I hastened along the main St. Quentin Road, troops and transports were as usual everywhere. We passed through the ruined villages of Foscaucourt and Estrées and brought our car to a standstill about two kilometres from the village of Villers-Carbonel, it being impossible owing to the fearful road conditions to proceed further.

We left the car and started off to explore the unknown. On either side of the road I noticed many troops in their trenches; they were looking down at us as if we were something out of the ordinary, until I turned to him and said:

"Is there anything funny about us? These chaps seem to be highly interested in our appearance, or something. What is it?"

"I don't know," he said, "let's enquire."

So, going up to an R.A.M.C. officer, who was standing outside his dug-out, I asked him if there was any news—in fact I enquired whether there was a war on up there, everything seemed to be so absolutely quiet.

"Well," he said, "there was up to about three hours ago; Bosche has fairly plastered us with 5.9 and whizz-bangs. These suddenly ceased, and, as a matter of fact, I began to wonder whether peace had been declared when your car came bounding up the road. How the devil did you manage it? Yesterday evening the act of putting one's head over the parapet was enough to draw a few shells; but you come sailing up here in a car."

"This is about the most charming joy-ride I have had for many a day," I replied, "but let me introduce myself. I am Malins, the Official Kinematographer, and my friend here is the Official 'still' picture man. We are here to get scenes of the German retreat, but it seems to me that one cannot see Bosche for dust. That is Villers-Carbonel, is it not?" I said, pointing up the road in the distance.

"Yes," he replied.

"Right," I said, "we are going there and on our way back we'll tell you all the news."

With a cheery wave of the hand he bade us adieu, and we started on our journey.

The once beautiful trees which lined the sides of the road were torn to shreds and, in some instances, were completely cut in half by shell-fire and the trunks were strewn across the road. These and the enormous shell-holes made it difficult to proceed at all, but, by clambering over the huge tree trunks, in and out of filthy slime-filled shell-holes, and nearly tearing oneself to pieces on the barbed wire intermingled with the broken branches, we managed at last to reach the village. Not a sound was to be heard. I turned to my companion.

" This is an extraordinary state of affairs, isn't it ? In case there are any Bosche rearguard patrols, we'll keep this side of the ruins as much as possible."

The village was practically on the top of a ridge of hills. I stood under the shadow of some tree-stumps and gazed around. What a scene of desolation it was. I got my camera into action and took some excellent scenes, showing what was once a beautiful main road : broken trees flung over it in all directions like so many wisps of straw, and an unimaginable mass of barbed wire entanglements. Then, swinging my camera round, I obtained a panoramic view of the destroyed village. Dotted here and there were the dead bodies of horses and men : how long they had lain there Heaven knows !

While examining the ruins of a building which used to be a bakehouse I received a startling surprise. I was bending down and looking into an empty oven when, with a rush and a clatter, a fine black cat sprang at my legs with a frightened, piteous look in its eyes, and mewed in a strange manner. For a moment I was startled, for the animal clung to my breeches. The poor creature looked half-starved. In its frenzy, it might bite or scratch my leg or hand. Blood-poisoning would be likely to follow. I gently lowered my gloved hand and caressed its head. With a soft purr it relaxed its hold of my leg and dropped to the ground. Feeling more comfortable I unfastened my satchel and, taking out some biscuits, gave them to the poor brute. It ravenously ate them up. My second surprise was to come. A faint scratching and mewing sound came from behind some bread bins in a corner and, as I looked, the black cat sprang forward with a biscuit in its mouth in the direction of the sound. I followed and gently moved the bin aside. The sight there almost brought tears into my eyes. Lying upon some old rags and straw were three tiny kittens. Two were struggling around the mother cat, mewing piteously and trying to nibble at the biscuit she had brought. The other was dead.

The mother cat looked up at me with eyes which were almost human in their expression of thanks. I took out some more biscuits, and breaking them up in an empty tin I picked up from the floor, I poured some water from my bottle on to them, placed it beside the starving group and, leaving a handful near the mother cat, I made their retreat as snug as possible.

Making our way again to the main road I stood by some ruins and looked away in the distance where the Germans had disappeared. What a difference. Here were green fields, gorgeous woods, hills, and dales with winding roads sweeping away out of sight. It reminded me of the feeling Moses must have experienced when he looked upon the Promised Land. Here were no shell-torn fields, no woods beaten out of all semblance to anything, no earth upon which thousands of men had poured out their blood ; but, here in front of us, a veritable heaven.

" Come along," I said, " let's explore. If there are any Bosches about they'll soon let us know of their presence. Let's get on to that other ridge ; the Somme river should be there somewhere."

We left the village and cautiously followed the road down one hill and up the next. The Germans had disappeared as completely as if the earth had swallowed them up. Not a soul was to be seen ; we might have been strolling on the Surrey hills !

I gradually reached the brow of the next ridge.

AN UNCANNY ADVENTURE

The sight which met my eyes was the most stimulating one I had ever seen from a picture point of view. There, in front of us, at a distance of six hundred yards, was the river Somme—the name which will go down to history as the most momentous in this the bloodiest war the world has ever known.

There it glistened, winding its way north and south like a silver snake.

"Come along," I said, "I shall get the first picture of the Somme," and we raced away down the road.

In calmer moments at home I have admitted that we were mad. Nobody in their right senses would have done such a thing as to rush headlong into country which might have been thick with enemy snipers and machine-guns. But the quietness of the grave reigned—not a rifle-shot disturbed the silence.

Evidence of the German retreat met our gaze as we ran down the road. On either side were discarded material and, in a quarry on the left, a German Red Cross sign was stuck up on a post, and several dug-outs were burning—smoke was pouring up from below, showing that the Hun was destroying everything.

I was brought to a standstill at the sight of a mass of wreckage near the river. Smoke was issuing from it. I looked on my map and saw that it was the village of Brie; a small section was this side of the river, but the main part was on the other side. The whole place had been completely destroyed, partly, I ultimately found out, by our gun-fire, and the remainder burnt or blown up by the Germans.

The river had developed into a swampy marsh; in fact it was very difficult to say precisely where the river and canal finished and the marshes began.

I again got my camera into action and filmed, for the first time, the Somme river which was directly in our line of advance.

The bridges were blown up ; huge masses of stone and iron, twisted and torn and flung into the morass of weeds and mud and water, forming small dams, thus diverting the river in all directions. Several scenes on this historic spot I filmed, then, wishing to push forward, I attempted to cross the broken bridges. By careful manœuvring I managed to cross the first, then the second, but a large gap blown in the roadway about forty feet across, through which the water rushed in a torrent, brought me to a standstill, so reluctantly I had to retrace my steps.

Except for the sound of rushing water the quietness was almost uncanny—the excitement of the chase was over. Then I began to realise our position.

We were in a section of ground which the enemy had occupied only a few hours before and had apparently abandoned—vanished into thin air ! We were at least two kilometres in *front* of our infantry, in fact we had, of our own accord—keen on obtaining live scenes for the people at home—constituted ourselves an advance patrol, armed, not with machine-guns, swords, or lances, but with cameras. There was every possibility of our being taken for Germans ourselves by our men from a distance ; the real advance guard coming up would undoubtedly open fire and enquire into credentials afterwards. The ruins across the bridge might hide enemy rifles ; they might open fire any moment. I explained the situation to my companion, who had also presumably reached a decision very similar to my own, which was to return to the village of Villers-Carbonel as quickly and as carefully as possible.

Keeping to the side of the road we trudged back, and half-way up the hill we ran into one of the things I expected—an advance party. An officer came forward and said in astonished tones :

" Where the devil have you fellows come from ? "

" We've been getting photographs of the German

retreat," I replied. "We're the official photographers and have been half-way across the Somme, but owing to the bridge being blown up we have come back. The Germans seem to have vanished entirely, not a sign of one about anywhere."

"Well, I'm ——," he said, "this is the funniest thing I've ever known. Will our advance patrols constitute the official photographers for the future? If so, it will save us any amount of trouble."

"Well?" I said, "you can go on—devil a Bosche is over there anyway."

"Well," he said, "these troops I am taking down will be the first across the Somme."

"Right," I said, seeing immediately the scoop it would be for my film. "I will come back and film your men going over; it will make a unique picture."

With that we retraced our steps, and laughing and chatting about our adventure, we once again reached the Somme river.

I fixed up my camera, and, when all was ready, a rough bridge was hastily made of several planks lashed together to bridge gaps in the fallen stonework, and I filmed the first troops to cross the Somme during the great German retreat.

The light was now failing, so, packing up my apparatus, and waving farewells to the C.O., I turned back again. B—— joined me; the day had been a great one for us, and we mutually agreed that it was a fitting sequel to the first British battle that had ever been filmed which I took at Beaumont Hamel on July 1st, 1916.

Weary in body, but very much alive mentally, we returned via Villers-Carbonel to our car.

On my way back I wondered how the cat and her kittens were getting on.

The black cat had certainly brought me luck.

CHAPTER XXVII

THE GERMANS IN RETREAT

The Enemy Destroy Everything as They Go—Clearing Away the Débris of the Battlefield—And Repairing the Damage Done by the Huns—An Enormous Mine Crater—A Reception by French Peasants—" Les Anglais ! Les Anglais ! " Stuck on the Road to Bovincourt.

TO keep in touch with all the happenings on that section of the front for which I was responsible, and to obtain a comprehensive record of events, it was necessary to keep very wide awake. Movements, definite and indefinite, were taking place in scores of different places at the same moment. To keep in touch with the enemy, to work with our forward patrols, to enter upon the heels of our advance guard into the evacuated villages—and, if possible, to get there first and film their triumphal entry, film our advance infantry and guns taking up new positions, the engineers at work remaking the roads, building new bridges over the Somme, laying down new railways and repairing old ones—the hundred and one different organisations that were working and straining every muscle and nerve for the common cause. Only the favoured few have the remotest idea of the enormous amount of work to be done under such conditions.

The road (which was No Man's Land yesterday morning) to the village of Villers-Carbonel was now swarming with men clearing away the accumulated débris of the battlefield. Tree trunks were moved off the road, shell-holes were being filled up with bricks and branches, trenches, which crossed the road, were being filled in, a Tank trap at the entrance to the village, the shape of a broad, deep ditch, about thirty by twenty feet wide by fifteen feet deep, was being loaded with tree trunks and earth. I filmed these scenes; then hurried as fast as possible in the direction of Brie to cover the advanced work on the Somme, and then to cross to the other side and get in touch with our cavalry patrols.

What an extraordinary change in the place! Yesterday a ghostly silence reigned; now men and material and transport were swarming everywhere. I reached the river. The engineers had thrown up light, temporary bridges—six in all. Huge iron girders had arrived from back behind; they had been made in readiness for " The Day." Our H.Q. had known that the Germans in their inevitable retreat would destroy the bridges, so, to save time, duplicates were built in sections, ready to throw across the gap.

I managed to arrive in time to film several squadrons of the Duke of Lancaster's cavalry hurrying forward to harass the enemy. Cyclist patrols were making their way over. I hurried as fast as possible through the ruins of Brie and on to the ridge beyond. In the distance I watched our cavalry deploying in extended order and advance towards a wood to clear it of the enemy rearguards. Motor-cyclists, with their machine-guns, were dashing up the hill anxious to get into contact with the flying enemy. I filmed many scenes in this section.

I looked along the road which was the main one into St. Quentin; it stretched away as far as the eye could see. The condition is certainly excellent, I thought. There would be a greater possibility of obtaining exciting scenes if it were possible to proceed in my car; the only question was whether the temporary bridges across the Somme were capable of sustaining the weight. The possibility of getting into villages just evacuated by the Germans spurred me on, so retracing my steps, I reached the river again.

"Do you think the bridge will take the weight of my car?" I asked an officer in charge of engineers.

"What is it?"

"Daimler," I replied.

"Well," he said, "there is a risk, of course, but our G.S. wagons have been across and also the artillery, so they may take your bus—if you don't bounce her in crossing."

"Right-o!" I said. "I will get it down. Hurrying across I had just reached the last bridge when, with a sudden snap, one of the main beams gave way. All traffic was, of course, stopped, and engineers quickly got to work replacing the broken girder.

"It will be at least another hour, sir," said a sergeant in answer to my enquiry. So there was nothing for it but to curb my impatience and wait, and I stood my apparatus down and watched the proceedings.

At that moment a car came to a standstill alongside me.

"What's wrong?" called out one of the occupants.

"Broken bridge," I said. "I'm waiting to cross with my car to get films of the villages and the occupants."

"That's good," said the speaker, a captain. "I am going up to them as well. Intelligence I heard from our airmen this morning that they saw civilians in one or two villages a few miles out—so I'm off to investigate. Would you care to come? We shall be the first there."

"Yes, rather," I replied. "It will be a fine scoop for me to film the first meeting of British troops in the liberated villages. I will follow in my car."

FILMING OUR GUNS IN ACTION DURING THE GREAT GERMAN RETREAT TO ST. QUENTIN. MARCH, 1917.

THE GERMANS IN RETREAT

The bridge was again complete, so, dumping my camera aboard, I followed in the wake of the captain. Up the hill we dashed and spun along the road at the top, passing beyond the outskirts of Brie. We were now beyond the extreme limit of the shelling which we had subjected the Germans to during their months of occupation.

I was now beginning to see the sights and view the atrocious system and regularity of wilful destruction which had obviously been planned months before by the Huns to carry out Hindenburg's orders and make the whole land a desert. Not a tree was standing; whole orchards were hewn down; every fruit tree and bush was destroyed; hedges were cut at the base as if with a razor; even those surrounding cemeteries were treated in the same way. Agricultural implements were smashed. Mons en Chaussé was the first village we entered; every house was a blackened smoking ruin, and where the fiends had not done their work with fire they had brought dynamite to their aid; whole blocks of buildings had been blown into the air; there was not sufficient cover for a dog.

The car suddenly came to a standstill; my driver jammed on his brake and I hurried forward. There, at the middle of the village cross-roads was another enormous mine-crater—one hundred feet across by about sixty feet deep. It was quite impassable, but the sight which astounded me was to see about twenty old women and children running up the road the other side of the crater shouting and waving their arms with joy. " Les Anglais ! Les Anglais ! " they yelled. I got my camera into position and filmed the captain and his companions as they clambered round the jagged lip of the crater and were embraced by the excited people. For the first time since their captivity by the Germans they had seen " les Anglais." Liberators and captives met !

Several scenes I filmed of the enormous crater and of the cut-down fruit trees. Not a single tree, old or young, was left standing. To blow up roads, and hew down telegraph poles was war, and such measures are justified; but to destroy every tree or bush that could possibly bear fruit, wilfully to smash up agricultural implements; to shoot a dog and tie a label to its poor body written in English :

> "Tommies, don't forget to put this in your next communique—that we killed one dog.   (Signed)   THE HUNS."

To crucify a cat upon a door and stick a cigar in its mouth, to blow up and poison wells, to desecrate graves, to smash open vaults and rob the corpses which lay there, and then to kick the bones in all directions and use the coffins as cess-pools—these things I have seen with my own eyes. Is this war? It is the work of savages, ghouls, fiends.

I wondered where these people had come from and where they had been as the whole village was burnt out. I enquired and found that the Germans, two days before, had cleared the village of its population and distributed them in villages further back, and had then set fire to the place, leaving nothing but a desert behind, and taking with them all the men who could work and many girls in their teens to what fate one may guess.

These few villagers had wandered back during the day to gaze upon the wreckage of their homes and arrived just in time to meet us at the crater.

"We will get along," said my companion. "I want to visit Bovincourt and Vraignes before night-fall, though I am afraid we shall not do it. By making a detour round these ruins I believe we shall strike the main road further down."

I followed him through the ruins and, after

bouncing over innumerable bricks and beams, we reached the main road. We passed through Estrées-en-Chaussée. One large barn was only standing; everything was as quiet as the grave; columns of smoke were still rising from the ruins.

Another jamming on of brakes brought us to a standstill at a cross-roads; another huge mine-crater was in front of us and it was most difficult to see until we were well upon it. There was nothing to do but to take to the fields—our road was at right angles to the one we were traversing.

I examined the ground, it was very soft, and the newly scattered earth and clay from the mine made it much worse.

"If we get stuck," I thought, "there is nobody about to help us out." The captain tried and got over.

I yelled out that I would follow; they disappeared in the direction of Bovincourt. Backing my car to get a good start I let it go over the edge of the road into the field. It was like going through pudding. The near wheels roared round without gripping. Then it happened! We were stuck! A fine predicament, I thought, with prowling enemy patrols about and no rifle.

"All shoulders to the wheel," I said. By digging, and jamming wood, sacking and straw under the wheels we managed, after three-quarters of an hour, to get it out. Jove! what a time it was! And so on the road again.

"We will get into Bovincourt," I said. "Let her go; I may meet the others."

The feeling was uncanny and my position strange, for all I knew Bosches were all around me (and later on this proved to be the case).

Night was falling, and ere I reached the village it was quite impossible to take any scenes.

At the entrance to the village I ran into several

people who crowded round the car, crying and laughing in their relief at seeing the British arrive. Old men and women who could barely move hobbled forward to shake hands, with tears in their eyes. They clambered in and around the car, and it was only by making them understand that I would return on the following day that they allowed the car to proceed. The sight was wonderful and I wish I were able to describe it better.

I could not find the other car, so, assuming it had gone back, I decided to return as far as Brie and stay the night. As I was leaving the village a burst of machine-gun fire rang out close by followed by violent rifle-shots.

" Let her go," I said to my chauffeur. " I am not at all anxious to get pipped out here. My films must not fall into enemy hands."

The car shot up the road like a streak ; the mine-crater was ahead and the possibility of getting stuck again whilst crossing made me feel anything but easy. Full tilt, I told my driver, we must trust to speed to get across. On went the lower gear ; a right-hand twist of the wheel and we were on the field ; the speed gradually grew less, the back wheels buzzed round but still gripped a little.

" Keep her going at all costs," I yelled, " if the car sticks here it will have to be left." To lighten her a little I jumped out and pushed up behind for all I was worth. Mud was flying in all directions ; we were nearly across ; another twenty yards. With a final roll and screech she bounded off on to the road. I jumped aboard again and up the road we shot towards Mons. If the Hun patrols had been anywhere near they must have thought a battalion of Tanks were on their track, for the noise my old " bus " made getting across that field was positively deafening. On I went through Mons, into the ruins of its houses, still glowing red and, in some places, flames were licking around the poor skeletons of its once prosperous farms.

One more mine-crater to negotiate; then all would be plain sailing. It was now quite dark. I dared not use lights, not even side lamps, and going was decidedly slow and risky in consequence. I sat in the bonnet of the car and, peering ahead, called out the direction. Shortly a lightish mass loomed up only a few yards distant.

"Stop!" I yelled.

On went the brakes, and only just in time. We came to a standstill on the outer lip of a huge crater. Another two yards and I should have been trying to emulate the antics of a "tank" in sliding down a crater and crawling up the other side. In my case the sliding down would have been all right, but coming up the other side would have been on the lap of the gods. A hundred men with ropes and myself—well, but that's another story.

"Back the car to give it a good run," I said, "and let us lighten it as much as possible," and soon all was ready.

"I will go ahead and put my handkerchief over my electric light; we must risk being seen—you head direct for the glow."

I went into the muddy fields.

"Let her go," I shouted. With a whir and a grind I could tell it had started. I stood still. It was coming nearer. Ye gods! what a row. Then, suddenly, the engines stopped and dead silence reigned.

"It's stuck, sir," came a voice from the darkness.

I went to the car and switched my lamp on to the near wheels. The car was stuck right up to the axel.

"We shall never get out of this unaided," I said. "Put all the stuff back inside and get the hood up; we shall have to sleep here to-night.

Then, to add to the discomfiture of the situation, it began to rain, and rain like fury, and in a few minutes I was wet through to the skin. The hood leaked badly and had convenient holes in alignment to one's body, whether you were sitting lengthways or otherwise inside. I had resigned myself for a dismal night out. Two hours had passed when I heard the clatter of hoofs coming towards me in the distance and, by the direction of the sound, I could tell they were our men. I tumbled out and ran as fast as possible to the other side of the crater and reached there just as the horsemen arrived.

"Hullo!" I shouted.

"Hulloa!" came the reply, "who is it?"

"I am badly stuck, or rather my car is—in the mud in the field here. Can you hitch two or three of your horses on and help me out on to the road?"

"Certainly, if we can, sir."

"I will guide you with my lamp—by the way, where are you going?" I said.

"We are trying to get into touch with the Bosche."

"I have been in Bovincourt," I said, "but there are none there, though I heard a lot of rifle-fire just outside the village."

We arrived at the car and, quickly hitching on a rope, the engine was started up and, with a heave and a screech, it moved forward and was eventually dragged on to the road.

"Thank Heaven," I thought. Then, thanking the men, and warning them of the other delightful mine crater further down, I started off again, sitting on the bonnet.

As I neared Brie I switched on my lamp as a head-light and got held up by two sentries with their bayonets at the ready. They did not understand why a motor-car should be coming back apparently from the German lines, and their attitude was decidedly unfriendly till I assured them I was not a German, but only the Official Kinematographer out for pictures.

CHAPTER XXVIII

THE STORY OF AN "ARMOURED CAR" ABOUT WHICH
I COULD A TALE UNFOLD

Possibilities—Food for Famished Villagers—Meeting the Mayoress of Bovincourt—Who Presides at a Wonderful Impromptu Ceremony—A Scrap Outside Vraignes—A Church Full of Refugees—A True Pal—A Meal with the Mayor of Bierne.

TO keep hard upon the heels of the retreating Germans and so obtain scenes, the character of which had never been presented before to the British public, was my chief aim. I had no time for sleep. I arrived at my base wet through, the rain had continued throughout the whole of my return journey. Changing into dry underwear, I refilled my exposed spool-boxes and packed up a good surplus supply, sufficient to last for several days, then packing my knapsack with the usual rations, bully and bread, condensed milk and slabs of chocolate, I was ready to start out once more. My clothes had by this time dried. Daylight was breaking, the car arrived and, with all kit aboard, I started out again for the Somme, wondering what the day would bring forth.

I stopped on the way to pick up the "still" photographer.

"Where for to-day?" he asked.

"Bovincourt and Vraignes," I replied, "and, if possible, one or two of the villages near by. I must get into them before our troops, so as to be able to film their entry. Does that suggest possibilities to you?" I said, with a smile, knowing that he, like myself, would go through anything to obtain pictures.

"Possibilities," he said, "don't, you make my mouth water. How about food? Shall we take some to the villages?"

"Excellent idea," I said.

We stopped on the way and purchased a good supply of white bread and French sausages, thinking that these two commodities would be most useful.

Through Foucacourt Estrées and Villers-Carbonel the roads were lined with troops, guns, and transport of every description, all making their way forward. Engineers were hard at work on the roads; shell-holes were filled in and road trenches bridged. Work was being pushed forward with an energy and skill which reflected great credit upon those in charge; traffic controls were at cross roads which forty-eight hours before had been " No Man's Land." Hun signboards were taken down and familiar British names took their place. The sight was wonderful. En route I stopped and filmed various scenes. Arriving again at Brie on the Somme the change in affairs was astounding. The place was alive with men; it was a veritable hive of industry; new lines were being laid to replace the torn and twisted rails left by the Germans; bridges were being strengthened, roads on both sides were widened, and, to make it possible to continue the work throughout the night, a searchlight was being mounted upon a platform.

Crossing the bridges of Brie we mounted the hill and were once again upon the ridge. Great gaps had been made by our men in the huge line of barbed wire entanglements which the Huns had spent months of laborious work to construct. It stretched away over hill and dale on both sides as far as the eye could see.

AN " ARMOURED CAR " 277

To pick up further information I stopped a cyclist officer coming from the direction of Mons.

" Any news ? " I enquired. " Where is Bosche ? "

" We were in touch with his rearguards all last night," he said. " They have made several strong points round the villages of Vraignes, Haucourt, and Bierne. They were scouting around Vraignes, but we quickly put the wind up them," he said, with a smile. " Several villages were seen burning during the night and the enemy put a little shrapnel around some patrols near Pouilly, but no damage was done."

" Vraignes, of course, is quite clear ? "

" Yes, as far as we know. Our patrols reported it clear late last evening, but possibly Bosche returned during the night. We captured three Bosches and they have an extraordinary tale of seeing two armoured cars yesterday evening near Bovincourt, and they insist upon it although I am quite aware there were none at all near there. They say that about six o'clock they were on the outskirts of Bovincourt when two armoured cars came in sight. Not having a machine-gun with them they decided to hide and so took cover in the ruins of a house. Later on they say they was only one car leave in the direction of the main road. That's their tale and they seem quite serious about it."

" Well," I said, with a grin, " do you think this car of mine would look like an armoured car at a distance ? "

" Well, yes, possibly, in a failing light. Why ? "

" Well, this must be one of your excellent prisoner's so-called armoured cars, because I was in Bovincourt with —— of the Corps Intelligence, hence the two cars. I missed him through getting stuck in the mud, and entered Bovincourt about six o'clock and left by myself later as a skirmish was taking place somewhere near by, and not being armed with anything more dangerous than a camera,

I decided to quit. I am much obliged to the Bosche for taking this bus of mine for an armoured car."

With a laugh and a cheery adieu the officer bade me good luck and pedalled off.

I could not help thinking that I had had a lucky escape.

On again, and reaching the first mine, the scene of the previous night's adventure, I put the car to the field at a rush and by some extraordinary means got her round.

I was just entering the village when, with a shriek and a crash, a shell burst near the church. I stopped the car and, under cover of the ruins, reached a distance of about three hundred yards from where it fell. If any more were coming over I intended, if possible, to film them bursting.

Carefully taking cover behind a wall, I fitted up my camera. Another shell came hurtling over and dropped and burst quite near the previous spot. Showers of bricks flew in all directions, liberally splattering the wall behind which I was concealed. The débris cleared, up went my camera, and, standing by the handle, I awaited the next.

It came soon enough, I heard the shriek nearer and nearer. I turned the handle and put my head close behind the camera with my eye to the view-finder. Crash came the shell, and, with a terrific report, it exploded. The whole side of a house disappeared, and bricks, wood, and metal flew in all directions. I continued to turn when, with an ugly little whistle, a small piece of something struck my view-finder and another my tripod. Luckily nothing touched the lens. I awaited the next. It was longer this time, but it came, and nearer to me than the previous one. I was satisfied. I thought if they elevated another fifty yards I might get a much too close view of a shell-burst, so scrambled aboard the car, and made a detour round the mine on to the road beyond.

"Those scenes ought to be very fine," I said. "It's one of those lucky chances where one has to take the risk of obtaining a thrilling scene."

By the balls of white smoke I could see that shrapnel was bursting in the near distance.

"That's near Pouilly," I said. "We are turning up on the left, let's hope the Huns don't plaster us there."

Reaching the village of Bovincourt, the villagers were there eagerly awaiting our arrival. They again crowded around the car, and it was with difficulty that I persuaded them to let us pass into the village. Cheering, shouting, and laughing they followed close behind. I stopped the car and asked an old man who, by his ribbons, had been through the 1870 war:

"Where is the Mayor?"

"There is no Mayor, monsieur, but a mayoress, and she is there," pointing to a buxom French peasant woman about fifty years of age.

I went up to her and explained in my best French that I had brought bread and sausages for the people, would she share them out?

"Oui, oui, monsieur."

"I would like you to do it here, I will then take a kinematograph film of the proceeding, so that the people in England can see it."

"Ah, monsieur, it is the first white bread and good French sausage we have seen since the Bosches came. They took everything from us, everything, and if it had not been for the American relief we should have starved. They are brutes, pig-brutes, monsieur, they kill everything." And, with tears in her eyes, she told me how the Huns shot her beautiful dog because, in its joyfulness, it used to play with and bark at the children. "They did not like being disturbed, monsieur, so they shot him—

poor Jacques! They have not left one single animal; everything has gone. Mon Dieu, but they shall suffer!"

I changed the painful subject by saying that now the British had driven back the Bosche everything would be quite all right. With a wan smile she agreed.

I set up my camera, and telling my man to hand over the food, the Mayoress shared it out. One sausage and a piece of white bread to each person, men, women, and children. The joy on their faces was wonderful to behold. As they received their share they ran off to the shelter of some ruins, or up into the church, to cook their wonderful gifts. I filmed the scene, and I shall never forget it.

The last of the batch had disappeared when up the road came hobbling a woman whose age I should say was somewhere about forty-five. I could see she was on the point of exhaustion. She had a huge bundle upon her back and a child in her arms, another about seven years clinging to her skirts. They halted outside the ruins of a cottage, the woman dropped her bundle, and crouching down upon it clung convulsively to the babe in her arms and burst into tears.

I went up to her and gently asked her the cause.

"This, monsieur, was my house. Two days past the Germans drove me away with my children. My husband has already been killed at the front. They drove me away, and I come back to-day and now my home, all that I had in the world, monsieur, is gone. They have burnt it. What can I do, monsieur? And we are starving."

The babe in her arms began to send forth a thin lifeless wail. I helped the poor woman to her feet and told her to go to the church, and that I would bring her bundle and some food for her.

God above, what despair! The grim track of war

in all its damnable nakedness was epitomised in this little French hamlet. Houses burnt, horses taken away, agricultural implements wilfully smashed, fruit trees and bushes cut down, even the hedges around their little gardens, their cemetery violated and the remains of their dead strewn to the four winds of heaven. Their wells polluted with garbage and filth; in some cases deliberately poisoned, in others totally destroyed by dynamite. Their churches used as stables for horses and for drunken orgies. All the younger men deported, and the prettiest of the girls. In some cases their clothes had been forcibly taken away from them and sacks had been given in exchange to clothe themselves with. They were robbed of every penny they possessed.

But when the wonderful sound of the British guns and the tramp of our soldiers crept nearer and nearer, terrifying, relentless, and irresistible, the Germans left, fleeing with their ill-gotten spoil like demons of darkness before the angels of light, leaving in their trail the picture I have unfolded to you.

Wishing to push on further I scouted round the outskirts of the village. In a wood a short distance away it was evidently that our patrols were in contact with the Huns. Volley after volley of rifle-fire rang out, and now and then a burst from the machine-guns. A horseman was heading straight for me. Was he British or Hun ? In a few minutes I could see he was one of our men—evidently a dispatch-rider. He swept down into a hollow, then up the road into the village. He was riding hard ; his horse stumbled, but by a great effort the rider recovered himself. He dashed past me and, clattering over the fallen masonry, disappeared from sight.

I looked around. Not a sign of life anywhere, so I decided to make for Vraignes about a kilometre distant south-east of Bovincourt. I had previously heard from one of the villagers that there were about one thousand people left there.

Strapping my camera on my back I tramped away, my man following in the rear. The " still " man, who had left me after feeding the villagers, had been prowling around getting pictures. Accidentally he ran into me, so together we trekked off.

Taking advantage of every bit of cover possible, as German snipers were none too careful as to where they put their bullets, we eventually reached the outskirts of Vraignes. Not a sign of Germans, but crowds of civilians. Things here were the same as at Bovincourt, but a few more houses were left standing owing to the fire not completely doing its work. The people were in the same state. We had just got into the village, and near the Mairie, when a commotion round the corner by the church attracted my attention. The men and women who had crowded around us shouting with joy, turned and rushed up the road.

" Vive les Anglais ! Vive les Anglais ! " The cry was taken up by every one. Hands and handkerchiefs were waving in all directions. " Vive les Anglais ! Vive les Anglais ! "

" Our boys are there," I said.

My camera was up and turned on to the corner where the crowd stood and, at that moment, a troop of our cyclists entered, riding very slowly through the exultant people—the first British troops to enter the village. I turned the handle. The scene was inspiring. Cheer after cheer rent the air. Old men and women were crying with joy. Others were holding their babies up to kiss our boys. Children were clinging and hugging around their legs, until it was impossible for them to proceed further. The order was given by the officer in charge to halt. The men tumbled off their machines, the people

AN "ARMOURED CAR" 283

surged round them. To say the men were embarrassed would be to put it mildly. They were absolutely overcome. I filmed them with the crowd around. And then an order was given to take up billets. Patrols were thrown out, sentries posted, the men parked their cycles and rested.

On a large double door of a barn the Huns had gone to the trouble of painting in huge letters the hackneyed phrase "Gott strafe England," and immediately our men saw it one of them, with a piece of chalk, improved upon it.

They gathered the children round them and formed a group beneath the letters with German trophies upon their heads; I filmed them there, one of the happiest groups possible to conceive.

I left them and went to find the officer in charge, and asked him for the latest news from other sections.

"I couldn't say," he replied, "but my men were well in touch with them early this morning, but you seem to know more about it here than anyone else. When on earth did you arrive in the village?"

"Just before you," I replied. "I came from Bovincourt."

"Well, you have got some job. I certainly didn't expect to find anyone so harmless as a photographer awaiting our arrival."

The conversation was abruptly stopped by a warning shout from one of the observers on a house-top close by.

"Germans, sir."

The officer and I rushed to a gap in the buildings and looked through our glasses, and there, on a small ridge a thousand yards off, a body of horsemen were seen approaching, riding hard, as if their very lives depended upon it.

An order was immediately given to the machine-gun company who had taken up a most advantageous position and one that commanded most of the country near by.

I placed my camera in such a position by the side of a wall that I could see all that was taking place and if seen myself I could easily pull it under cover.

Nearer and nearer they came. They were too far away to photograph. Excitement was intense. Were they coming into the village? If they did, I thought, in all conscience they would get a warm reception, knowing as I did the arrangements for its defence. My eyes were fixed upon them.

The officer close by was on the point of giving the order to fire when a burst of machine-gun fire rang out in the distance.

" Our cavalry have got them," said the officer. " We have some strong posts just here, Bosche has fairly run into them. Look! They have their tails up."

And they had, for they were running back for all they were worth in the direction of Bierne.

Our men were positively disappointed, and I can honestly say I was myself, for the possibilities of a wonderful scene had disappeared.

The tension relaxed; most of the men returned to their billets and quickly made themselves at home with the people.

Noticing people going into church, I went up the hill to investigate. As I entered the outer gate an officer clattered up on horseback, swung himself off and walked up to me.

" Hullo," he said, " I am the doctor. Anything doing here? "

" Well," I said, " there might have been just now."

I related the happenings of the last ten minutes.

" Have you been to Bovincourt? "

" Yes, but the poor devils are too ill for me. I haven't sufficient stuff with me to go round."

Another officer ran up, " I say, Doctor, for

Heaven's sake look in the church here. The place is packed and half of them are ill, God knows what with, and one or two are dead."

"Well, I will look, but I can do nothing until this evening. I have no stuff with me."

We went into the church. Heavens! what a sight met our eyes; the atmosphere was choking. It was like a charnel-house. Crowds of old men, women, and children of all ages were crowded together with their belongings. They had been evacuated from dozens of other villages by the Huns. Women were hugging their children to them. In one corner an old woman was bathing the head of a child with an old stocking dipped in water. The child, I could see, was in a high fever. There must have been at least three hundred people lying about in all directions, wheezing and coughing, moaning and crying.

The doctor spoke to one old woman, who had hobbled forward and sank down near a pillar. The doctor bent down and told her that he would bring medicine in the evening. Everybody there seemed to hear that magic word, and scrambled forward begging for medicine for themselves, but mostly for the children. The scene was pitiable in the extreme.

I asked one women where they had come from. She told me from many villages. The Bosche had turned them all out of their homes, then burnt their houses and their belongings. They had walked miles exposed to the freezing cold rains and winds, they had been packed into this church like a lot of sheep without covering, without fires. She was begging for medicine for her three-months-old babe.

"She will die, moniseur, she will die!" And the poor woman burst into a flood of tears.

I calmed her as much as possible by telling her that everything would be done for them without delay, and that medicine, food, and comfort would be given them.

I turned and left the building, for the air was nearly choking me. Outside I met the doctor, who was arranging to send a cyclist back for an ambulance.

"They cannot be treated here, it's impossible. I've never seen such a sight."

I left him and went into the house where the cyclist C.O. had made his temporary headquarters.

"I want to get on further, is there any other village near by?"

"Yes," he said, "there is Haucourt, but I believe Bosche is in part of it, or he was this morning. It's about two kilos from here. I shouldn't go if I were you unless you get further information; I am expecting another patrol in from there. If you care to wait a few minutes you may learn something."

I agreed to wait, the "still" man came in just then, and he agreed to come with me.

"We may as well risk it," I said. "I will take my old bus into the place. If Bosche sees it he may mistake it again for an armoured car."

So, packing the cameras aboard, I waited for the expected patrol to turn up. Half an hour passed; no sign. Daylight was waning.

"I am going on," I said to the "still" man, "we cannot wait for the patrol, there's not time. Will you come?"

"Yes," he said.

I told the C.O. of my intention.

"It's thundering risky," he said. "You're going into new ground again."

I left Vraignes and advanced at a cautious pace in the direction of Haucourt. Rifle-fire was proceeding in the distance, which I judged was the other side of the village. A destroyed sugar refinery on the left was still smoking. It had been blown up by the Huns and the mass of machinery was flung and twisted about in all directions.

In the village I stopped the car close by a crucifix, which was still standing.

"Turn the car round," I said to my driver, "and keep the engine going, we may have to bolt for it."

Then, shouldering the camera, I made my way up the main street. The place was a mass of smoking ruins; absolutely nothing was left. A huge mine had been blown up at a cross-road; all trees and bushes had been cut down. A piano, curiously enough, was lying in the roadway; the front had been smashed, and no doubt all the wires were hacked through by some sharp instrument, and the keys had all been broken. The Huns had evidently tried to take it away with their other loot, but finding it too heavy for quick transport had abandoned, then wilfully destroyed it to prevent its being used by others.

The place was as silent as the grave. I filmed a few scenes which appealed to me, and was on the move towards the further end of the road when two of our cyclists suddenly came into view. I hurried up to them.

"Any news?" I asked. "Where's Bosche?"

The men were half dead with fatigue. Their legs were caked inches thick in mud, and it was only by a tremendous effort that they were able to lift their feet as they walked. They were pushing their cycles; the mud was caked thick between the wheels and the mudguards forming in itself a brake on the tyres. Fagged out as they obviously were they tried to smile at the reply one made.

"Yes, the Bosche is about here outside the village," said one. "We had a small strong point last night over there," pointing in the distance, "myself and two pals. We were sitting in the hole smoking when nine Bosches jumped in on us. Well, sir, they managed to send my pal West, but that's all. Then we started and six Fritzes are lying out there now. The other three escaped. It made my blood boil, sir, when they did in my pal. I'm going to make a wooden cross, and then bury him. We had been together for a long time, sir, and—well—I miss my pal, but we got six for him and more to come, sir, more to come before we've finished."

I thanked the man and sympathised with him over his loss and complimented him on his fight.

"But it's not enough yet, sir, not enough."

The two then struggled away, bent on their errand of making a cross for a pal. And as they disappeared among the ruins I wondered how many men in the world could boast of such a true friend. Very few, worse luck!

. . . . . .

The sharp crack of a rifle quickly brought me back to earth. A bullet struck the wall close by. I dived under cover of some bricks dragging my camera after me. Another came over seeming to strike the spot I had just vacated. I decided to keep the ruins between myself and the gentle Bosche. Scenes were very scarce, no matter where one looked it was just ruins, ruins, ruins.

I wandered on until I came to a long black building, evidently put up by the Huns. It was quite intact, which to me seemed suspicious. It might hide a German sniper. I put my camera behind a wall then quietly edged near the building. Not a sound was audible. In case anyone was there I thought of a little ruse. The door was close to me and it opened outwards, so picking up a stone I flung it over the roof, intending it to fall the other end and so create a diversion. With a sudden pull I opened the door alongside me, but with no result. I peered round the door; nobody there. I entered and found the building had been used as a stable,

Straw was lying all over the place; feed-bags had been hastily thrown down, halters were dotted here and there, and a Uhlan lance was lying on the ground, which, needless to say, I retained as a souvenir. The rearguard of the enemy had evidently taken shelter there during the previous night and had made a hasty exit owing to the close proximity of our boys.

Evening was drawing on apace, so I decided to make my way back to the car. The "still" man was awaiting my return.

At Bovincourt I met an Intelligence Officer and told him of my experiences. He seemed highly amused and thanked me for the information brought. I told him that wishing to be on the spot if anything interesting happened during the night or early next morning I had decided to sleep in my car in the village. I was going to hunt up a place to cook some food.

"I will take you somewhere," he said. "There is the old Mayor of Bierne here. He has been evacuated by the Bosche. He's an interesting old fellow and you might have a chat with him. He is in a house close by with his wife. Come along."

We found the old man in one of the half-dozen remaining houses left intact by the Huns.

We entered the kitchen and my friend introduced us to Paul Andrew, a tall stately French farmer of a type one rarely sees. He had dark curly hair, a shaggy moustache and beard, blue eyes and sunken cheeks, sallow complexion and a look of despair upon his face, which seemed to brighten up on our entrance.

I asked him if his good wife would cook a little food for us, as we wished to stay the night in the village.

"Monsieur," he said, "what we have is yours. God knows it's little enough—the Bosche has taken it all. But whatever monsieur wishes he has only to ask. Will monsieur sit down?"

I bade adieu to the officer who had brought us there, had the car run into the yard, and then returned to the cosy kitchen, and sat by the fire whilst the old lady prepared some hot coffee.

"These are more comfortable quarters than we expected to-night," I said. "I must make a note of all my scenes taken to-day. Have you a light, Monsieur Andrew?"

"Oui, Monsieur, I have only one lamp left and I hid that as the Bosche took everything that was made of brass or copper, even the door handles."

He brought in the lamp, a small brass one with a candle stuck in it. I proceeded with my record, then we supped on bread, sardines, and bully, sharing our white bread with Andrew and his wife. They had not seen or tasted such wonderful stuff since the Bosche occupation, and their eyes sparkled with pleasure on tasting it again. I had brought copies of the *Echo de Paris*, *Journal*, *Matin* and other French papers, and these were the first they had seen for two years. The farmer declared it was like a man awakening from a long sleep.

"We'll turn in," I said.

Gathering up my coat I opened the door. The freezing cold seemed to chill me to the bone, and it was snowing hard. I flashed on my torch and we found our way to the car. Quickly getting inside, I unfolded the seats which formed two bunks, and struggling inside our sleeping-bags we were soon asleep.

I awoke with a start. It was pitch dark. I rubbed the steam from the door window and looked out; it was still snowing. I had an extraordinary feeling that something was happening, that some danger was near. If anybody had been there near the car I should have seen them; the snow made that

THE QUARRY FROM WHICH I CRAWLED TO FILM THE GERMAN TRENCHES IN FRONT OF ST. QUENTIN, 1917. IT WAS ALSO THE POINT OF LIASON BETWEEN THE BRITISH AND FRENCH ARMIES

possible. But there was not a sign of movement. I got out of my sleeping-bag, thinking that if any prowling Bosche patrol ventured near I should be able to do something. Nothing happened, and for quite half an hour I was on the alert. Several rifle-shots rang out quite near, then quietness reigned again, and, as nothing else happened, I wriggled into my bag again and dozed.

In the morning I told one of our patrol officers of my experience.

"You were right," he said. "Uhlan rearguard patrols sneaked in near the village, and must have passed quite close to your place. My men had some shots at them and gave chase, but owing to the confounded snow they got away."

I decided that if I slept there again that night it would be with a rifle by my side.

CHAPTER XXIX

BEFORE ST. QUENTIN

The "Hindenburg" Line—A Diabolical Piece of Vandalism—Brigadier H.Q. in a Cellar—A Fight in Mid-air—Waiting for the Taking of St. Quentin—*L'Envoi*.

STILL the great German retreat continued. Village after village fell into our hands; mile after mile the enemy was relentlessly pursued by our cavalry and cyclist corps. Still the Germans burnt and devastated everything in their path although, in some instances, there was evidence that they were shifted from their lines of defence with far more force and promptitude than they imagined we would put up against them in this particular section. The enemy had arranged his operations, as usual, by timetable, but he had failed to take into consideration the character of the British soldier, with the result his schemes had "gone agley." To save men the German high command gave orders for a further retirement to their Hindenburg defences, a fortified line of such strength as had never been equalled.

If this line was not impregnable, nothing could be. It was the last word in defence system and it had taken something like two years to perfect.

The barbed wire, of a special kind, was formidable in its mass; three belts fifty feet deep wound about it in an inextricable mass in the form of a series of triangles and other geometric designs. The trenches themselves were constructional works of art; switch lines were thrown out as an extra precaution; in front of the most important strategical positions, machine-gun posts and strong points abounded in unlimited quantities. It was the Hun's last and most powerful line of defence this side of the Franco-German frontier. This "Hindenburg" line stretched from a point between Lens and Arras where it joined the northern trench system, which had been occupied for the past two years, down to St. Quentin, passing behind the town at a distance of about five kilos, with a switch line in front to take the first shock of the Allies' blow when it came.

Behind this trench the Huns thought they could safely rest and hold up the Allies' advance. But, with their wonderful and elaborate system of barbed-wire defence which they anticipated would keep us out, they probably forgot one point—it would certainly keep them in—tightly bolted and barred. Therefore, under such conditions, it was the side which had the predominance in guns and munitions that could smash their way through by sheer weight of metal, and force a passage through which to pour their troops, taking section by section by a series of flanking and encircling movements, threaten their line of communication, finally cracking up the whole line and compel a further extensive falling back to save their armies.

Against the front portion of this line we thrust ourselves early in March, 1917, and our massed guns poured in the most terrible fire the world had ever known. Lens was practically encircled—the Vimy ridge was taken by assault, and dozens of villages captured, resulting in the capture of eighteen thousand prisoners and over two hundred guns. Hindenburg threw in his divisions with reckless extravagance; he knew that if this section gave way all hope of holding on to Northern France was gone. Time and again he sent forward his "cannon fodder" in massed formation—targets which our guns could not possibly miss—and they were mown down in countless numbers; his losses were appalling. In certain places his attacking forces succeeded for a time in retaking small sections of ground we had gained, only to be driven out by a strong counter-attack. His losses were terribly disproportionate to his temporary advantage.

I moved down to the extreme right of the British line; St. Quentin was the goal upon which I had set my mind. In my opinion the taking of that place by a combined Franco-British offensive with the triumphant entry of the troops would make a film second to none. In the first place the preliminary operations pictorially would differ from all previous issues of war films, and in the second place it would be the first film actually showing the point of "liaison" with the French and their subsequent advance—making it, from an historical, public, and sentimental point of view, a film *par excellence*. Therefore in this section of the British line I made my stand.

I left my H.Q. early in April, 1917. I intended to live at the line in one of the cellars of a small village situated near the Bois de Holnon, which had been totally destroyed.

I proceeded by the main St. Quentin road, through Pouilly into Caulaincourt. The same desolation and wanton destruction was everywhere in evidence; but the most diabolical piece of vandalism was typified by the once beautiful Château of Caulaincourt, which was an awful heap of ruins. The Château had been blown into the Somme, with the object of damming the river, and so flooding the country-side; partially it succeeded, but our engineers were quickly upon the scene and, soon, the river was again running its normal course. The flooded park made an excellent watering-place for horses. The wonderful paintings and tapestries in the library on the Château had beeen destroyed. As I wandered among the ruins, filming various scenes of our engineers at work sorting out the débris, I noticed many things which must have been of inestimable value. Every statue and ornamentation about the grounds was wilfully smashed to atoms; the flower-pots which lined the edges of the once beautiful floral walks had been deliberately crushed—in fact a more complete specimen of purposeless, wanton destruction it would be impossible to find.

I filmed the most interesting sections; then continued my way through Bouvais on to see the General of a Division. This Division was working near the French left. After a very interesting conversation this officer recommended me to call on a Brigadier-General.

" He is stationed at —— " he said. " I will ring him up and tell him you are on the way. He will give you all the map references of the O.P's in the neighbourhood. Anyway, you can make your own arrangements, I suppose, about views ? "

" Oh, yes, sir, certainly, so long as I can get very near to the place."

" Right. You go into all these details with General ——."

Thanking him I hurried away. I found the mines which Bosche had exploded at all cross-roads very troublesome, and on one occasion, in endeavouring to cross by way of the field alongside, I got badly stuck; so I had to borrow a couple of horses to get me out on to the road again.

\I duly arrived and reported to Brigadier H.Q. It was the cellar of a once decent house by the appearance of the garden. I went down six steps into a chamber reeking with dampness about six feet high by ten feet square; a candle was burning in a bottle on a roughly made table, and, sitting at it, was the General closely studying details on a map.

He looked up as I entered.

"Are you the Kinema man?" he enquired. "General —— told me you were coming; what do you want?"

"Well, sir," I said, "I want to obtain films of all the operations in connection with the taking of St. Quentin; if you have an observation-post from which I can obtain a good view it will suit me admirably."

"I am sure we can fix you up all right. But we are just going to have a meal; sit down and join us. We can then go into details."

Lunch was served in primitive fashion, which was unavoidable under such conditions—but we fared sumptuously, although on a rough plain table with odds and ends for platters, and boxes and other makeshifts for chairs.

During the meal I went into details with the General about my requirements. He quite understood my position and thoroughly appreciated my keen desire to obtain something unique in the way of film story.

"The taking of St. Quentin by the Allied troops, sir, would be one of my finest films."

"Well," he said, "the French are bombarding the suburbs and other places, so far as damage is concerned, to-day; our batteries are also giving a hand. I should advise you to go to this spot"—indicating a position on the map. "What do you think?" he turned to the Brigade Major. "Will this do for him?"

"Yes, sir, I should think so."

"Anyway, I can soon see, if you can put me on the road to find it. But a guide would save time."

"You had better take him," said the General to

BEFORE ST. QUENTIN

the Brigade Major; "you know the place quite well."

"Right, sir," he said.

So, getting hold of an extra orderly to help carry my kit, we started off, up through a wood and then for the first time I viewed St. Quentin.

"We had better spread out here," said my guide. "Bosche can observe all movements from the Cathedral tower, and he doesn't forget to 'strafe' us although no harm is ever done."

"He is crumping now by all appearances," I replied, noticing some crumps bursting about three hundred yards away.

"Yes, they are 'strafing' the place we are going to! That's cheerful, anyway. We will make a wide detour; he's putting shrapnel over now. Look out! Keep well to the side of the wood."

We kept under cover until it was necessary to cross a field to a distant copse.

"That's our O.P. We have some guns there, worse luck."

"Hullo, keep down," I said; "that's a burst of four." Crash—crash—crash—crash! in quick succession, the fearful bursts making the ground tremble.

"Very pretty," I remarked. "I will get my camera ready for the next lot."

They came—and I started turning one after the other; it was an excellent scene; but, as the enemy seemed to swing his range round slightly, the pieces were coming much too near to be healthy. So, hastily packing up, we made straight for the copse on the quarry top.

High shrapnel was now bursting, several pieces whistling very unpleasantly near.

"Let's get under shelter of the trees," said the Brigade Major, "the trunks will give us a lot of cover."

We made a run for it, and reached them safely, and, gently drawing near the outer edge, I was in full view of St. Quentin.

The Cathedral loomed up with great prominence—and shrapnel was exploding near the tower.

"That's to keep the Hun observers down," he said. "We are not, of course, shelling the place to damage it at all. Those fires you can see there are of Bosche making; he is systematically burning the place as a prelude to retreat. My Intelligence officer says that the Palace of Justice and the theatre are well alight, and airmen declare the town quite empty; they flew over it yesterday only about two hundred feet above the house-tops and they were not fired at once. Seems to me they've evacuated the populace entirely."

"Jove," I said, "the French are letting them have it over there," pointing in the distance.

"That is, of course, south of the town, very nearly running due east and west—it's an excellent barrage—and all H.E., too."

I soon got my camera into action and, carefully concealing the tripod behind a tree trunk or rather a little to one side, I began exposing.

The firing was very heavy. I continued exposing on various sections which gave me the most comprehensive idea of barrage fire.

"The French are bang up against the "Hindenburg" line there, and it's pretty deep in wire—as you know," said my guide, "but I think they will manage it all right; it's only a matter of time. Hullo! they are 'strafing' their confounded guns again with H.E. Look out! keep down!" And keep down we did. "Those 5·9 of brother Fritz's are not very kind to one; we had better stay for a few minutes; he may catch us crossing the field."

Ten minutes went by; things were a bit quieter, so, hastily packing up, we doubled back to the road.

BEFORE ST. QUENTIN

"I never did like getting near forward gun positions," I said, "but, curiously enough, my best view-points compel me on many occasions to fix up in their vicinity."

We got on to the road without casualties and in time to see the H.L.I. forming up to leave at dusk for the front line, or the series of strong points which comprised it in this section.

They were having the operation orders read out to them by their officer in charge. The scenes made very interesting ones for me—the men, alert and keen to the last degree, stood there in line, listening intently to the words until the end.

The next morning I had a wire from H.Q. asking me to take charge of two French journalists for a day or two; they were most anxious to see the British troops in action before St. Quentin. Towards midday they arrived—M. Gustave Babin, of *L'Illustration*, Paris—and M. Eugène Tardeau, of the *Echo de Paris*. I presented these gentlemen to the General, who kindly extended every facility to them.

I took them up to the observation post from which they could look down on St. Quentin.

"It will be a great moment for me," said M. Babin, "to obtain the first impression of the Allied entry in the town."

For myself the day was quite uneventful, beyond obtaining extra scenes of the preparatory work of our artillery. The heavy bombardment was continuing with unabated fury, the horizon was black with the smoke of bursting high explosives, huge masses of shrapnel were showering their leaden messengers of death upon the enemy. Towards evening the weather changed for the worse. It began with a biting cold sleet, which quickly turned into snow.

That night we slept in an old greenhouse which was open to the four winds of heaven. The cold was intense. I rolled myself up tight in my bag and drew my waterproof ground-sheet well over my body. It was a good job I did so for the snow was blowing in through the many fissures and cracks and settling upon me like fallen leaves in autumn.

The heavy shelling continued throughout the night. Several Bosche shells came unpleasantly near, shaking my rickety shelter in an alarming manner.

The next day the weather continued vile and the operations were indefinitely postponed. Therefore there was nothing further to do but to return to H.Q.

St. Quentin, for the present, was to me a blank, although I had continued for some time preparing all the scenes leading up to its capture.

The weather was changing, the ground was drying. Our line, just north of the town, was being pushed further forward. Holon-Selency, Francilly-Selency, Fayet and Villerete had fallen to our victorious troops, but the main attack was not yet.

To obtain scenes of our men actually in the front line trenches facing the town, I made my way through Savy and Savy Wood, in which not a single tree was left standing by the Bosche. Through the wood I carefully worked forward by keeping well under cover of a slight rise in the ground. I met a battalion commander on the way who kindly directed me to the best path to take.

"But be careful and keep your head down. Hun snipers are very active and he is putting shrapnel over pretty frequently. Although it doesn't hurt us—it evidently amuses him," he said, with a smile. "There is one section where you will have to run the gauntlet—for you are in full view of the lines. Keep down as low as possible."

I thanked the C.O. and went ahead. The weather was now perfect—a cloudless blue sky flecked here and there by the furry white balls of our bursting shrapnel around Hun aeroplanes, keeping them well above observation range.

I noticed a flight of our men winging their way over enemy lines. I could hear the rapid fire of the Bosche anti-aircraft guns, and see their black balls of shrapnel burst. But our birdmen went on their way without a moment's hesitation. I recalled the time when I was up among the clouds, filming the Bosche lines thirteen thousand feet above mother earth.

Suddenly a sharp crack, crack and whir of a machine-gun rang out. A fight was going on up there; our anti-aircraft guns ceased, being afraid of hitting our own men, but the Bosche still kept on.

It was impossible to see the progress of the fight; the whole flock was now directly overhead. Watching the "strafe" with such keen interest, this point quite escaped me until pieces of shrapnel began to fall around in alarming proportions, causing me to beat a hasty retreat out of range, though I still hung about in the hope of a Bosche machine being brought down, thereby providing me with a thrilling scene. But it did not happen. The airmen disappeared in a southerly direction, still fighting until the sharp cracks of the guns droned away in the distance.

In a few minutes I came in full view of one of our strong points in the shape of a disused quarry. Around the inner lip our Tommies had made a series of funk-holes, which looked quite picturesque in the bright sunlight.

Machine-gun parties were there ready for anything that might turn up; in the far corner a group of Frenchmen were chattering volubly to a knot of our men.

This certainly was a most interesting scene—the

point of "liaison" between the two great armies, France and Britain. I noticed by fresh shell-holes that Bosche had a rather bad habit of annoying the place with his pip-squeaks, but generally they only resulted in scoring a Blighty for more or one of the occupants—and, for others, they were a source of amusement in the shape of gambling on the spot the next one would fall.

I filmed various sections here, then, having partaken of a little tea, I wended my way to the trenches. I kept low, as the tower of the Cathedral was in full view. I had previously covered the aluminium head of my tripod with a sandbag to prevent it glistening in the sun. As I drew nearer to the trench, which I could now see quite distinctly, more and more of St. Quentin came into view. Such a picture gives one rather a queerish feeling. If a keen-eyed Hun observer spotted me, with my load, he would take me for a machine-gunner or something equally dangerous. But, fortunately, nothing happened.

I dropped into the trench of the —— Worcesters who were amazed and amused to see me there, as one of them said:

"Well, sir, I always thought all the War pictures were fakes, but now I know they're not.

"Will you take us, sir? We expect to go over to-night. Please do, sir; our people at home will then in all probability see us. Don't suppose I shall. I have an idea I shan't—but," he said, pulling himself together, "I hope so, yer know, sir."

I liked the man's spirit. It caused all the others to smile. I carefully fixed up my machine and filmed them, holding our front line.

"How close is this to the town?" I asked.

"About nine hundred yards, sir."

Whether or not Bosche had seen movement I

OUR OUTPOST LINE WITHIN 800 YARDS OF ST. QUENTIN. IT WAS TO THIS OUTPOST THAT I CRAWLED IN DAYLIGHT TO OBTAIN THIS SCENE

don't know, but suddenly a group of four 5·9 came crashing over. Everybody ducked—wise plan, rather, out here—they fell and burst about fifty yards behind us. I awaited the next lot; they came very shortly and fell in almost the same place.

"Before he shortens the range," I thought, " I'll move," and suiting the action to the word I moved out towards the Bois de Savy and was half-way there when another lot burst in my direction. This time I made for the Bois de Holnon, and fortunately the shells ceased.

As I reached the furthest side of the Bois de Savy several tear shells came whistling over and burst just behind me. Needless to say I had fallen flat, and, as I arose, the sweet smell of tear gas made itself evident. Not intending to risk a repetition of my previous experience at Beaumont Hamel, I closed my eyes and ran like—well, you couldn't see me for dust.

Yard by yard we continued to press back the enemy. For me the film story of the taking of St. Quentin is an obsession. It holds me as a needle to a magnet. And in this section, at the present, I remain—waiting and watching.

My leave is fast running out, and I am nearing the end of my story. In all the pictures that it has been my good fortune to take during the two and a half years that I have been kept at work on the great European battlefield, I have always tried to remember that it was through the eye of the camera, directed by my own sense of observation, that the millions of people at home would gain their only first-hand knowledge of what was happening at the front.

I have tried to make my pictures actual and reliable, above all I have striven to catch the atmosphere of the battlefield, and whilst I have dwelt as little as possible upon its horrors, I have aimed at showing the magnificent spirit which imbues our fighting men, from the highest in command to the humblest unit in the ranks.

I am proud to think that the task of doing this has been mine, and in doing it, I have tried " to do my bit " for the land that gave me birth.

THE END

INDEX

A
Albert, 172
Albert, King of the Belgians, 217
Alexander of Teck, Prince, 217
Amiens, 254
Andrew Paul, Mayor of Bierne, 289, 290
Anzacs, the, 211
Armentières, 108
Arras, 83, 108, 293
Aubers Ridge, 114
Australians, the, 197, 198

B
Babin, M. Gustave, of *L'Illustration*, 299
Bailleul, 52
Bapaume, 250
Basle, 41
Beaumont Hamel, 124, 129, 165, 208, 245, 265, 303
Bécourt Wood, 172, 176, 197
Belfort, 42
Belgians, Queen of, 217, 218
Bernafay Wood, 186, 188
Besançon, 42, 47
Biaches, 254
Biel, 41
Bierne, 277, 284, 289
Bizantin-le-Grand, 190
Bois de Holnon, 294, 303
Bois de Savy, 300, 303
Boulogne, 205-7, 253, 254
Bouleaux Wood, 240
Bouvais, 295
Bovincourt, 270, 271, 274, 275, 277, 279-84, 289
Brie, 263, 267, 269, 272, 274, 276
Brooks, Lieut., Official "Still" Photographer, 259-65, 275
Burstall, General, 218

C
Calais, 219-221
Cambrai, 259
Canadians, the, 52-60, 218
Carnoy Valley, 184
Caulaincourt, 294
Cavan, Earl of, 63, 76, 77
Clarendon Film Co., the, 5
Contalmaison, 199, 201-203

D
Delemont, 41
Delville Wood, 238
Dieppe, 48
Dijon, 47
Dinorah, S.S., the, 48
Dixmude, 31
Dunkirk, 111

E
Estrées, 259, 271, 276

F
Fayet, 300
Festubert, 108, 114
Foch, Gen., 215
Folkestone, 251
Foscaucourt, 259
Foucaucourt, 276
Francilly-Selency, 300
Fricourt, 171, 208, 209, 212
Fromelles, 114
Furnes, 6, 8, 13, 15, 21, 29, 30, 38

G
Gaumont Co., the, 5
George V—
  his approval of Somme film, 177
  arrival at Boulogne, 206, 207
  attends Divine Service, 217
  on Battlefield of Fricourt, 208-211
  being filmed, 216
  his departure from France, 220, 221
  greets Sir H. Rawlinson, 208
  at hospitals, 212
  inspects Canadians, 218

George V (cont.)—
  meets M. Poincaré and Gen. Joffre, 215, 216
  and puppy, 212, 213
  visits King of the Belgians, 217, 218
George, David Lloyd, Prime Minister, 177, 216, 217
Givenchy, 108
Gommecourt, 123
Gouerment, 122
Goumiers, the (Algerian Arabs), 15–17, 21
Guards' Division, the, 61, 63, 65–71, 76–79, 234, 241
Guillemont, 135, 234, 236, 238
Gully Ravine, 136

H

Haig, Field-Marshal Sir Douglas, 207, 208, 214–16
Haucourt, 277
Hawthorn Reboubt, the, 141, 159
Hill 60, 113
Hill 63, 56–58
Hindenburg, General, 293
"Hindenburg Line," the, 259, 292, 293, 298
Hohenzollern Redoubt, the, 108
Holon-Selency, 300

J

Joffre, General, 214–216
Josephine, Princess, 218
Jury, Mr. Will, 176

K

Keppel, Sir Derek, 207
Kinematograph Trade Topical Committee, the, 51
"King George's Hill," 209
Kitchener, Earl of, 206

L

La Bassée, 65, 72, 114, 115
La Boisselle, 171
La Gorgue, 61
La Maisonnette, Château of, 255
Lancashire Fusiliers, the, 127, 152, 157
Lancers, 17th, the, 214
Lens, 293
Les Bœufs, 234, 239, 245
London Scottish, the, 122, 234
Loos, 104, 108, 114
Lueze Wood, 238

M

Malins, Lieut. Geoffrey H., O.B.E.—
  appointed Official War Office Kinematographer, 51
  arrested in Switzerland, 41
  at Battle of St. Eloi, 85–92
  on battlefield of Neuve Chapelle, 72–79
  with Belgian Army, 6–13, 30–39
  in bombardment of Furnes, 31
  with Canadians, 52–60
  his description of preparation of film, 178–182
  experiences in aeroplane, 107–120
  films Battle of the Somme, 121–177
  with Goumiers, near Nieuport, 15–21
  with Guards' Division, 65–71
  his life before the War, 5
  narrow escapes of, 93–106, 142–146
  at Pozières and Contalmaison, 196–204
  and Prince of Wales, 77, 207, 212
  at Ramscapelle, 32–34
  reported dead, 38
  spends Christmas at the Front, 62–64
  and Tanks, 222
  on tracks of retreating Huns, 254–303
  in Trones Wood, 183–195
  views battle of sand-dunes, 22–29
  visits ruins of Guillemont and Mouquet Farm, 234–250
  on Vosges Mountains, 40–48
  on Western Front with the King, 205–221
  at Ypres and Arras, 80–84
Mametz, 171
Martinpuich, battle of, 234
Messines, 52, 54, 113
Middlesex Regt., the, 152
Mons, 136
Mons en Chaussée, 269, 272
Montaubon, 186
Morval, 234, 239, 245
Mouquet Farm, 245, 247, 248

N

Neuve Chapelle, 72, 73, 108, 114
Nieuport, 15, 31
Nieuport Bain, 22, 23
Norfolks, the, 234

INDEX 307

North Staffordshire Regt., the, 206
Northumberland Fusiliers, the, 218

O

Oost-Dunkerque, 22
Ostend, 111

P

Peronne, 254–258
Perrontruy, 41
Petite Douve, 56, 58, 60
Plœgsteert, 108, 114
Plœgsteert Wood, 53, 56
Plœgstrathe, 52
Poincaré, President, 214–216
Pouilly, 279, 294
Pozières, 197, 198, 201–203, 211, 245

R

Ramscapelle, 6, 12, 31–33
Rawlinson, General Sir H. S., 136, 208
Remiremont, 42
Richebourg, 108
Richebourg St. Vaast, 55
Royal Engineers, West Riding Field Co., 136
Royal Fusiliers, the, 136, 137, 152
Royal Welsh Fusiliers, the, 65

S

St. Dié, 40, 42, 43, 47
St. Eloi, 108, 113
St. Eloi, Battle of, 89–92, 218
St. Quentin, 259, 267, 293, 294, 296–303
Savy, 300
Somme, River, 255, 263, 265–267, 275, 294
Somme Battle, film of, 176–178, 183, 223

Stamfordham, Lord, 207
Suffclks, the, 234

T

Tanks, the, 225, 229–233, 237, 240
Tardeau, M. Eugène, of *Echo de Paris*, 299
Thiepval, 245
Thompson, Major, 207
Tong, Mr., 51, 52, 64
Trones Wood, 184, 186, 190, 192, 241

U

Uhlans, the, 32

V

Vernilles, 132
Villerete, 300
Villers-Carbonel, 259–266, 276
Vimy Ridge, 293
Vosges, the, 40, 47, 51
Vraignes, 270, 275, 277, 281

W

Wales, Edward, Prince of—
  his anxiety to avoid camera, 77, 212
  attends service on Christmas Day, 63
  cheered by Tommies, 211
  and General Foch, 216
  in German trench, 210, 211
  inspects gun-pits, 77
  meets King George at Boulogne, 207
  takes leave of King George, 220
Wigram, Lieut.-Col. Clive, 207, 216, 219

Y

Ypres, 55, 75, 80–83, 111, 112, 253

www.ingramcontent.com/pod-product-compliance
Lightning Source LLC
Chambersburg PA
CBHW032123160426
43197CB00008B/494